JULIA MORTIMER JUNE '00

Studies in Medieval Mysticism

Volume 1

ST BIRGITTA OF SWEDEN

Studies in Medieval Mysticism

GENERAL EDITORS
Anne Clark Bartlett and Rosalynn Voaden

ISSN 1465–5683

Studies in Medieval Mysticism offers a forum for works exploring the textures and traditions of western European mystical and visionary literature, from late Antiquity to the Reformation including both well- and lesser-known mystics and their texts. It particularly welcomes publications which combine textual and manuscript study with current critical theories, to offer innovative approaches to medieval mystical literature.

Proposals or queries may be sent directly to the editors or publisher at the addresses given below; all submissions will recieve prompt and informed consideration.

Professor Anne Clark Bartlett, Department of English, De Paul University, 802 West Belden Avenue, Chicago, IL 60614, USA

Professor Rosalynn Vpaden, Department of English, Arizona State University, PO Box 870302, Tempe, AZ 85287, USA

Caroline Palmer, Boydell & Brewer Limited, PO Box 9, Woodbridge, Suffolk, IP12 3DF, UK

ST BIRGITTA OF SWEDEN

Bridget Morris

THE BOYDELL PRESS

First published 1999
The Boydell Press, Woodbridge

ISBN 0 85115 727 0

The Boydell Press is an imprint of Boydell & Brewer Ltd
PO Box 9, Woodbridge, Suffolk IP12 3DF, UK
and of Boydell & Brewer Inc.
PO Box 41026, Rochester, NY 14604–4126, USA
website: http://www.botdell.co.uk

A catalogue record for this book is available
from the British Library

Library of Congress Cataloging-in-Publication Data
Morris, Bridget.
St. Birgitta of Sweden/ Bridget Morris.
p. cm. – (Studies in medieval mysticism ; v. 1)
Includes bibliographical references and index.
ISBN 0–85115–727–0 (hardback : alk. paper)
1. Bridget, of Sweden, Saint, c. 1303–1373. 2. Christian saints – Sweden – Biography. I. Title. II. Title: Saint Birgitta of Sweden. III. Series.
BX4700.B6M65 1999
271'.97
[B] – DC21 98–52188

This publication is printed on acid-free paper

Printed in Great Britain by
St Edmundsbury Press Ltd, Bury St Edmunds, Suffolk

CONTENTS

ILLUSTRATIONS

ACKNOWLEDGEMENTS

This book is the result of many years of research on St Birgitta of Sweden which began in Uppsala in 1976, under the supervision of Professor Lennart Moberg and Professor Sten Eklund. During that year and the years that followed I learned much from my Swedish colleagues and friends.

I am grateful to Professor Göran Dahlbäck and to Professor Alf Härdelin and Dr Monica Hedlund for kindly inviting me in 1994 to discuss parts of the book at their Medieval Research Seminars at Stockholm University and Uppsala University respectively. Dr Veronica O'Mara and Mr Gavin Orton have given much of their time in reading drafts of the book, and it is my pleasure to thank them for their patient help and encouragement, and for saving me from many errors. Dr Claire Sahlin has generously made available unpublished material from her Ph.D. thesis, and provided helpful comments on my work in its early stages. Dr Tore Nyberg kindly agreed to read the completed manuscript and made many valuable and constructive suggestions. Advice, help and information on specific matters was given by many other colleagues, but in particular I should like to acknowledge Dr Hans Aili, Dr Andrew Ayton, Roger Axelsson, Dr Jutta Baum-Sheridan, Dr Olle Ferm, Dr Judith Jesch, Dr Anders Piltz and Professor Jan Svanberg. I alone am responsible for the outstanding errors and omissions in this book.

The Librarian and staff of the Brynmor Jones Library of the University of Hull have shown unfailing support of my research over many years. Staff at the University Libraries of Uppsala and Lund and at the Royal Library in Stockholm have always been most accommodating during my research visits to Sweden, and I am grateful to them. I should also like to thank Professor Birger Bergh for allowing me access to his computerised Birgittine concordance, which has proved an invaluable research tool. My colleagues in the Department of Scandinavian Studies at the University of Hull shouldered extra teaching and administrative burdens during my periods of research leave, and I warmly thank them for their support.

A number of funding bodies have generously facilitated my research. The Swedish Institute, Stockholm, made it possible for me to spend time in libraries in Uppsala and Stockholm during the initial stages of my work. In 1991 I was honoured to receive a scholarship in support of my work from the Swedish Women's Educational Association International (SWEA). A grant from Torsten and Ingrid Gihls fond (administrated by Kungliga Vitterhets Historie och Antikvitets Akademien, Stockholm) enabled me to undertake research in Rome. I also gratefully acknowledge the Humanities Research

Board of the British Academy for its support under the Research Leave Scheme 1995–96, without which this book could not have been completed.

Grateful acknowledgement is made to the following for permission to reproduce the illustrations contained in the book: Antikvarisk–Topografiska Arkivet, Riksantikvarieämbetet, Stockholm; Danmarks Kirker (Nationalmuseet, Copenhagen); Kungliga Biblioteket, Stockholm; New York Public Library; Pierpont Morgan Library, New York.

My final, special, debt of gratitude is owed to my husband, Philip, who has so cheerfully and tolerantly lived with two Bridgets for so many years.

NOTE ON LANGUAGE, SPELLING AND REFERENCES

Because so many names are used from so many countries, the principle has been adopted of following national origins, and giving the modern-day equivalent in the language or country concerned, except where there are very commonly accepted anglicised forms, or where the written sources suggest a latinised form. I remain aware that this approach falls short of complete consistency.

References to the revelations are given by Book and chapter number (the Book of the *Revelaciones Extravagantes* is abbreviated as Ex., the *Sermo Angelicus* as SA, and the *Liber Questionum* (Book V) is referred to by its *interrogacio* (int.) and *revelacio* (rev.) numbers). The canonisation materials are referred to by the abbreviation AP, with page reference to Isak Collijn's edition, 1924–31. Excerpts from the sources are cited from the Latin text (unless it is otherwise stated) and quoted from the modern critical editions. The editions not yet in print are taken from Professor Birger Bergh's unpublished computer concordance of the entire Birgittine corpus. The translations from Latin, Old Icelandic and medieval Swedish are my own (unless it is otherwise stated).

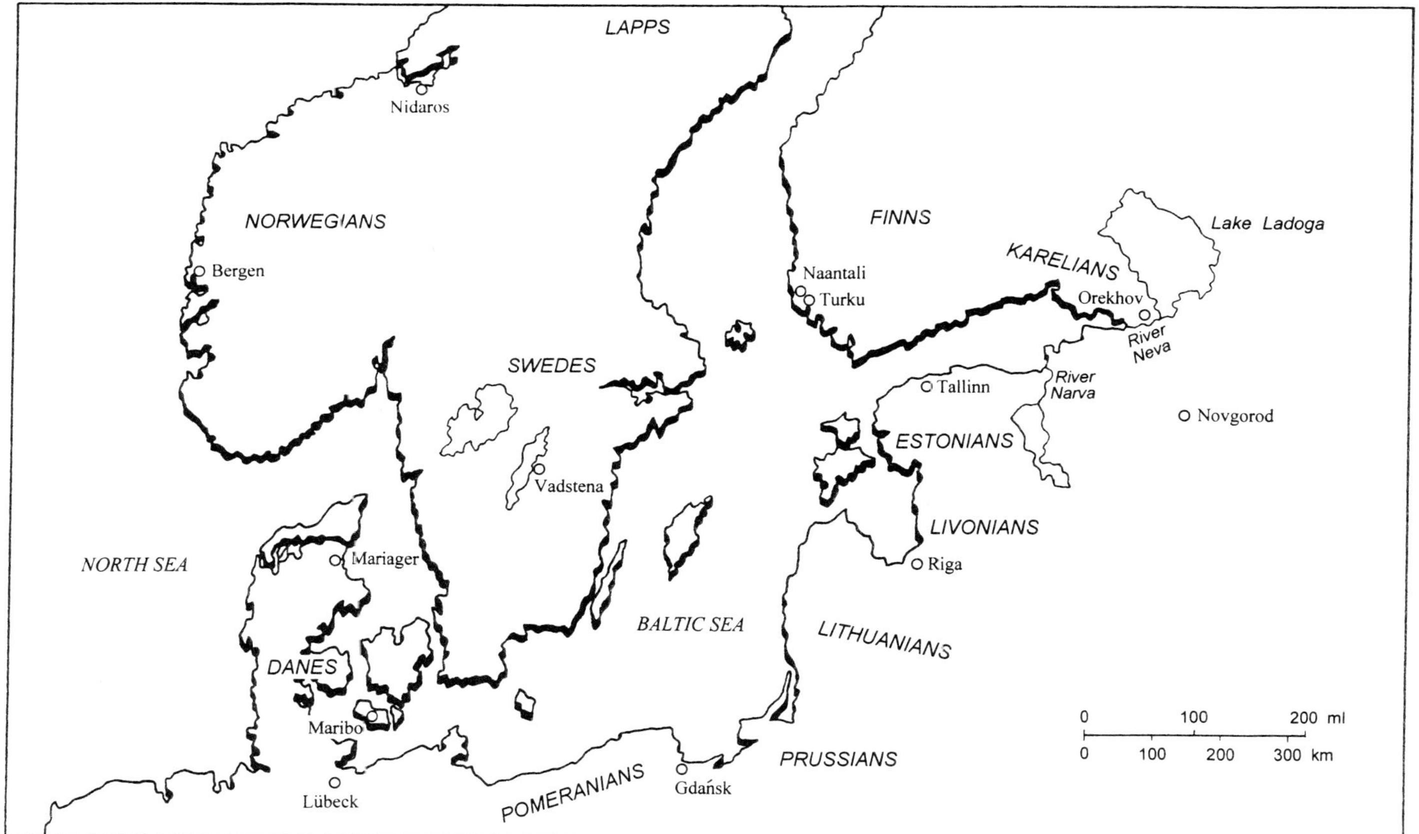

Map 1. The baltic Region in the Middle Ages

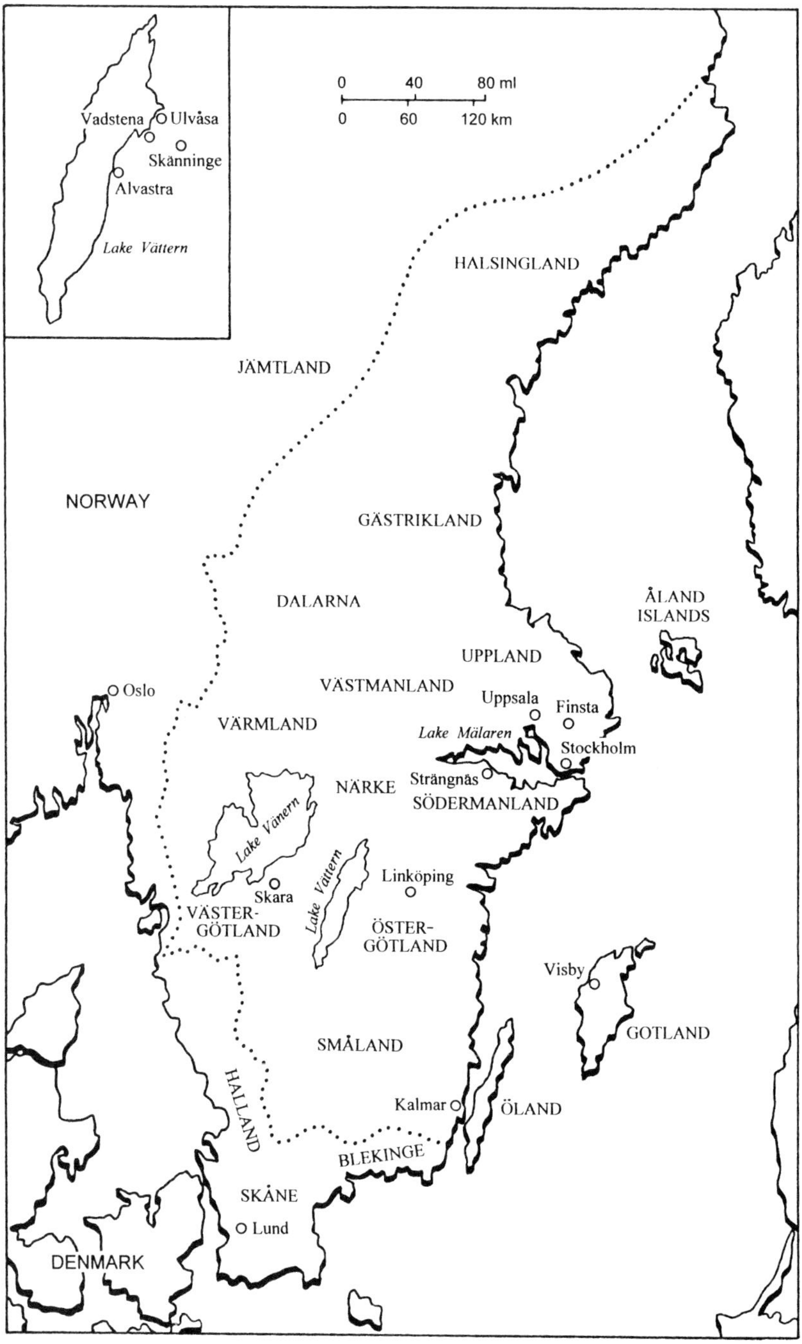

Map 2. Medieval Sweden

Introduction

> . . . in order that something good might come even from the North, this holy man visited his vineyard according to custom, and to participate in the further cultivation of the vineyard, he brought a strong woman from afar, from remote regions, a woman bearing her own reward, that is, the blessed widow Birgitta . . .
>
> . . . ut etiam ab Aquilone aliquid boni esset, ille cœlestis agricola eamdem vineam suo de more visitans, mulierem fortem procul et de ultimis finibus suum secum precium deferentem, ad hujusmodi vineæ culturam adduxit inesse, beatam scilicet viduam Birgittam . . .
>
> (Canonisation bull 1391, *Acta Sanctorum, Octobris*, vol. 4 p. 469)

ST BIRGITTA of Sweden is one of the most charismatic figures in the late medieval mystical tradition. She was the only woman in the fourteenth century to have been canonised, the only woman to have founded a monastic order of her own devising, an order which has had an unbroken history since its foundation and is still in existence today. She went as a stranger to Rome and succeeded in commanding prelates and popes and engaging in political secular intrigues in the courts of Europe. Even in the last decades of the fourteenth century she had acquired a formidable reputation in influential circles throughout the Christian world, and well into the fifteenth century she was widely revered, read, cited, emulated and debated. Only five years after her death there were artistic representations of her in churches in Rome and Naples, and the pope, Gregory XI, reportedly had a picture of her in his chamber.[1] She is often placed alongside the other great fourteenth-century mystic, Caterina of Siena (c.1347–80), and although the two women never met, there is evidence of contact between their confessors.[2] An early fifteenth-

1 This information is given by her daughter, Katarina Ulfsdotter, who wrote to the archbishop of Sweden in 1378, expressing surprise that her mother was not better known in her native country; see Ekwall 1965, pp. 99, 129–30.

2 Birgitta's confessor, Alphonso of Jaén, was sent by the pope to Siena in c.1373, where he met Caterina; see Colledge 1956, p. 34. Several clerics who knew both women are discussed by Collijn 1929, pp. 21–38. One of Caterina's secretaries who assisted in writing down her *Dialogo* was Ser Cristofano di Gano Guidini who was the copyist of an Italian translation of Birgitta's Revelations in 1389. Both women are compared

century English manuscript, possibly from Yorkshire, contains a defence by a hermit named Thomas Basset of the English mystical writer Richard Rolle against his critics, and quotes St Birgitta in evidence.[3] Margery Kempe (c.1373–1439), the middle-class housewife and religious enthusiast from King's Lynn in Norfolk, regarded the Swedish saint as her mentor and model, and made a pilgrim's journey to the Holy Land and Rome where in 1415 she visited the room in Birgitta's house in which she had died, and was told by one of her servants that she 'was kind and meek to every creature and that she had a laughing face'.[4] Cicely, duchess of York and mother of Edward IV and Richard III of England, had one of her granddaughters, to whom she was godmother, named Bridget, and bequeathed her copy of the Revelations to another granddaughter, Anne de la Pole, who became prioress of the English Birgittine house of Syon.[5] With the foundation of the Birgittine order, her cult spread rapidly throughout Europe, as far as Bohemia, where, alongside the Bible, St Birgitta's Revelations were said to have been the favourite reading of Emperor Wenceslaus IV.[6] Compilations of Birgittine prophecies, such as the *Onus mundi*, of 1433, by the Leipzig theologian Johannes Tortsch, were disseminated in Germany; and in Italy, where *de luxe* manuscripts were produced in the last decades of the fourteenth century, revelations also found their way into pamphlets and apocalyptic treatises and were quoted and counter-quoted in support of religious and political causes.[7]

Yet for all her popularity in some quarters, Birgitta also had her detractors. There were rumblings of discontent, for instance, at the fact that she was canonised. In 1415, Jean Gerson, chancellor of the University of Paris, wrote a treatise in which he obliquely referred to Birgitta as an example of the dangerous practice of excessive religious fervour among 'unlettered women'.[8] During negotiations in 1439 between the English and French in Oye, near Calais, Birgittine prophecies and those of a devout hermit were competitively cited in discussions between the two sides, which prompted cardinal Henry Beaufort wryly to comment that a convenient solution might be for these two holy people to be married off to each other![9] Even Martin Luther in the sixteenth century acknowledged the popularity of the Birgittine prophecies,

during Caterina's canonisation process in the fifteenth century. See also Vauchez 1993, pp. 243–53.

3 MS Cod. Ups. C621; see further Hedlund 1989–90, p. 94.

4 'was goodly & meke to euery creatur & þat sche had a lawhyng cher'. Meech 1940, p. 95.

5 Armstrong 1983, p. 151.

6 Undhagen 1978, p. 32 note 145, and p. 64 note 2.

7 See for example, on *Onus mundi*, Montag 1968; on the prophecies, Reeves 1969, pp. 338–40; and on the influence in England, Ellis 1982. Only in France is the cult lacking; see Vauchez 1991.

8 See Boland 1959, pp. 25–38.

9 Allmand 1972, p. 116.

dismissing them as satanic illusions by which he himself had almost been taken in when he was still a monk, and describing their author as 'die tolle Brigit', 'the crazy Birgitta'.[10]

The present book

This book provides an account of the life and achievements of this towering Swedish saint, and is aimed in particular at students, scholars and general readers with a keen interest in medieval female saints. My study seeks to place Birgitta in the context of the society from which she emerges, and to assess how a woman from a small country on the Christian fringes of northern Europe could succeed with so forceful a voice in making herself heard in papal circles in Rome. It also looks at the way in which her public voice is underpinned by a deep private spirituality at all stages of her life. These two approaches have been used to consider the fundamental question of how she succeeded in achieving the seemingly impossible: of gaining the status of saint, of reaching so great a recognition and following within Europe in the decades after her death, and of establishing a new monastic order, in an age when new foundations were proscribed. Birgitta's life is examined chiefly through the primary sources, but I have also sought to bring together the many threads of research that have been undertaken within Birgittine studies over the past thirty years, mostly in Scandinavia, where there has been a renewed interest in St Birgitta in the wake of the 600th jubilee celebrations of her death in 1373 and canonisation in 1391.[11]

The sources

The central body of biographical material is provided by the revelations themselves, which number approximately seven hundred in all. We are told that Birgitta wrote down many of her visions in her native tongue, before her confessors translated them into Latin.[12] Today only two autographs survive,

10 See Obrist 1984, p. 236.

11 Further biographical information can probably be sought in the Italian archives, which have not been extensively researched by Birgittine scholars since Collijn's studies in 1929. But see Bolton Holloway 1996 and Pezzini 1999 (forthcoming).

12 The procedure for recording the revelations is fully described in the *vita* written shortly after Birgitta's death: '. . . the words that were given her from God she wrote down in her mother tongue with her own hand when she was well and she had us, her father confessors, make a very faithful translation of them into Latin. She then listened to the translation with her own writing, which she herself had written, to make sure that not one word was added or subtracted, but was exactly what she had heard and seen in the divine vision. But when she was too weak she would call her confessor and another scribe, especially appointed as secretary, whereupon with great devotion and fear of God and sometimes in tears, she spoke the words in her native language in a kind of tense, ecstatic trance as if she were reading from a book;

Plate 1. One of two surviving fragments written by St Birgitta in 1361, in which she incites four noblemen to rise up against King Magnus Eriksson if he cannot be persuaded to mend his ways.
Source: B-autograph, MS A65 Kungliga Biblioteket, Stockholm.

which provide the most valuable source of information about Birgitta as a scribe.[13] They are written in a cramped, angular script, which, though competent, lacks fluency and is prone to errors and inconsistencies, suggesting that she may have been unused to holding a pen and that she may have dictated her revelations more frequently than written them down herself. Moreover, the sheer volume of revelations and the exceptional length of some of them may have meant that she frequently made draft notes, perhaps on wax tablets, which were later expanded upon in Latin by consultation with her confessors.[14]

During her lifetime most of the revelations probably had a limited readership and were treated as private documents or letters directed at particular individuals.[15] These texts in Latin, none of which survives, were gathered in bundles and booklets, which by the end of her life must have grown into a vast and unwieldy body of material.[16] Towards the end of her life, she asked her confessor, Alphonso of Jaén, to gather all the revelations into Books and

and then the confessor dictated these words in Latin to the scribe, and he wrote them down there in her presence. When the words had been written down she wished to hear them and she listened very carefully and attentively.' '. . . illa verba diuinitus ei data scribebat in lingua sua materna manu sua propria, quando erat sana, et faciebat illa translatari in lingua latina fidelissime a nobis confessoribus suis et postea ascultabat illa cum scriptura sua, quam ipsa scripserat, ne vnum verbum ibi plus adderetur uel deficeret, nisi que ipsa in visione diuinitus audierat et viderat. Si vero erat infirma, vocabat confessorem et scriptorem suum secretarium ad hoc specialiter deputatum, et tunc ipsa cum magna deuocione et timore Dei et aliquando cum lacrimis referebat ei verba illa in uulgari suo cum quadam attenta eleuacione mentali, quasi si legeret in libro, et tunc confessor dicebat illa verba in lingua latina illi scriptori, et ille scribebat illa ibidem in sua presencia, et postea cum erant verba conscripta, ipsa volebat illa ascultare et ascultabat valde diligenter et attente.' AP p. 84.

13 See Högman 1951, who also provides facsimiles of the autographs.

14 However, such an assertion would contradict the statement in the *vita* quoted above, that she recorded every word in full. See further on this question Morris 1993. A number of visions are specifically said by witnesses in the canonisation process to have been written down in her native tongue (see AP pp. 270, 328, 384, 509, 512, 518), and the prologues to certain individual Books, which are attributed to Alphonso of Jaén, also suggest that she wrote her visions down in Swedish: the prologue to Book VIII, known as the *Epistola solitarii;* Book V, which says that the vision was engraved on her mind as vividly as on a 'marble tablet' and that she wrote it down immediately in her native tongue before her confessor translated it into Latin; and the prologue to the *Sermo Angelicus* states that after she had read her hours and prayers each day, she sat expectantly with a writing tablet, paper and pen in her hand.

15 On the revelations as letters, see Öberg 1969. Because of the extensive editorial reworking, revelations which were originally letters have usually lost their letter form.

16 The piecemeal collection of texts is suggested by the words 'in scedulas et sexternos', 'leaves and booklets' given in Ex. Prologue. See Hollman 1956, p. 116.

publish them.[17] He became editor-in-chief after her death, and he divided the material into books with headed chapters.

The textual history of the work begun by Alphonso is complex and there were a number of editions before the final canonisation edition of 1391.[18] Alphonso's first redaction was prepared in 1377–78 and contained the following: a Prologue to the whole œuvre; Book I (containing 60 chapters); Book II (30 chapters); Book III (34 chapters); Book IV (130 chapters); Book V, known as the *Liber Questionum*, which is in dialogue form with sixteen interspersed revelations; Book VI (109 chapters) and VII (32 chapters). A second redaction was completed in 1380, which contained further material: the *Epistola solitarii* by Alphonso, which is an introduction to a further Book, Book VIII, consisting of some sixty-one revelations excerpted mainly from other Books. Book VIII deals solely with kings and political affairs, as is suggested by its title, *Liber celestis imperatoris ad reges*. Other works are the *Sermo Angelicus*, the daily readings for the Birgittine nuns, and the *Quattuor Oraciones*, four major prayers.

After a number of setbacks during the 1380s, the canonisation commission was established in 1391, and following the examination, Pope Boniface IX was presented by the confessor general at Vadstena, Magnus Petri, with a luxury copy of the Revelations and the *Liber attestacionum*, containing the official documents and testimonies relating to the canonisation: this 'canonisation edition' was in all likelihood identical with Alphonso's first redaction.[19]

Alphonso's work in arranging the revelations into Books did not provide a chronological ordering (with the possible exception of Book VII), although some Books (such as Book V) are arranged thematically, and there are certainly lesser thematic groupings within each Book. In general it can be said that Books I, II and V date from the 1340s; Book III contains revelations directed at the priesthood, and many date from the Rome period (1349–73); Book VII contains revelations received in the Holy Land (1372–73); and Books IV and VI comprise a wide mixture of revelations on assorted topics from different periods. In his second redaction, Book IV ends at chapter 130, but later it came to be supplemented by five revelations on the morals of the clergy (known as the *Tractatus ad sacerdotes*) and nine further chapters (some in letter form) which urge a return of the papacy to Rome (known as the *Tractatus ad pontificcs*).[20]

Some material, such as these two tracts, was considered unsuitable by Alphonso for inclusion in the canonisation submissions, probably on sensitive political grounds. Other material was excluded because it was obscure or cast

17 AP p. 98, Ex. 49, Book VII 31.

18 For a useful account of the various stages in the history of the Latin text, see Undhagen 1978, pp. 1–37.

19 Undhagen 1978, p. 37.

20 See further Aili 1992, and Jönsson 1997, who discusses the uncertain status of this group of revelations.

a negative light on Birgitta, or else it was potentially controversial. Other material, again of minor significance for the canonisation application, may not have passed through Alphonso's hands because it was never taken from Sweden to Rome. Gradually, these rejected or half-forgotten texts came to be incorporated into later editions, either as *additiones* and *declaraciones* – explanatory and circumstantial information which glossed existing revelations – or as a separate book, known as the *Revelaciones Extravagantes*, consisting of some 116 revelations on disparate topics.[21]

As the Birgittine cult grew, copies of the Latin texts were made at the end of the fourteenth century and in the course of the fifteenth century. Today about 150 Latin manuscripts of the Revelations exist in libraries around the world. One of the main manuscript traditions is represented by manuscripts that were copied at Vadstena, of which MS 'Codex Falkenberg' in Lund University Library, and a manuscript formerly held by Kalmar Stifts- och Gymnasiebiblioteket, are the most complete and best preserved copies; and among the *de luxe* copies is the large folio Harley 612 in the British Library, which was written at the Birgittine House of Syon in England around 1440.[22] The first printed text of the Revelations was produced in Lübeck in 1492 at the press of Bartholomaeus Ghotan, and after his edition there were some eight later editions: two printed in Nuremberg in 1500 and 1517, two in Rome in 1557 (edited by Olaus Magnus) and 1606 (edited by Consalvo Durante, who made an attempt to amend some of the mistakes in Ghotan's edition), the others in Antwerp in 1611, Cologne in 1628, Rome in 1628 and Munich in 1680.[23]

Distinct from the Latin text corpus there is a Swedish tradition. When the Birgittine monastery at Vadstena was inaugurated in 1384 it was considered a priority to procure a vernacular text for use by the newly professed nuns, and during the 1380s a translation of the complete corpus from Latin to Swedish was undertaken. Today there are altogether fourteen extant manuscripts in medieval Swedish, the earliest of which dates from c.1385.[24] For the most part this is a literal, pedantic and unidiomatic translation of an unidentified Latin text. However, there are some individual revelations which give reason to argue that there were several text versions available to the Swedish translators, who in theory may have had access to Birgitta's own autographs, early drafts in Swedish and Latin or details which existed in oral tradition but were never committed to writing.[25] There are proverbs and images, for instance, where the detail stands out more sharply in the Swedish than the Latin text

21 Hollman 1956.

22 On these three manuscripts see further Undhagen 1978, pp. 92–113, 182–5.

23 On these editions see further Hollman 1956 and Bergh 1991.

24 See Wessén 1976. On a recently-discovered fragment of Book IV, see Wiktorsson 1998, pp. 94–8.

25 Westman 1911, pp. 47–72, was the first scholar to raise the question of the Swedish original texts. As new work is done on the Latin critical editions, a more nuanced picture is coming to light, and it is increasingly apparent that individual revelations

and suggests that the translator may have been drawing on more than one source.[26] Thus the Swedish tradition cannot be disregarded in considerations of the revelations, and sometimes the Swedish text may bring the reader closer to Birgitta's utterance than the Latin text. In the end, however, scholars are agreed that the original formulation of her vision cannot easily be prised out of the existing texts or her voice heard through all the editorial levels of textual transmission.

The second major source is the *vita*, written shortly after Birgitta's death by her two Swedish confessors, Peter Olafsson of Alvastra (referred to in this book as Prior Peter), and his namesake, Peter Olafsson of Skänninge (referred to as Magister Peter). There are two principal redactions: the so-called 'Process' *vita*, and a shorter version, MS Cod. Ups. C15, both of which have provoked a lively and continuing debate about priority.[27] A number of biographies were also written in the wake of Birgitta's death and incorporated into offices in her honour. Those by Archbishop Birger Gregersson and Nikolaus Hermansson are best known.[28] A life in Swedish was produced around the same time as the Latin *vita*, which although based on the Latin text, is markedly independent of it, especially in its arrangement of material.[29]

Another valuable repository of information is found in the materials relating to the canonisation process, and here again, the sources are extensive. The documents are presented in the form of a judicial inquisitorial procedure, and follow twelve stages. During the official *processus*, an account of the candidate's life was broken down into articles, and witnesses were called to confirm or deny the articles in turn; if the articles were proven, the canonisation might be successful.[30] By its nature, this was a negative procedure, to block rather than facilitate canonisation; and it was important that the witnesses were carefully chosen, and their accounts presented in such a way that they would maximise hopes for a successful outcome. Thus the witness testimonies, while not insincere, are not always impartial.

The Birgittine tradition that flourished at Vadstena after the saint's death also produced a variety of biographical materials. There is an abundance of miracle stories associated with Birgitta, in two main collections.[31] Many

need to be looked at critically in order to ascertain the extent of 'mixed' textual traditions. See further, for example (on Book IV 24) Aili 1986 and (on Book V) Morris 1991, pp. 33–52.

26 There are proverbs, for instance, in Books I 19, V int. 15, VI 54. The Swedish texts which without doubt have priority over the Latin text are the so-called 'Julita fragment' (Liedgren 1961), the 'Birgittiner-norske' text, written in Swedish mixed with Norwegian (Wessén 1968, pp. 73–152), a part of the *Quattuor Oraciones* (Eklund 1983–84), and some of the *Extravagantes* (Hollman 1965, p. 104).

27 See Ekwall 1965 and Jönsson 1989, pp. 90–7.

28 Collijn 1946 and Schück 1893.

29 See Wollin 1999 (forthcoming).

30 See Collijn 1924–31.

31 See Fröjmark 1992.

contain supernatural events connected with historical reality, which throw a light on the social and cultural background and demonstrate the spread of the saint's cult. As well as miracle stories, the vast collection of sermon texts from Vadstena monastery provides information concerning the image of the saint and the cultural climate of the order which she founded.[32] In the fifteenth century, a colourful genealogical account of Birgitta's forebears and children was written, in Swedish, by the abbess of Vadstena, Margareta Clausdotter (died 1486).[33] Background information about the history of the monastery can be obtained from the *Diarium Vadstenense*, the Memorial Book which covers the period 1344–1545.[34] Entries for the early decades of the monastery's history are sparse, and apart from events of major significance, they consist mainly of death notices of its benefactors; but in the fifteenth and sixteenth centuries there is much detailed information relating to Swedish history as well as internal events at the monastery. Besides the monastic sources, Swedish diplomatic materials also give a skeletal account of Swedish history and include scattered references to Birgitta, her family and entourage; and they underpin and occasionally corroborate some of the hagiographical materials.

Between history and myth

In their study of sainthood in its social context, D. Weinstein and R. Bell observe that most hagiographical material lies somewhere between the extremes of spurious legend and richly ornamented character portrayals: 'But the problem remains: facts are relatively few and tend to be subordinated to myth; therefore they are to be treated with skepticism.'[35] Although the known facts in Birgitta's case are far more abundant than for most other medieval saints, their interpretation is no less slippery and her historical life remains elusive. The revelations present difficult material, which is highly coloured, often sensational and dramatic, never purely historical, but always essentially concerned with her visionary calling. In number they are voluminous and in content they are frequently repetitive or obscure. They are the saint's uncontrolled outpourings, the phantasmagoria of her imagination, committed to writing in their raw form and lent an idiosyncratic quality in their verbal expression. In their language they contain a mixture of stereotypical mystical

32 The range of sermons (which run to some 7000 lines) is well illustrated in the catalogue of the C-collection of manuscripts from Vadstena; see Andersson-Schmitt et al. 1990, vol. 3, although very few of them have so far been edited. Vadstena sermons are a productive area of research which is currently opening up in Sweden; see further the publications of the project, based at Uppsala University, 'Vadstenabrödernas predikan. Meddelanden 1994–   '.

33 See Annerstedt 1876.

34 Gejrot 1988.

35 Weinstein and Bell 1982, p. 8.

commonplaces and startlingly homely and sensational imagery, for which she draws directly on her personal experience.

By their intensely personal nature, her visions are to a considerable extent autobiographical, and give her the means to express in words the attitudes and beliefs that shaped her life and empowered her to take a role as a public figure on the European stage at the heart of Christendom. The visions are often prompted by simple, everyday events, and provide the means of spontaneous confession and self-analysis. They also provide the resolution of initial uncertainties or problems with which she had been confronted, and they articulate the reactions of her innermost mind.[36]

In spite of their appearance as personal documents, however, the revelations are transmitted through many layers of editing and the final text leaves many of the visions cleansed by conscientious confessors and promoters of her cause for canonisation, with the result that it is difficult to hear the original utterance of the saint herself. Furthermore, her own words are constantly interwoven by borrowings from other sources – biblical, patristic, legal and encyclopaedic writings, for instance – to lend weight and authority to her visions. Never is this process of reworking the revelations consistent, however, and in some revelations, especially those that were of minimal interest to the editors, there is clearly much less editing than in other more important ones. Thus there is an unevenness in the editorial activity which adds to the difficulties of interpretation. The process of interpretation is further complicated by the fact that individual revelations seldom contain circumstantial details with respect to date, places and persons involved, and only rarely can they be corroborated from non-Birgittine historical sources.

Although the source materials have to be read with caution, they nevertheless provide an extraordinarily full account of the different facets of Birgitta's life. The sources collectively highlight the spiritual and moral characteristics of St Birgitta as they are perceived by her biographers and acquaintances in their efforts to display their notion of sainthood. Her supporters have good reasons to present her in a favourable light, whether to suit the strict protocol laid down in the papal court, or the secular advocates of the saint who used her for political advantage, or the pious devotees among the women of her monastic order, who wished to perpetuate her name and reputation by embellished and often tendentious anecdotes of her life. Particular and fresh, and sometimes contradictory, perspectives emerge kaleidoscopically from the

36 E. Petroff 1986, pp. 22–3, writes of the mystics in general that: 'the autobiographical impulse . . . cannot be separated from the visions; visions constitute a vehicle for the transformation of the self . . . Visions are also responses to real-life situations: they may be compensatory or offer creative solutions to difficulties or provide images for identity, but they always come in response to something, and they always set in motion a new relationship to the original event that called them forth.' See also on autobiographical elements in visionary writing, Greenspan 1991.

sources, and there is not always a consistent picture of Birgitta in her different roles, as woman, wife and mother, and as saint and monastic founder. The historical Birgitta is different from Birgitta as mystic or theologian; Birgitta as wife and mother is markedly different from Birgitta as politician and kingmaker, or Birgitta as idealised by her followers after her death or revered in the company of saints after her canonisation.

In this book I have sought to present St Birgitta in the light of these varying perspectives and thereby to demonstrate the breadth of her achievement. In such a narrative biography as this, therefore, there has not been space to discuss single perspectives in detail; but in the notes and bibliography references are given for readers wishing to pursue debates further. The material is arranged chronologically rather than thematically (although occasionally there are thematic discussions which are tangential to the descriptive narrative). In this way it is hoped that the reader will see the development of Birgitta's spirituality, from her Swedish background and initial uncertainties, to her outspoken and strident calls for reform in her later life, and to the practical embodiment of her piety, the founding of a monastic order primarily for women.

I

The Swedish Roots

Tunc aves rapaces preoccupaverunt cacumina moncium

That was a time when birds of prey rested on the mountain tops

(*Diarium Vadstenense* 1365)

ST BIRGITTA marks the continuation of a long visionary tradition in Scandinavia which had produced poetic masterpieces like the *Völuspá (The Wise Woman's Prophecy)* and literary figures like the sibyl in *The Saga of Eirik the Red*. The tradition is continued after her in Sweden with the philologist and mystic Johannes Bureus (1568–1652), the scientist and theologian Emanuel Swedenborg (1688–1722), the literary giant August Strindberg (1849–1912) and perhaps even the film-maker Ingmar Bergman (1918–), in whose work one can trace a grim intensity and hallucinatory imagination as well as a tender lyricism.

She emerged in the fourteenth century from a society on the periphery of Christendom which was in the process of change, from a small country still rooted in Germanic custom and tradition towards a more fully integrated European nation which drew influences from Roman and continental ideas of government and law. Coming as she did from the traditional aristocracy, she was by instinct opposed to the new wind of change that was blowing across Scandinavia. Members of her class had traditionally been given a considerable voice and an active role in matters of state; and in addition, women of her background were accorded a status which extolled their co-operation and vigorous involvement in public as well as private enterprises to a greater extent than elsewhere in Europe at this time.[1]

1 Carol Clover has argued (mainly with reference to Old Norse society) that 'the one-sex or single-standard system . . . is one that advantages men. But it is at the same time a system in which being born female was not so damaging that it could not be offset by other factors. A woman may start with debits and a man with credits, but any number of other considerations – wealth, marital status, birth order, historical accident, popularity, a forceful personality, sheer ambition, and so on – could tip the balance in the other direction. . . . to the extent that we can speak of a social binary, a set of categories into which all persons were divided, the fault line runs not between males and females per se, but between able-bodied men (and the

To understand Birgitta's public and private voice and how successful she was in making her message heard, it is necessary first to examine Swedish society at the time. What sort of society was it that produced a woman of such towering stature as Birgitta? How was her attitude shaped by the society from which she emerged? The prosperous years of the viking age were long since past, and the next few centuries saw the country's prolonged and painful birth as a nation state. Sweden's development as an emerging country was slow-paced and in many ways out of step with its continental neighbours. Christianity came late, even later than to Norway and Denmark, and was introduced piecemeal in the early eleventh century. There was no common law before the mid-fourteenth century; there was no vernacular literary tradition as there was in Norway and Iceland; the first proper capital, Stockholm, was not founded until the mid-thirteenth century, and the first University, Uppsala, was not inaugurated until 1477, on St Birgitta's feast-day. But unlike other European countries at the same time, society was relatively static and not rocked by strife between Church and monarchy, or religious heresy of the kind that affected other parts of Europe. During the post-viking period, Sweden was occupied with internal colonisation and with consolidating her national boundaries, containing inter-dynastic strife and turmoil, strengthening the Church and managing a struggling economy. In short, the Swedish middle ages, from the close of the viking age in the eleventh century until the election of King Gustav Vasa in 1523, was an undistinguished period in Swedish history.[2]

Geography

The boundaries of medieval Sweden were different from today's, and the country had a squarer shape with its perimeters extending across the Baltic Sea to the inhabited regions of southern and western Finland, and south as far as Blekinge, Halland and Skåne, which for parts of the period belonged to Denmark, while the western provinces of Bohuslän, Härjedalen and Jämtland were part of Norway. It was a vast land with a varying geography; it had a mild climate and a flat, arable landscape in the south but a cold, mountainous terrain in the north, where the winters were dark and long. The north was only inhabited by the nomadic Lapps and *birkarlar*, traders who

exceptional women) on the one hand and, on the other, a kind of rainbow coalition of everyone else (most women, children, slaves, and old, disabled, or otherwise disenfranchised men).' Clover 1993, pp. 379–80. On the role of women in later medieval Sweden, see Gunneng and Strand 1981, and Sawyer and Sawyer 1993, pp. 188–213.

2 For survey accounts of medieval Swedish history, see Carlsson and Rosén 1962, Scott 1977 and Lindkvist and Ågren 1985. On specific subjects, see articles in the twenty-volume encyclopedia of the Scandinavian Middle Ages, KLNM, or, in one volume in English, *Medieval Scandinavia*, ed. P. Pulsiano, 1993.

acknowledged the sovereignty of the Swedish king and who, according to tradition, were granted the privilege by King Magnus Ladulås (Barnlock) (1275–90) to collect royal taxes from the Lapps. The large tracts of inhospitable mountain terrain, lakes and forests provided natural boundaries which separated one community from another, and above all it was water and forestland that determined daily life and living conditions in Sweden. The central regions were dominated by the two great lakes, Vättern, in the province of Östergötland, and Vänern in Västergötland (the entire region of Götaland being the original home of the Götar, or Geats), and by Lake Mälaren in the heart of Uppland (the original home of the Svear, or Swedes). In this vast country water was the most rapid means of transport; and access was provided not only by the coastal routes and inland waterways but also by the frozen lakes in winter which made movement possible. There was an extensive network of established land routes especially across the inhabited central regions, and there were routes north into Norway which led through Dalarna, Hälsingland and Jämtland, such as the route suggestively described by the great Swedish Renaissance historiographer, Olaus Magnus, whose *Historia de gentibus septrionalibus* was published in 1555:

> In summer the natives and foreign travellers journey from Jämtland by a route that is no less frightening than dangerous across the lofty mountains . . . whereas in winter they make their way whenever they wish by short cuts and footpaths over frozen marshes, lakes and rivers. For these mountains are enormous and hardly to be paralleled in Europe. On the eastern side they have at the entrance to the foothills gates or openings of the hardest flint, some cloven by Nature, some hewn out or pierced through for the use of the people and paid for by monarchs in the past. Beyond these, within the flanks of the mountains, such cold is felt even in the middle of summer that, unless the travellers fortify themselves in winter fashion by wearing many layers of clothing, they encounter an almost fatal hazard from the sudden change in air temperature, which lasts until they are able to quit these bowels of the mountains and freezing valleys.[3]

This may have been the route taken by St Birgitta on her pilgrimage from somewhere in central eastern Sweden to Nidaros (modern day Trondheim) around 1340 to visit the shrine of St Olof, the Norwegian king who was killed in 1030 at the battle of Stikklastaðir, and was widely venerated as a saint throughout Scandinavia. Very little is known about Birgitta's pilgrimage though her daughter Katarina testifies that she made the journey (of some seven hundred kilometres) on foot, rather than on horseback, and that the pilgrimage lasted thirty days.[4]

3 Translation from Foote 1996, p. 109.
4 AP pp. 14, 309, 579, mention the pilgrimage. See further Eklund 1975, p. 22. The journey can be compared with that undertaken from Vadstena to Nidaros by the

Where water could facilitate movement, forestland could obstruct it. Dense forests surrounded settlements, and there were vast tracts of forestland inhabited only by bandits and outlaws, such as those depicted in Ingmar Bergman's *Jungfrukällan* (*Virgin Spring*), a story that calls to mind one of the posthumous miracles associated with St Birgitta. The miracle tells of a bandit who had lived in the forest for six years, and who abducted two women from Denmark who were returning from the Birgittine abbey of Vadstena. He forced them to walk for a whole day through the 'dense, sharp, and thorny thicket' forest until they reached a well where he intended to drown them, but he took flight when he saw two women from a neighbouring farm walking nearby.[5] The unfriendly nature of the forest is also reflected in another miracle in which a seven-year-old girl in Finland gets lost in the forest 'where she wandered for ten days without food, and among wild animals like bears, wolves and different types of snakes, which she lay amongst at night'.[6] Another contemporary account of hostile forest terrain is given in the Old Norse *Sverris saga*. When the Norwegian king Sverri is forced into exile in 1177 he travels on foot from the Norwegian border to Dalarna in central Sweden, and later, having failed in an attempt to cross a lake on a makeshift raft, he and his companions wandered around in the forest living on a diet of birch twigs, sap and berries:

> In all these forests they could find no food other than fowl and elk. Much during this journey was difficult and troublesome for they travelled for long through uninhabited regions, and suffered hunger, cold and fatigue. They could not obtain horses or other means of faster transport; because it was the worst time of year when the snow was melting in the forests and the ice on the lakes. Sometimes they travelled over moorland or large marshes, and through impenetrable forest or dense woodland.[7]

More of the country was undeveloped than developed and most of the meagre population was chiefly engaged in farming, in the central and southern regions, near coasts, lakeshores and rivers. On the flat plains around lakes Mälaren and Vättern cereals were produced from the eleventh century onwards: barley, which was used for bread and beer-making, rye, and to a lesser extent, wheat; and oats was cultivated for horse fodder. In animal

Venetian pilgrim Pietro Querini in June–July 1432, which took forty days. See KLNM s.v. 'reiser'.

5 AP pp. 126–7.

6 AP pp. 138–9.

7 'Á þessum skógum öllum var engi fæðsla nema fugla hold ok elgja. Í þessari ferð gerðust margir hlutir erfiðligir ok þungligir, því at þeir fórun um óbyggðir mjök lengi ok þoldu bæði hungr ok kulða ok mikla mæði. Mátti þar ok ekki hesta við njóta eða annarra fararskjóta, því at í þann tíma váru verstar ferðir, er snjó leysti af skógum, en ísa af vötnum. Þeir fara stundum um mosa eða stórar mýrar ok þröngar merkr eða brota stóra.' Jónsson 1965, p. 23.

husbandry there were dairy cows and oxen for ploughing and for use as draught animals, but horses, pigs, sheep and goats were also reared. The varying terrain also offered a range of berries and fruits such as cowberry, bilberry, cranberry and cloudberry. The forests yielded timber, bark, charcoal and tar, as well as game such as elk, fallow deer, red deer and wild reindeer. Hare, fox, beaver, squirrel, marten, ermine and other creatures provided skins for clothing, many of which would have made valuable exports. Margareta Clausdotter's fifteenth-century life of St Birgitta contains an exotic description of the saint's worldly son Karl appearing before the pope at Montefiascone in 1370 dressed in a cloak made entirely of ermine skins. Round the head of each ermine was a bell, and as he moved the animals shimmered as if they were alive.[8] Other animals that were hunted included bears, which were treated as a nuisance because they caused great damage, and farmers had a statutory obligation to join in bear hunts. For catching wolves each farmer owned a net of a specified size; according to the provincial laws, bears and wolves could also be tamed if desired. Fishing was another key element in the medieval economy. Freshwater and seawater fish of all kinds were caught: perch, bream, pike, salmon, burbot, flounder, cod, herring, and catches were often preserved by salting, or especially in the north, by drying. Several of the Birgittine miracle stories give realistic glimpses of some of the hazards of fishing, especially in winter, through holes drilled in the ice.[9] One relates how Lake Vättern had an unusual tendency to swell violently at the time the ice was melting, and the water, driven by the wind, surged up causing small cracks to form in the ice, which could become very wide even when the ice was still more than one metre thick. One day when ten men and a little boy were fishing on the ice it began to crack and although six of the men got to shore the remaining men and the boy were stranded. Praying to St Birgitta, they suddenly saw the ice shift together again and ran to safety but the boy was unable to keep up with the men and fell in. Praying again for his deliverance, but fearing he was drowned, they suddenly saw him lifted safely to the surface.[10] Another miracle contains a similar story about a boy called Holmsten, who was stranded while fishing on thin ice, and as the ice broke up around him he seemed to be standing on the water for four or five hours until a boat could rescue him.[11] Another miracle story tells of a Norwegian couple who fell through the ice but when the woman prayed to St Birgitta, she was lifted miraculously to the surface and made her way to shore; and a further one tells of three Scandinavians in Tallinn who went fishing on the Baltic Sea and were blown towards a redoubt called Kaberneeme in heathen territory, where they were seized, stripped of all their possessions except their cloaks,

8 Annerstedt 1876.
9 On the Birgittine miracles see further Fröjmark 1992, pp. 31–43.
10 AP p. 114.
11 AP pp. 131–2.

and stones were tied round their necks and their hands tied behind their backs. They were taken far out to sea where one was thrown overboard. But his rope came loose from the stone and he floated calmly to the surface of the water, whereupon the heathens tried to kill him with their sticks; eventually, after hearing their pleas to St Birgitta for intercession, the captors agreed to free all three men. Their boat was transported back to land before darkness fell, without need of sail or oars.[12]

Besides agriculture, animal husbandry and fishing, another complementary source of wealth in medieval Sweden was mining. In Östergötland and Västergötland there were thriving centres of iron production and processing. The central region of Bergslagen was the largest producer of quarried iron; but the island of Utö in the Stockholm archipelago and the provinces of Närke, Uppland and Värmland and the Baltic islands of Åland were also producers of pig-iron. Birgitta's father, Birger Persson, owned iron mining lands in Järnberg (Iron hill) in Närke, which he bequeathed to his son-in-law, Birgitta's husband, in 1328.[13] Copper was mined in Stora Kopparberget (Great Copper hill), at Falun in Dalarna, which is first mentioned in 1288 and from where there are surviving privileges from 1347 and regulations from 1360; and later there is evidence of copper production at Åtvidaberg in Östergötland.[14] Small deposits of silver were found at the end of the twelfth century and by 1510 a significant amount was being mined in Sala in Västmanland. Birgitta shows an acquaintance with mining activities when she describes the sufferings of a soul in purgatory by means of three stages of metal processing, an image which has been interpreted as a real description, rather than an imagined metaphor, of a blast furnace or gold workshop.[15] She uses technical imagery on many other occasions, drawing no doubt in part on her actual experience, but also from the vast repository of learned and popular tradition, which included encyclopaedic writings and travellers' tales as well as visual images. God is described as a glazier in Book VI 44, who makes vessels out of ashes, just as God makes angels out of impure beings. Another image is the mechanical clock in Book VIII 48, which she may have borrowed from the German mystic Henry Suso's *Horologium sapientiae*.[16]

As the mining industry became established, more densely populated centres emerged and there was a steady growth of towns. The viking towns of Helgö and Birka in Uppland were replaced in the eleventh century by Sigtuna, the oldest existing medieval town, and followed in the twelfth century by Lödöse (near present-day Gothenburg), Visby on the Baltic island of Gotland, and the fortress settlements of Kalmar, Skara, Strängnäs, Uppsala, Västerås,

12 AP pp. 133–5.
13 DS no. 2658.
14 DS no. 964.
15 Book VI 7; see Götlind 1990.
16 See further Klockars 1966, pp. 228–33, and Götlind 1990.

Arboga and Örebro. The place-name element *köping* suggests a place where trading was conducted, and is seen in a number of towns like Köping, Norrköping, Söderköping and Linköping. By the end of the middle ages there were some forty towns, the largest being Stockholm and Visby which are estimated to have had over six thousand inhabitants each.[17] Some of the towns had been ancient assembly sites and some developed in conjunction with the spread of Christianity and became ecclesiastical centres; but they were also centres of trade and administration, each subject to strict control of trading conditions and regulation of weights and measures, and their trade monopolies were guaranteed by the prohibition of any form of trade outside the towns. Urban growth was also accelerated by the growth of the Hanseatic league, a loose federation of towns, trading posts and colonies, with Lübeck at its centre, which opened up commercial links with the entire Baltic region. Many arguments about relations between Sweden and the Hanseats still remain unresolved. The Swedes had an ambivalent relationship with these German traders who were in many ways superior to them in their administration, trading skills and vessels (especially the cog, which had an increased loading capacity, and better speed and safety for bulk cargoes).[18] The Germans stimulated trade but at the same time they had a monopoly which led to price fixing and they were more prosperous than the native traders and thus a cause of hostility and resentment. Swedish resignation to the economic pre-eminence of this merchant empire and the widescale export of Swedish commodities have been explained in terms of mutual interdependence: in exchange for privileges from the Swedes the Germans guaranteed necessary financial support. German merchants came to form as much as a third of the population of Stockholm, and they dominated the economic activity of the town. However, protection for Swedish traders was eventually enshrined in *Magnus Erikssons stadslag* (Magnus Eriksson's Town Law) c.1340, which stipulated that not more than half of the leading positions in the town could be held by Germans. As far as it is possible to identify nationality by names, it has been estimated that in Uppsala 40 per cent of the *borgare* (traders or craftsmen who owned town land) at the beginning of the 1350s were German, but one hundred years later the figure reached no more than 10 per cent.[19] German influence left its mark also on political and administrative institutions: town planning and administration was based on German models as was the establishment of trade guilds, and the Hanseats are also credited with new building and architectural techniques, such as the introduction of bricks, which, as Olaus Magnus noted in 1555, were used in the construction of Vadstena castle.[20] At the same time the Swedish language was overwhelmed with an

17 Lindkvist and Ågren 1985.
18 See further Kumlien 1953.
19 Lindkvist and Ågren 1985, p. 53.
20 Olaus Magnus 1555, Book XII ch. 1.

influx of Middle Low German words which affected all levels of discourse, and are still greatly in evidence today.

Exports from Sweden during the middle ages included iron, copper and animal products, and imports included salt, clothing, and luxury items such as spices and wine. For the funeral of Birgitta's father, Birger Persson, in 1328, three types of wine were obtained by the Stockholm merchant Konrad Arxö: a barrel of white wine costing 4 marks, a barrel of Rhine wine costing 8 marks and a red wine from La Rochelle costing 12 marks.[21] Wine was not, it seems, a major import and beer was more commonly drunk, even among the upper classes, as is suggested by the purchase of German beer for the Norwegian queen Margarethe in 1370.[22] Swedish beer was normally flavoured with bog myrtle or hops, as is illustrated at Vadstena monastery which received thirty 'handfuls' of myrtle in tithes in 1477 from a farm in Södermanland. Birgitta shows an intimate knowledge of brewing in some of her revelations, describing on one occasion the way in which a vat of ale rises and sinks as it is brewed, and how those who get too close to the vat are caused to sneeze fiercely or get a headache from the fumes.[23]

Houses in the medieval period probably consisted of a number of buildings arranged in a rectangular or square shape within an enclosure. Each of the buildings had its own function and the laws distinguish between locked and unlocked 'houses' or between the main house, the cook-house and cold-house, which Birgitta describes allegorically in a vision:

> But you, my bride, since you are made mine by divine law, should have three houses. In the first, there should be necessary things which benefit the body. In the second, clothes which cover the body externally. In the third the necessary tools for the upkeep of the house. In the first there should be three things: first bread, second drink, and third provisions. In the second house there should also be three things: first, clothes made of linen, second, wool and third, the work of silkworms. In the third there should also be three things: first, tools and vessels which should be filled with liquids, second, livestock with which physical objects may be transported, namely horses and donkeys and such animals, and third, equipment which sets in motion the living things.[24]

21 Nelson 1925–26.

22 Authén Blom 1992, p. 476.

23 Book IV 24. In an interesting example of editorial emendment, Swedish 'beer' is given as 'wine' in the Latin version of this vision, presumably to accommodate the different drinking preferences of a continental readership. See further Aili 1986.

24 'Tu ergo, sponsa mea, quia iure diuino mea facta es, oportet te habere tres domos. In prima debent esse necessaria, que intrant in corpus; in secunda vestes, que vestiant corpus exterius; in tercia necessaria instrumenta ad utilitatem domus. In prima debent esse tria: primo panis, secundo potus, tercio edulium. In secunda domo debent esse eciam tria: primo vestimentum lineum, secundo laneum, tercio, quod fit de opere vermium. In tercia domo eciam tria: primo instrumenta et vasa, que

There follows a lengthy exposition on these houses and their symbolism, illustrating the careful use of material things for spiritual gain, and there are again details which must reflect Birgitta's own experience of life in a noble household: drink is good for the digestion; meat and cheese add flavour to plain bread, and are better for the body and improve the blood; linen is comfortable against the skin and does not lose its colour in the wash; silk is expensive to buy; the vessels in the outhouse should contain water, oil and wine, and the other pots are for mustard and flour. She then continues:

> Can you understand what these things mean? The liquids signify indeed the good and evil thoughts of the soul. The good thought is namely like a choice oil and like a pleasant wine, but the evil thought is like a bitter mustard, for it makes the soul bitter and unquiet.[25]

Birgitta's revelations are a valuable source of information about life in medieval Sweden, and the above descriptions can be extensively supplemented by further examples: in Book I 33 her soul is described like a cheese in a vat which will grow into the shape of the vat, an echo of Job 10.10. She likens God to a washerwoman in Book III 30, a magpie in Book II 29 and to a chicken and goose in Book IV 16, an aquavit still in Book IV 24 and Book VIII 48, wine dregs in Book I 22; there are flowers and gardening in Book V int. 20 and Book VII 28, the rising of dough in Book IV 28 and Book IV 66; and fish spawning in Book II 19. Many of these images, in which she draws a metaphorical meaning out of a mundane detail, are not paralleled in the writings of other mystics, and they are an indication of the unrefined immediacy with which she expresses her visionary ideas, as well as a reflection on the lack of a vocabulary of mystical discourse available to her.[26] With such imagery Birgitta also shows with a sharply observant eye her proximity to nature and life at all levels, and she provides insights into the life of women of her class in fourteenth-century Swedish society.

Society

It is generally assumed – although there is no positive evidence – that Sweden was originally a tribal society with a clannish structure based on agnatic

implenda sunt liquore, secundo instrumenta viuencia, quibus promouentur corporalia, utputa equi et asini et similia, tercio instrumenta, que per viua mouentur.' (Book II 24) (Quotation from Bergh's concordance.)

25 'Numquid potes tu intelligere, quid ista significant? Liquores certe significant cogitaciones anime bonas et malas. Cogitacio enim bona est sicut oleum dulce et sicut vinum delectabile. Cogitacio vero mala est sicut sinapis amara, quia amaram facit animam et turbidam.' (Book II 27) (Quotation from Bergh's concordance.)

26 Compare, for example, the rich metaphorical language of the English mystics; see Riehle 1981.

kindred relationships. The extended family was the corner-stone of society and there was a strong sense of kindred solidarity, which had a practical impact in matters of inheritance and land tenure, consent in marriage, and legal disputes involving wergilds and blood vengeance. Corporate kinship was strong and the family remained a unifying social and political force until the end of the medieval period. But gradually a more differentiated state with discernible social hierarchies emerged, as is suggested even by the early eleventh-century runic inscriptions which commemorated not only the activities of wealthy yeoman farmers, or *bönder,* and leaders of military bands, but also of their 'house carles' who took part in viking expeditions to Russia and Byzantium. In this largely pre-literary period, Sweden was probably a federation of separate small kingdoms or provinces, referred to as *land* or *landsagor,* which were rather like the Anglo-Saxon kingdoms, each with its own laws and administrative organisation, and each at various points in the ascendancy. The provinces were in turn divided into smaller units, called the *härad* in Götaland and *hundare* in areas around Lake Mälaren (but later also called *härad*); and there are traces of further land divisions down to the *socken,* which eventually became identical with the parish division. As political communities grew, they developed their own laws and legal administration. Legal matters were dealt with at district and provincial *thing* or assemblies, a term which Birgitta uses in refererence to the Last Judgement, which she calls *placitum generale, allmännelikit thing,* demonstrating her ability to draw from her own experience of the law and transfer into a spiritual context.[27] The lawman, or *lagman,* had a key role at the *thing*; he was the guardian of the law and responsible for memorising and reciting it, for interpreting it in areas of dispute, and, with other members of the *thing,* proclaiming judgement on offenders. His office was one of the most prestigious in the land and held in very high esteem. Provincial laws are preserved from eleven districts of jurisdiction. They fall into two broad groups: the laws of the Svear, which comprised those from the central, northern and eastern areas, that is, the laws of Uppland and Södermanland, Västmanland, Hälsingland, Finland and Dalarna; and the laws of the Götar, which governed the southern regions of Östergötland, Västergötland and Gotland. From the Tiohärad district in Småland only the ecclesiastical section exists, and another provincial law, that of Närke (where Birgitta's husband Ulf was lawman) is mentioned in sources although no manuscript of it survives. It has been widely assumed that the provincial laws were passed down orally for several centuries before they came to be written down in the thirteenth and fourteenth centuries, and that consequently they reflect a continuity with ancient Germanic legal tradition. But this view has been challenged in recent years, and more emphasis has

[27] Books I 25 and VI 23. Birgitta's influences from Swedish law, and the extent of influence from Roman law, have not yet been examined in depth. See Klockars 1966, pp. 139–49.

been placed on the influence from Mosaic, Roman and canon law, and the way in which the provincial laws must have been codified less out of a desire to preserve ancient tradition and more as instruments of political expediency for the lawmakers and kings themselves.[28] The codification of the laws marked a stage in the transfer of an oral to a written culture and was done at the instigation of the king or of leading magnates in society, as is suggested by the letter of confirmation granting royal assent to *Upplandslagen* in 1296: according to the preface, Birger Persson, who was lawman of the district of Tiundaland in Uppland, had asked the king on several occasions to allow him to undertake a rationalisation of the existing law codes which were in use across the province; and after his commission, consisting of representatives from the Church, nobility, yeomen and spokesmen for the law, had 'assessed and scrutinised ancient law and formulated, compiled and overseen a new law, it was made known at the *thing* in the hearing of all whom it concerned'.[29] The laws had a unifying quality and each province had a sense of local distinctiveness, which is illustrated in the law of Västergötland which stipulated that the fine for homicide would be highest for the killing of a man from Västergötland, with a sliding scale downwards of fines for killing a man from Svealand or a man from Småland, a Dane or Norwegian, and a German or Englishman. There were also significant differences between the laws of the Svear and Götar, reflecting the two main power and political bases in the country; the Svear laws for instance are dominated by the supremacy of the noble classes, while those of the Götar share more in common with other Scandinavian laws outside Sweden.

The provincial basis of society, no doubt reinforced by geographical factors, continued to be reflected in the political, social and legal organisation throughout the entire medieval period and beyond, and the existence of strong and powerful provinces circumscribed the king's powers and made it difficult for central monarchic authority to be established. Royal power was weak also because, unlike the combined sacral and secular office of the pagan kings, it required the support of the Church, whose interests sometimes ran contrary to those of the crown. Furthermore, the king's power was checked by the people itself whose assent was required before a king could be accepted. This ancient tradition is described in Rimbert's ninth-century life of St Ansgar, the first missionary to Sweden, who had come to the viking town of Birka in 830 and 850.[30] Rimbert observes that the power of the Svear lay with the voice of the people, and what the people decided, the king must embody and confirm. As he suggests, the early Swedish people probably held the

28 Sjöholm 1988. Sjöholm's conclusions are, however, not uncontested; see reviews by T. Lindkvist in *Historisk tidskrift (Sweden)* 1989:3, pp. 413–20, and by S. Bagge in *Historisk tidskrift (Norway)* 1989:4, pp. 500–07.

29 Henning 1967, p. 11.

30 See for references *Medieval Scandinavia*, ed. Pulsiano, 1993, s.v. 'St Ansgar'.

traditional Germanic view of kingship, whereby the king was not sovereign, and the source of the law was the custom of the people. It was his function to declare and formulate this custom, to apply it in judicial decisions, and to enforce it by executive power, but in no way to override it. Thus the king was not absolute but his power was supported by his nobles who owed him certain well-defined duties and services, although it was not in his power to determine what these duties should be; indeed, he himself was bound by reciprocal obligations to them. Populist kingship never died out throughout the medieval period in Sweden and it was not until Gustav Vasa was elected in 1523 that a new outlook of absolutism and a descending theory of kingship became established.

Although the monarchy was elective, in general the royal succession followed dynastic lines. The first king of a united Sweden was Olof Skötkonung in the early eleventh century; after him followed a succession of weak rulers from the leading families of Svealand and Götaland, the Sverkers and the Eriks, who were locked in dynastic strife. The Folkung dynasty traditionally begins with Birger Jarl, who took the Swedish throne in 1250, and after him there were several decades of unrest, strife and fratricidal wars which reached a head in 1317 with the famous Banquet of Nyköping to which King Birger Magnusson invited his two brothers, Erik and Valdemar, ostensibly for a feast of reconciliation and rejoicing, but treacherously slaughtered them. The event is dramatically portrayed in the rhymed chronicle *Erikskrönikan*, written c.1320. Birger asks his brothers whether they remember how at Håtuna eleven years earlier they had deprived him of his power:

> Do you remember anything of the battle of Håtuna?
> Full well I remember it!
> This meeting will be no better than that!
> Now this time you shall follow me.
> Then they bound them both by the hands
> And led them both together
> Barefoot into the tower.[31]

The chaos that ensued, with Birger forced into exile, led to the nobles and commoners attempting to restore order and electing Magnus, the infant son of the murdered prince Erik, king in 1319.

In the early medieval period the Swedish kings supported themselves from the so-called Uppsala *öd*, the income from their estates, which were scattered throughout the country; and being the highest representatives of the law, they were also entitled to a share of the fines incurred in legal disputes. Originally, they were itinerant rulers who were accompanied by their *hird*, or retinue, and

31 'Mynnes jder nakot aff hatuna leek/ fulgörla mynnes han mik/ Thenne er ey bätre än hin/ j wardhin nw följia mik om sin/ The bundo tha beggis thera hender/ ok leddo them tha badha sender/ jnnan tornit barfötta.' Pipping 1963, pp. 220–1.

could demand hospitality of right from their subjects wherever they travelled. They could also muster the *ledung*, or levy, a primitive naval force, which was probably made up of weapon-bearing farmers and provided the means of defending the kingdom. But in the thirteenth century the levy ceased to be effective and it became necessary to have more regular armies of armed knights on land; and rather than equip them himself, the king offered exemption from taxation to all men who could supply themselves with armour and horses. Armed knights who had military obligations to the king in exchange for tax exemptions came to be included in the new class of nobility which was formally established in c.1280 when Magnus Ladulås issued the Alsnö statute which confirmed the economic standing of the nobility and defined its legal relationship to the crown.[32] The nobility, however, was probably the least cohesive group in society, and its members represented different factions whose interests often conflicted with each other – the old provincial aristocracy, the spiritual nobility, as well as the emerging military group of knights, some of whom came from the wealthy allodial farming class.

Apart from the king's retinue, there was originally little formal royal administration, and the only recognised office was held by the *jarl* (earl) whose status was almost equal to the king's and who acted as his official representative in Svealand, since the king had his residence chiefly in Götaland. However, during the thirteenth century, as a centralisation of power took place, the key offices of state came to resemble more closely those found elsewhere in Europe. The *jarl* was replaced after Birger Jarl's death in 1266 by *hertig* (duke), and reserved for men closely related to the king. The *rådsman* (councillor) presided over the *riksråd*, the council of state, which helped establish central royal power; and other offices of state included the *kansler* (chancellor) and *drots* (steward) who was in charge of royal legislation, and *marsk* (marshall) who had responsibility for military activity and command in war time. The class of free yeoman farmers, the *bönder*, was probably the largest social grouping, and they remained a powerful influence with a strong sense of their own freedom and equality in law, and a status in society that was publicly recognised by their having their own estate in the parliament, the Riksdag, when it was founded in the late fifteenth century. This class of tax-paying farmer-proprietors was a cornerstone of medieval society; it owned more land than any other class, took an active part in matters of local administration and justice, could participate in the election of the king and *lagman*, judges and clergy; its members could carry weapons, swear oaths and bring their own cases to the *thing*. As a class it was strong enough to influence the constitutional struggles between monarchy and nobility, and whereas in other countries the natural allies of the crown would have been the burghers, in Sweden support often came from the farmers. The strength of the farming

32 On the knight-class see Löfqvist 1935 and KLNM s.v. 'riddare'.

class was due in part to the fact that Sweden had never strictly been a feudal country, and the farmer never lost his position of free equality even when his social and economic status was at its most depressed. The fief system, which is so central to European feudalism, appears from the thirteenth century but without significant political and legal implications, because the fiefs could not be inherited and therefore fief holding remained temporary. Furthermore, between the nobility and the farmers there were initially few intermediate social gradations of any consequence, and therefore a tenurial pyramid never came into existence. Society was divided into those who paid taxes, mainly the free farming class, and those who did not, mainly the nobles, their tenants, and the crown's tenants.[33] Slavery had been abolished by fiat at the conversion to Christianity although in practice it continued to a limited extent for long after and was not formally abolished until 1335, when Magnus Eriksson on his royal progress, the *Eriksgata,* proclaimed that no child of a Christian parent should be a slave.

The Church

Simultaneously with the emerging secular organisation, the Church was also establishing itself, although the pace of conversion was slow. For a long time in the eleventh century small pockets of Christian communities lived alongside pagan Swedes; indeed, in his ecclesiastical history of the archbishopric of Hamburg–Bremen written in c.1070, Adam of Bremen records that the pagan temple in Uppsala was still being used for worship.[34] The new faith was introduced piecemeal, with some of the early kings vacillating between the old and the new faith, and foreign missionaries having only limited success. Some missionaries died as martyrs, including St Botvid, born in Södermanland, who became a Christian while on a journey to England, and worked towards converting his native province until his death around 1120 at the hand of a Wendish slave whom he had freed from captivity and intended to send back to his own land to preach the gospel.[35] Botvid appeared to Birgitta while she was in prayer in c.1340 and prophesied that she would experience spiritual things: 'Together with other saints, I have obtained God's grace for you to hear, see and feel spiritual things, and God's spirit will light up your soul.'[36] Brynolf, bishop of Skara 1278–1317, was another saint whose cult was growing in the fourteenth century. Birgitta compares Brynolf's saintliness to the alleged saintliness of his political opponent, King Magnus Ladulås, whose

33 See further Roberts 1967, p. 5, and *Medieval Scandinavia,* ed. Pulsiano, 1993, s.v. 'Feudal influences and tendencies'.
34 See further Foote and Wilson 1970, pp. 387–433.
35 For a study of the medieval Swedish saints see Lundén 1983.
36 AP pp. 81, 486, 619, and Ex. 72.

cult and credentials for sanctity she clearly does not accept.[37] The most celebrated native saint was the Swedish lawgiver, King Erik Jervardsson, who engaged on a crusade to convert the Finns, and was killed by a Danish pretender to the Swedish throne in 1160.[38] St Erik became a popular saint in the thirteenth century onwards, and was used as a symbol by the aristocracy's uprisings against some of the monarchs in the thirteenth century. In one of Birgitta's visions Christ tells her how the king – presumably Magnus Eriksson – was not worthy to build a house in his name – presumably Vadstena – and that his memory for posterity would not be like that of the Norwegian St Olof (d.1030) and St Erik.[39] Erik's name is also mentioned in the alliterative and rhythmic marriage formula given in *Upplandslagen*, which would have been used by Birgitta at her own marriage. The bride's nearest kinsman would give her away 'for honour and wife, for lock and keys, for half the bed, for her third legal share [i.e. her legal right at marriage], and for all that he owns in chattels, and for all that he can produce, apart from gold and servants, and for all the justice contained in Uppland's law and which St Erik gave; in the name of the Father, Son and the Holy Spirit'.[40] Another saint whom Birgitta would have known of and to whom she was distantly related was Ingrid of Skänninge, the aunt of Birger Persson's first wife, Kristina Johansdotter. Ingrid founded the Dominican nunnery of Skänninge, at the instigation of Petrus of Dacia, a Dominican cleric who had studied under Thomas Aquinas, and became interested in mysticism and allegory when he entered into correspondence with the German beguine Kristina of Stommeln in 1277.[41]

Under Pope Urban II bishops ceased to have a missionary role and the territorial Church was established. The Scandinavian metropolitan see in Lund was founded in 1104, and under Archbishop Eskil (1137–78), the nephew of the first archbishop of Lund and friend of St Bernard of Clairvaux, there were five fixed sees in Sweden – Skara, Linköping, Uppsala, Strängnäs and Västerås, followed by Turku (Åbo) in 1200 – and in 1164 Sweden got its own archbishopric in Uppsala. However, the Church of Rome was a remote power that exercised an influence which sometimes militated against national interests and as the Church in Sweden became established, it began to seek dispensations from lay authority in matters of finance and law, especially in areas where there was a conflict between common law and and canon law. During the course of the middle ages, the delicate balance between state and Church

37 Book II 30, Ex. 108.

38 On St Erik, see Cross 1957–61 and Nyberg 1995–96.

39 Ex. 27.

40 'til hedhers och hussfrudomis, til lasa ok nykla, til halwra siäng ok til lagha thridiungx i. allu han a. i. løsørum oc han afflæ fa utæn gull och hemæ hion. oc til allæn þæn ræt uplænzk lagh æru. oc hin hælghi erikær kungunger gaff. i. nampn faþurs ok sons ok þæs hælghæ andæ.' Henning 1967, pp. 81–2.

41 See further Morris 1999.

tilted back and forth; and alternately compromises were reached and concessions gained by one side at the expense of the other.

The Church gradually became one of the most powerful institutions and largest landholders in the country as bequests and donations poured in from all sections of the community. The Cistercians contributed much to the development of land, and their possessions reached their height in the early Folkung period. Their first monastery, a Cistercian house at Alvastra in Östergötland, with which Birgitta had close links during her formative years as a mystic, was founded in 1143 under Archbishop Eskil and received support from the Sverker dynasty; King Karl Sverker is alleged to be buried there. The Benedictines, Augustinians and Cluniacs had made no inroads into Sweden, but the mendicant orders became a major force in the thirteenth century. The Dominicans came to the episcopal sees, where they contributed to urban growth and town administration, and their principal Swedish foundations were at Sigtuna and Skänninge. Dominican tradition saw a cultural awakening and the establishment of closer ties with the continent; and the Dominicans were instrumental among other things in introducing the missal into Sweden and for promoting the cult of the eucharistic host. The Franciscans, who played a role in encouraging the development of lay piety, laid down roots mainly in the trading centres, such as Söderköping, Enköping and Stockholm – where indeed Magnus Ladulås was buried at the monastery of Gråmunkeholm (Grey Friars' Isle). At the end of the medieval period a Carthusian house was established in 1493 at Mariefred.

Sweden's spiritual awakening is glimpsed only fragmentarily in the written sources; but artworks and richly ornamented wall paintings in parish churches throughout the country provide an important reflection of the piety of the period.[42] Theology was taught to the people by means of preaching in the vernacular, instruction in the central tenets of faith and liturgy, and by the example of the saints. Individuals' part in salvation history was made clear by emphasising their part in the universal Church and in the scheme of creation; and the individual's part in the Christian scheme of things was underpinned by the seven sacraments. A small insight into early fourteenth-century debate on the sacraments is seen in the trial of a farmer named Botulf of Gottröra, a parish not far where Birgitta was born, who was burned as a heretic in 1311 for his denial of the real presence of God in the Eucharist. The story of this 'heretic' may have left an impression on the eight-year-old Birgitta.[43]

The Church brought Sweden into closer contact with Europe, as most of its clerics received their education in the universities and monastic centres of Europe: until the mid fourteenth century most Swedes went to Paris, after which Prague became the favoured university.[44] The clerics brought back with

42 On the wall paintings see *Medieval Scandinavia*, ed. Pulsiano, 1993, s.v. 'painting'.
43 See Aili, Ferm and Gustavson 1990, pp. 110–17.
44 On education abroad see Lindroth 1975.

them to Sweden new intellectual impulses, which are reflected in the early library collections, and which provided a foundation-stone for an emerging literature in the vernacular.

The early fourteenth century

By the beginning of the fourteenth century, the spiritual and lay aristocracy were fully established and their relationship to the crown was more or less fully defined. Much of the subsequent period covers the struggles between the crown, nobility and Church in their attempts to improve their stake in the limited financial resources of the country. Magnus Eriksson became king not just of Sweden in 1319 but also he inherited Norway and its dependencies on the death of Håkon V on 8 May 1319, and his neighbours – Russia, Scotland, Denmark and the Baltic states – all had political and economic interests to defend in the northern region.[45] The vastness of his kingdom and the fact that Norway had traditionally looked west in its foreign policy whereas Sweden had looked east, meant that his difficulties in consolidating the union were enormous. Yet with his election there appears to have been a genuine hope that a new era had dawned. His minority, 1319–32, was presided over by a council drawn from the aristocracy and Church; initially it was led by the regent Mats Ketilmundsson and then by *drots* Knut Jonsson of Aspenäs, who was Birgitta's uncle. Later, in 1348, Birgitta's brother Israel Birgersson took over the office. Magnus's mother, Ingeborg, took an active part in political intrigue during the minority, with her Danish favourite, Knut Porse; and although it was a period of relative quiet, political instability and factional disputes simmered and occasionally erupted into open hostility. Magnus was crowned 'king over Sweden, Norway and Skåne' in Stockholm on 22 July 1336. He inherited serious financial difficulties caused essentially by an imbalance between the nation's income and its expenses. Denmark – which was in even greater financial disarray at this time until Valdemar Atterdag (Day-Again) restored its fortunes in the 1340s – was forced to mortgage some of its territories, and the people of Skåne and Blekinge asked Magnus to take over the rule of the unpopular Johan of Holstein who was governing them. Magnus paid Johan 34,000 marks, pleased to gain a wealthy region with about 350,000 inhabitants, but to help raise the money to pay for the provinces, he taxed the nobility and Church savagely. A number of Swedish noblemen, including Israel Birgersson, were taken as hostages to live in Holstein during this financial enterprise. As he ran into further financial difficulties of his own, in 1336 Magnus was forced to mortgage Kalmar castle and district, and all of the provinces of Östergötland, Hälsingland, Gästrikland, Fjädrundaland, Dalarna, Närke and Värmland. The fragile economic system was further

45 Authén Blom 1992.

unable to support the newly developed state and military institutions and the king continued to increase taxes, and to bring more of the nobility under the tax-paying umbrella, to tax exports, to raise further loans – from the papacy, the Hanseats and German magnates – and to centralise trade and impose greater state controls on fiscal life.

Notwithstanding the financial uncertainties and the fragile political structures which threatened the kingdom's stability, Magnus undertook his rule when conditions seemed favourable for the setting up of a united and fully consolidated kingdom, and the early decades of Magnus's reign were quiet and marked by a number of legal reforms and a cultural awakening. He was responsible for the codification of all the provincial laws into a single, national law, *Magnus Erikssons landslag*, in c.1347, which became the embodiment of the constitutional basis of society. He also developed closer contacts with Europe. In marrying Blanche of Namur in 1336, the daughter of a Flemish duke, he was forging a bond with one of the most politically developed and advanced states in Europe; and the new queen no doubt brought with her new continental ideas about kingship and government. Magnus's political programme may have been influenced by the treatise on kingship, written c.1280 by Giles of Rome for Philip the Fair of France, and paraphrased in Swedish c.1345 under the title *Um styrilse konunga ok höfdhinga* (*On the government of kings and leaders*). It is one of the most important monuments of early Swedish pre-Birgittine prose, and is thought to have been written for Magnus's two sons, Erik and Håkan.[46] It argues for absolutism rather than group government by an aristocracy; and shows how kingship by inheritance is to be preferred to kingship by election. It also contains a moralistic discourse on how the prospective king should be educated, listing virtues to be pursued and vices to be avoided, and it discusses what demands should be made on the court and the king's subjects.

The Swedish Church and magnates were prepared to give the new king a chance to show he was a *rex iustus* and for the earliest years of his reign at least he succeeded in some of the aims for which the regency government had prepared him. But without a strong power base, a fixed court, a healthy economy, a loyal aristocracy and a supportive Church, it was difficult for him unconditionally to establish his authority. Although he did appear to be attracted by European political ideas of government, Magnus Eriksson was too weak or simply too unlucky to reform the institution; and the Swedish monarchy continued to follow the elective principle based on mutual consent on the part of the king and those who elected him. The old aristocratic families, such as Birgitta's, whose members included *lagmän* and leading ecclesiastics, had powerful positions in society, and the king was beholden to them; if he was not in a strong enough position, politically or economically, the aristocracy

46 It is edited by Moberg 1984.

could legitimately overthrow him, as indeed was the case with Magnus in 1362. He had divided his kingdom between his two sons, and when the younger son Håkan reached his majority in 1355 he was declared king of Norway, leaving his brother without power or influence, and thus lured into conspiracy with the leading magnates against his father. In particular there was opposition among the magnates to the king's favoured adviser, Bengt Algotsson, which led to open conflict in 1356, in which Erik, aided by Magnus's brother-in-law, Albrekt of Mecklenburg, forced his father to relinquish parts of his Swedish kingdom. Bengt Algotsson was banished from Norway and Sweden, and a council of state, consisting of members of the aristocracy, was from then on consulted in matters involving both kings.[47] Other parts of the kingdom were further weakened in this power struggle: Albrekt of Mecklenburg gained control of parts of the south, and thereby a political foothold in the country, and the Danish king, Valdemar Atterdag, who was anxious to regain the southern territories which formerly had been under the Danish crown, entered an alliance with Magnus and his son Håkon, against Erik and Albrekt. Erik however died shortly afterwards, in 1359, and during the following political negotiations, Magnus found himself isolated when Albrekt and Valdemar agreed terms. Sweden lost the southern provinces in the ensuing conflict, and Valdemar then turned his attention to the rich Baltic island of Gotland.

Danish influence in Sweden had increased significantly, and Magnus's position looked more and more vulnerable. His relations with the aristocracy grew increasingly bitter, especially since the nobles had cherished the possession of the southern provinces. By his ill-fated alliance with Valdemar, Magnus had lost the southern region, and the aristocracy now criticised him openly for what they regarded as his deceitful policy. They sided with his son, Håkan, and deposed Magnus in 1362. But shortly afterwards father and son were reconciled and they sought support from Valdemar, which was cemented by the marriage of Håkon with Valdemar's daughter Margarethe. Magnus, king of Sweden, and Håkan, king of Norway, had established a formal tie with Valdemar, king of Denmark, and in doing so, they obtained protection from the opposition of the Swedish magnates, but more importantly, their alliance meant that the long-term dynastic preconditions for the union of the three Scandinavian countries under one ruler were created.[48] The unhappy events at the end of Magnus's reign heralded a new period of upheaval which led to Margarethe taking over the crown of a unified Scandinavia in 1397 which was to last for over a hundred years.

47 On Bengt Algotsson see further Klockars 1976, pp. 129–33.
48 This point is made by Carlsson and Rosén 1962, p. 215.

Birgitta's parentage; her date and place of birth

During the early years of her life, Birgitta witnessed far-reaching changes in the government, law and spiritual life of her country. Her own family was actively involved in many of these changes and her life is therefore firmly rooted in her Swedish background. Birgitta's forebears were from Uppland and they had a reputation for piety, strict devotion and generous endowments to the Church. Some had close ties with the Uppsala archbishopric and cathedral school: her father's uncle, Jakob Israelsson, was archbishop of Uppsala, and his brother, Israel, and cousin, Andreas And, both held the post of provost at Uppsala cathedral, and there were other cousins who were canons and bishops in the Uppsala diocese.[49]

Birgitta's father, Birger Persson, was probably born around 1265. The first mentions of him are in 1280, and the sources refer to him as knight, councillor of state and *lagman*. He was a major author of the codification and revision of *Upplandslagen*, the law of his province, which was confirmed by the king in 1296, and he appears to have held the office of *lagman* from around the beginning of the fourteenth century, with a break between 1316 and 1318; and in 1319 in this office he took part in the election of three-year-old Magnus Eriksson as king. He was pious in his devotions; he confessed every Friday and was a generous benefactor to the Church.[50] His first wife, Kristina Johansdotter, who came from another godfearing noble family, died childless in 1293; and on her deathbed she is said to have granted freedom to several male and female slaves.[51] Birger then married Ingeborg Bengtsdotter, daughter of *lagman* Bengt Magnusson, whose family came from Östergötland and belonged to the so-called 'lawman's branch' of the Folkung dynasty.[52] The fact that *Margareta Clausdotters krönika* suggests that Ingeborg's father was the king's brother, though wrong, is suggestive of the close links between this family and that of the king and it may partly explain why Birgitta is sometimes referred to as *princessa* in the source materials.[53] Ingeborg's forebears were also eminent magnates; her father was *lagman* in Östergötland, and a member of the king's council in 1288; he undertook a pilgrimage in 1289 and died c.1294. Her mother, known as Sigrid the Fair (apparently Birger Jarl had been entranced by her beauty), died in 1289 and was buried in Skänninge. Ingeborg is first mentioned on 20 February 1301, which is the date of her

49 See Klockars 1976, on the context of her Swedish background.

50 AP p. 472.

51 DS no. 1095.

52 Ingeborg's name is given erroneously as Sigrid in the canonisation materials (AP p. 74) which is in fact the name of her mother. On all the genealogies see Wernstedt 1957–65.

53 She is also referred to by Alphonso of Jaén as being descended from 'the Goths', to highlight her royal birth and connections. See Undhagen 1978, p. 6.

marriage to Birger Persson.[54] On her deathbed in 1314 she left bequests to Uppsala cathedral and a number of monasteries. Both Birger, who died on 3 April 1327, and Ingeborg were buried in Uppsala cathedral, where they founded a chantry chapel and asked for three masses to be said each week; they also made gifts to religious houses.[55]

The official account of Birgitta's life, in the *vita* and canonisation documents, relates incidents presaging her birth and future spiritual gifts. When her maternal grandmother visited the Cistercian convent of Sko in Östergötland she was treated disdainfully by one of the nuns because of her apparent pride; the nun subsequently had a dream in which she was told that the woman's progeny would be imbued with divine grace. Again, when her mother Ingeborg was pregnant with Birgitta, she was miraculously rescued from a shipwreck by the king's brother, Duke Erik Magnusson.[56] The next night a person in shining garments appeared in Ingeborg's dream and told her she had been saved because of the good she bore in her womb. On the night of her birth an elderly priest in a parish near to where her parents lived received a vision in which the Virgin, holding a book, told him that a daughter had been born to Birger Persson 'whose wonderful voice will be heard throughout the world'.[57]

The exact date and place of her birth have been the subject of debate. Birgit Klockars has examined a letter written by Birger Persson's brother, Israel, on 20 May 1302, in which he bequeaths an estate to his cousin Andreas And. After Andreas's death the estate was to fall to Birger Persson; but in the event that Birger died childless before Andreas – 'quod absit' ('which may not happen') – Andreas could give it away for the benefit of all their souls.[58] Klockars argues that the phrase 'quod absit' suggests that Birger was still childless at the time the letter was written but was expecting a child. She further refers to the story of the ship in which Duke Erik and Ingeborg were travelling together when it was wrecked, suggesting that they may have been travelling to celebrate the coronation of the duke's brother, Birger, which took place in the late autumn, 1302. She concludes, reasonably, that Birgitta was born some time soon after this, around New Year 1303.[59]

Tradition has always associated the place of her birth with Finsta in the parish of Skederid in Sjuhundra district in Uppland; *Margareta Clausdotters krönika* mentions her birthplace as Finsta; in the fifteenth century there was a chapel to the saint there; and today Finsta is firmly placed on the tourist map

54 DS no. 1336.
55 DS no. 2586.
56 This event is portrayed in a wall-painting in Tensta church, Uppland. See Lindgren 1991, p. 24.
57 AP pp. 74–5, 473–4.
58 DS no. 1364.
59 Klockars 1976, pp. 29–33.

of Sweden. Finsta was certainly one of several estates belonging to Birger Persson, who was one of the foremost landowners in Sweden at the time. But it was not his main patrimony and Klockars has cast doubt on whether he did in fact live there at the time of Birgitta's birth.[60] He allegedly purchased the estate from a cousin by the name Ragnhild Erlandsdotter in 1283; but in 1296 he exchanged the main property and a mill, with a property and mills belonging to a certain canon Rörik Matsson at Skällnora, in the neighbouring district of Fresta. In 1301 Birger sealed the will of a member of his household at Finsta, suggesting that at least part of the estate at Finsta was still in his possession on this date, and also in 1301 the king donated a portion of the estate to him 'for loyal service'. Thus it is unclear exactly how much of the entire estate was in Birger Persson's possession in 1303, and there remains an element of doubt that Birgitta was indeed born there. This doubt is further compounded in the canonisation documents where the place of birth is given as 'Frastad', which might be interpreted as Fresta, the name of the property Birger acquired in 1296.[61]

Like all Swedes of the time Birgitta's life is closely related to nature and the seasonal cycle; she knows all aspects of life on a large estate from first hand knowledge; she knows the geography of her native province of Uppland as well as Östergötland where she married; she knows the political tensions and intrigues between the magnates in these regions, which were the heart of the old power bases; her family background meant that she was immersed in legal practice and custom at a time when it was undergoing enormous reform; she represented the traditional aristocracy and lent support to group government by the aristocracy, but she was on close terms with the monarchy. Her family ties with the Church were good, and she was receptive to the new currents of religious thought and lay piety which were reaching Sweden in the fourteenth century. Brought up by, and among, the leading political, legal and Church magnates of her day she was uniquely prepared for her life as a reformer and prophet and as the woman who would put Sweden on the European map.

60 Klockars 1976, p. 33. See too Rahmqvist and Skoglund 1986, pp. 162–4.
61 AP p. 11. One manuscript gives 'Fristad'.

II

Childhood, Marriage and Motherhood

. . . quasi aquila prouocans ad volandum pullos suos et super eos volitans . . .

. . . like an eagle, encouraging her chicks to fly and soaring over them . . .

(Birger Gregersson's *Vita;* Collijn 1946, p. 17)

BIRGITTA was the second oldest of seven children born to Birger and Ingeborg, but only she, her younger sister Katarina, who was born shortly after her, and the youngest child, Israel, grew to maturity.[1] The event of major significance in her childhood was the death of her mother on 21 September 1314, when she was aged about eleven. She and her sister then moved away from Uppland to live with their aunt, Katarina Bengtsdotter, at Aspenäs in Östergötland. Katarina was married to Knut Jonsson, a leading magnate from the Aspenäs family who had a position of influence at court and who was for some period *drots*. She appears to have had a considerable role in Birgitta's upbringing; having nurtured and educated her 'from infancy', which suggests that she might have fostered Birgitta as a young child even in the years before her mother's death.[2] Whether or not this was the case, the loss of her mother must have been keenly felt and strengthened Birgitta's desire to seek maternal comfort vicariously in the Virgin Mary.[3]

1 The name Birgitta (Latin Birgitta, Brigida), from the Irish saint Brigid of Kildare (d.525), had probably entered Scandinavia through Norway, which had early missionary contacts with the Celtic and Anglo-Saxon Church. Although there are some mentions in pre-fourteenth-century sources, including a runic inscription in Västergötland and the name of the wife of Earl Birger Brosa of the Folkung dynasty, it was not, it appears, an especially common name; and it was only after Birgitta's death that the name grew in popularity.

2 AP p. 473.

3 For further examples of personal deprivation see Bynum 1992, p. 197.

Plate 2. A childhood vision depicted on a panel of the reredos of Appuna church, not far from Vadstena, by a German artist, c. 1450–75. Christ appears to the ten-year-old Birgitta, saying 'Dochter su wo ik gheplaget byn' (Daughter, see how tortured I am') and she replies: 'O leue her we hattet . . .' (O dear Lord, who has [done this to you?]' Source: Photo: M. Bratt-Gustafsson, 1964, Antikvarisk-Topografiska Arkivet, Stockholm.

Childhood visions

A number of stories about Birgitta's childhood in the *vita* testify to her special gifts and supernatural endowment, the various stages of her spiritual awakening at specific ages, and her gift for prayer and humility:

> *How she was as if mute for three years.* And so, as the girl Birgitta advanced in age, she was as if mute for three years and did not have the use of speech. Her parents were in much doubt about this, believing that she was mute; but at the end of the third year, she so fully obtained the use of speech that she did not speak in the babbling manner of infants, but, contrary to what is natural at such an age, she pronounced the words perfectly.

. . . *How, as a girl, she saw wonderful things.* And so, when the girl Birgitta, the bride of Christ, was six years old, she once saw, while wide awake, an altar just opposite her bed and a lady in shining garments sitting above the altar. The lady had a precious crown in her hand and said to her 'Birgitta, come!' And hearing this, she got out of bed, running to the altar. The lady said to her: 'Do you want to have this crown?' She nodded, and the lady put the crown on her head so that Birgitta then seemed to feel the crown touching her head. But when she returned to bed, the vision disappeared; and yet she could never forget it.

How she saw Christ crucified. Round about her tenth year, on a certain occasion she heard a sermon preached in church about the Passion of our Lord Jesus Christ. The following night she saw, in a dream, Christ as if he had been crucified in that same hour, and he said to her: 'In such a way I was wounded.' And she thought that this had happened at that hour and answered in her sleep: 'Lord, who has done this to you?' Jesus Christ answered: 'Those who scorn me and neglect my love: they have done this to me.' Then she came to herself; and from that day, she felt such affection for the Passion of Christ that she could rarely recall the memory of it without tears.

How an unknown girl was seen sitting beside her. Moreover, one day in her twelfth year, she was intent upon some handiwork involving silk and gold in the company of other girls of her own age; and she felt much anxiety because she could not do her work as she wished. Her maternal aunt – a very devout and praiseworthy lady into whose keeping Birgitta had come after her mother's death – walked into the house and saw an unknown girl sitting beside Birgitta and doing the same piece of work with her. And since, at her entrance, that unknown girl had disappeared, the aunt then asked Birgitta who the girl was that had been working with her. Birgitta answered that she had seen no one. Her aunt, however, inspected the work and found that it was so finely done that anyone looking at it might well understand that it was not the work of a girl of such a tender age but was something divine. Therefore this lady herself used to preserve it among her relics as something from God.

How her aunt found Birgitta praying at night. One night, the aunt secretly entered the bedroom of the young girls and found Birgitta kneeling naked before her bed and praying with tears. The aunt, suspicious of girlish frivolity, ordered someone to bring a stick. But when she had begun to extend the stick to strike Birgitta, at once it broke into tiny pieces so that the aunt, when she saw this, wondered greatly and said: 'What have you done, Birgitta? Have the women taught you some fallacious prayers?' The young girl answered with tears: 'No my lady; but I arose from bed to praise him whose custom is always to help me.' And her aunt said: 'Who is he?' To which the young girl said: 'The Crucified One whom I saw.' And because of this, from that day her aunt began to love and venerate her more fervently.

How she saw the devil. Not long after, when Birgitta was wide awake and playing with other girls, the devil appeared to her with a hundred hands and feet and most deformed in every way. Completely terrified, she ran to her bed, where the devil appeared to her again and said to her: 'I can do nothing unless the Crucified One were to permit it.' Since the women had seen and were asking what it was that had happened to her and why she was so completely terrified, she answered: 'A certain anxiety seized me.' And those women asked nothing more of her. But after some years, her aunt came and heard from her the whole truth and instructed her to hide her visions in silence and to be of good hope, to love God intimately and to beware of all frivolity.[4]

4 '*Quomodo tribus annis quasi elinguis erat.* Puella igitur Brigida etate proficiens quasi elinguis erat per triennium, non habens vsum loquendi, de quo multum dubitabant parentes credentes, quod esset muta, sed illa in fine tercij anni sic plene obtinuit loquendi vsum, vt non balbuciendo more infancium loqueretur, sed perfexte contra naturam tante etatis verba resonaret. . . . *Quomodo adhuc puella vidit amiranda.* Puella igitur Brigida, sponsa Christi, cum iam septimum annum attigesset etatis, vidit semel vigilans ex opposito lecti sui altare et quandam dominam super illud vestibus fulgidis sedentem et habentem in manu preciosam coronam, que dixit ei: "O Brigida, veni!" Illa autem hoc audiens surrexit de lecto currens ad altare, cui dixit domina: "Visne habere istam coronam?" Cui annuenti dicta domina imposuit coronam in capite, ita quod sensit tunc Brigida quasi circulum corone caput suum tangere. Redeunte vero ea ad lectum, disparuit visio, quam tamen numquam poterat obliuisci. *Quomodo vidit Cristum crucifixum.* Circa dedicum annum cum quadam vice audiuisset predicari de passione Domini nostri Jhesu Christi in ecclesia, nocte sequenti vidit in sompnis Christum quasi eadem hora crucifixum et eii dictentem: "Taliter plagatus sum," et illa putans, quod ea hora hoc factum esset, respondit in sompno: "O Domine, quis tibii fecit istud?" Respondit Jhesus Christus: "Illi, qui me contempnunt et negligunt caritatem meam, ipsi michi hoc fecerunt." Tunc illa rediens ad se ipsam tantum affectata ab illa die ad passionem Christi, vt raro sine lacrimis recordaretur memoriam eius. *Quomodo puella ignota fuit visa considere illi.* Jtem duodecimo anno cum vna dierum intenderet labori manuum de serico et auro cum suis puellis coeuis et multum anxiaretur animo, quia opus suum facere nequiret ad votum, matertera sua, in cuius custodia post mortem matris deuenerat, domina multum deuota et laudabilis, ingressa domum vidit virginem ignotam considentem Brigide et facientem idem opus cum ea, cumque ad introitum suum disparuisset illa puella ignota, quiesiuit tunc matertera ab ea, quenam esset puella illa, que laborabat simul cum ea. Respondit Brigida se neminem vidisse, matertera vero intuens opus sic subtiliter illud factum jnuenit, vt cernentibus daret intelligi non esse opus puelle tam tenere etatis sed diuinum. Jdeo domina ipsa illud inter reliquias suas tamquam duiunum aliquid solebat obseruare. *Quomodo matertera jnuenit Brigidam orantem de nocte.* Nocte quadam predicta matertera ingressa latenter cubiculum virginum jnuenit Brigidam nudam flexis genibus stantem ante lectum et cum lacrimis orantem. Que suspicata de leuitate virginis jussit afferri virgam, quam cum illa extendere cepisset, vt Brigidam percuteret, statim virga comminutata est in frusta minima, jta quod dicta matertera hoc videns vehementer admirata dixit: "Quid fecisti, Brigida, numquid docuerunt te mulieres aliquas fallaces oraciones?" Respondit virgo cum lacrimis: "Non, domina mea, sed surrexi de lecto, vt laudarem eum, qui me semper adiuuare solet." Et matertera dixit: "Quis", inquit, "est ille?" Cui virgo ait: "Crucifixus ille, quem vidi." Et propter hoc ex illa die matertera eius cepit eam feruencius diligere et venerari. *Quomodo vidit diabolum.* Non longe post, cum Brigida staret ludendo cum puellis, vidit vigilando diabolum quasi habentem

Such stories are extremely stereotypical, and probably have little historical content. They serve to a large degree as prefigurations of her later life, and convey standard hagiographical patterns showing her gradual progression from infant to adolescent. Furthermore, they encapsulate themes and motifs that later came to play an important part in her mystical life. Already at the age of three she is distinct from other children, the 'old child' who shows gravity and verbal maturity, her initial muteness having caused her parents concern for her normality.[5] She has her first vision proper at the traditional age of seven, an age at which she probably would have received her first communion and been made aware of the social roles expected of her, having on the one hand the model of her mother to follow, to make a good marriage and become mistress of a large household, but also perhaps glimpsing the spiritual life as a possible alternative, with the Virgin as the female role model. The image of the Virgin placing a crown on her head in this first vision can be seen as a call to the spiritual life, with the crown representing the crown of virginity; this is a motif that she uses frequently in her revelations, and is represented symbolically in the characteristic head-dress of the Birgittine nuns. In this experience it is also emphasised that she is wide awake, thus indicating that her special gift cannot be confused with dream. Her next preternatural experiences coincide with the age of puberty, and perhaps also the time of her mother's death. They include another dominant subject for her, that of the suffering Christ. This time the experience takes the form of a dream, but with all the immediacy of the present time, such that she becomes a participant in the drama itself. We see too in this experience how it is provoked by a sermon, an anticipation of the great importance Birgitta comes to attach to preaching later in her life. Clearly she had little difficulty in becoming rapt in spirit, and her experience of the Passion was accompanied by tears, a feature she shares with other mystics.[6] Night-time prayer is another activity that recurs throughout her adult life, and the sources tell how she often spent whole nights deep in devotion. A further adumbration of her future life is reflected in the reaction of

centum manus et pedes in omnibus deformissimum, que perterrita cucurrit ad lectum suum, vbi iterum apparens illi diabolus dixit ei: "Nichil possum facere, nisi permiserit crucifixus." Cum vidissent mulieres, quidnam esset querentes quod sibi accidisset aut cur sic esset perterrita, respondit illa: "Quidam dolor cordis apprehendit me." Et ille mulieres nichil amplius ab ea requirebant. Post aliquos vero annos matertera sua veniens audiuit ab ea totam veritatem et precepit illi, vt visa silencio tegeret et esset bone spei, et intime Deum diligeret et caueret sibi ab omnj leuitate.' AP pp. 75–7. Translation based on A.R. Ketzel in Tjader Harris 1990, pp. 72–4.

5 On the motif of the 'old child' and other childhood manifestations of sainthood, see Weinstein and Bell 1982, pp. 19–47.

6 Tears are presented as a sign of her devotion, and as part of her penitential observance, but they are never mentioned excessively, unlike, for example, Marie of Oignies, for whom they are her nourishment, or the perpetually tearful Margery Kempe. See Atkinson 1983, pp. 59–65. Birgitta has revelations on types of tears in Books IV 13 and IV 81.

her aunt to her childhood experiences. It reflects a genuine initial scepticism, fear and awe, and an intuition that the experiences should be kept secret; eventually, however, Katarina becomes the young girl's confidant and mentor, in the same way as her male confessors, who initially showed caution, later gave her their wholehearted support.

However stereotyped the childhood experiences may be, in a real sense they highlight the tension between the worldly and the spiritual life. From an early age young girls of noble birth would have been aware of the expectations offered by the life that lay ahead of them – marriage and motherhood at an early age, the risks of childbirth, having to manage large households and estates, and the possibility of early death or widowhood. The prospect of escaping the rigours of the secular life and of finding solace in religion and a retreat into a cloistered life must have had its appeal; but if a girl did choose this path, there were many years of hard preparation – curbing her natural instincts, learning self-mortification, humility and obedience, denying herself food, drink and ordinary material comforts, and renouncing her family and home. Neither the secular nor the spiritual life was easy if it was pursued at its ideal level, and although most girls enjoyed the worldly life, yet some clearly felt the call to asceticism in early childhood.[7] In Birgitta's case, although she felt such a call, as is suggested by her childhood visions, it could only be acted upon within the framework of the worldly life for which she was prepared, and this meant marriage.

Marriage

In 1316, Birgitta and her sister Katarina, aged thirteen and twelve respectively, were both given in marriage to two noble brothers, Ulf and Magnus Gudmarsson, sons of Gudmar Magnusson, a knight and councillor of state who was also lawman in Västergötland.[8] Their mother, like Birgitta's, was distantly related to the royal Folkung family. Although there is no record of a close friendship between the two families, both fathers are mentioned in state

7 Weinstein and Bell 1982, p. 45, have written: 'to a girl just beginning to grope toward femininity the ideal of sainthood was a siren call beckoning her to a life so extreme that even contemporaries were prone to look upon it as madness, unless and until she could demonstrate that here was a divine madness confounding the wisdom of the world. She did this through the sheer force of her personality – sometimes, but not always supported by miracles and signs – which turned her antagonists into supporters and the rest of the world into believers.'

8 The date 1316 is suggested by Klockars 1976, p. 43, on the basis of the stipulation of twelve years minimum in canon law, the age Birgitta's younger sister must have reached by that year. Birgitta must therefore have been at least, and possibly not more than, thirteen at her marriage. Apart from a four-line testimony by Katarina's and Gudmar's daughter Ingeborg (AP p. 65), nothing is known – surprisingly perhaps – of this couple's subsequent life. The present factual account draws largely on Klockars' important archive work.

affairs together on occasion in early fourteenth-century documents, and both probably thought it expedient to consolidate their political and financial interests by a double marriage between their children.

Ulf, who was the younger of the two sons, and who had lost his father at about the same time as Birgitta lost her mother, was five years older than his bride. The occasional glimpses of him in the political domain, given in diplomatic materials throughout the first decades of the fourteenth century, record his involvement in property deals and affairs of state and describe him as a leading member of the council of state and lawman of Närke province. They are insufficient to build a portrait of him, as are the descriptions of him in the canonisation materials which are sparse and stereotypical and portray him as a good and godfearing husband: 'a powerful, wealthy and prudent nobleman', a 'handsome knight' and a 'leader in the king's court'.[9]

Birgitta must have known from her earliest years that marriage was an inevitability for her: the marriage of the only two surviving daughters of one of Sweden's most eminent families would have ensured protection of Birger Persson's wealth and interests and brought the promise of new generations who would perpetuate the family name. Certainly her childhood visions do not suggest any opposition to marriage, but her daughter, Katarina Ulfsdotter, giving a predictably traditional and retrospective response, later testified that her mother repeatedly told her that she had entered into marriage reluctantly, that her family had 'compelled, coerced and forced her', and that she would have preferred death to marriage.[10] If Birgitta was a reluctant bride, other witness accounts do not say so, and there is no suggestion that she came into conflict with her parents or prospective husband over the marriage.

Katarina's expedient response about her mother's desire for chastity belies the gradual erosion in the later middle ages of the traditional perception of marriage as necessarily an inferior state, which was in particular a result of the upsurge in the female mystical tradition, and was forcing the Church to modify its attitude towards devout married women. The traditional view of the three states of womanhood, virginity, marriage and widowhood, placed special emphasis on virginity as the only state in which a woman could hope to achieve true union with the divine and at the same time recognition by the Church. Marriage, which involved sexual activity, was regarded by the Church as incompatible with a woman's aspirations to live a godly life of the highest kind. But where a girl was married, she could be a candidate for sainthood on certain conditions: if her marriage was not consummated, or if she lived with her husband in continence, or indeed, if she was forced into marriage and sexual activity against her will. Those girls who were compelled into marriage normally demonstrated their opposition by extreme physical

9 AP pp. 504, 64, 482.
10 AP p. 305.

behaviour, whether starvation, absconding or self-mutilation.[11] Married life, which necessarily involved sexual experience, *could* offer a path to sainthood, as is demonstrated by St Birgitta and by St Elisabeth of Hungary, in whose canonisation process in 1234 there are statements to suggest that, far from being coerced into marriage, it was love that united her with her husband.[12] But since women were classified and judged by the Church in terms of their sexual condition – in other words, whether their chastity was preserved or not – it was harder for them to achieve saintliness than for men, and as saints their image was always likely to be tarnished for their having had carnal relations.[13] Although the married status was gaining acceptability and the Church was finding ways of refining its requirements for sanctity, greatest importance was nevertheless still attached to the higher state of virginity, as is suggested at the canonisation process of St Caterina of Siena in 1411–16, during which a Dominican advocate of the saint declared that she was superior to St Birgitta in not having been married.[14] In general terms, then, in spite of a brief acceptance of married female saints by the Church, which probably coincided with Birgitta's canonisation, marriage, whether it was willingly or unwillingly entered into, remained an obstacle towards sanctity for women.

Birgitta's views on marriage

Birgitta's attitude towards marriage – though not of course necessarily her own marriage – is articulated later in her life in her revelations.[15] She argues that the traditional hierarchy of virginity, marriage and widowhood are all worthy and virtuous states provided they are accompanied by spiritual purity, which is achievable in any state, and should be sought continually by all women and men, whatever their social standing.[16] In all human relations, at whatever level, purity of purpose, intention, and action are all essential precepts to follow, as is shown by the example of Peter who became an apostle while he was still married.[17] She broadly echoes St Paul's teaching that marriage is a concession to human weakness, and that although it is the most lowly of the three states, it is necessary since it regulates carnal impulses. Because chastity of mind is more important than physical virginity, a married woman can be better than a virgin if she lives a spiritually chaste life; thus

11 The most obvious fourteenth-century example is Caterina of Siena. See further on this point Weinstein and Bell 1982, pp. 73–99, and in particular on Birgitta, Børresen 1991, pp. 63–6.
12 Vauchez 1993, p. 185.
13 See further on these arguments Shahar 1983, pp. 65–125, Duby 1994.
14 See Vauchez 1988, pp. 445–6.
15 See further Losman 1983, Nieuwland 1991, Fogelqvist 1993, pp. 233–9.
16 For example: Ex. 20, Books IV 53, V int. 12, VI 111.
17 Book VIII 1.

although a virgin would be ideal as abbess of Vadstena monastery, a widow with proven experience of life would be more pleasing to God than a proud virgin.[18] With utterances such as these, Birgitta elevates the status of married women and widows and equates them with the state of virginity.

In medieval writings, women were commonly presented as instruments of the devil, and symbolised by Eve, at once inferior and evil in her capacity as temptress and seducer.[19] Although Birgitta has examples of women in this role, she accords the role of tempter equally to men, and when she does mention the biblical Eve, it is in contexts other than those stressing the sinful nature of woman and more often connected with the Virgin Mary as fulfilment of the Old Testament in the New Testament. Her attitude is underpinned by constant reference to the exemplary marriage of the Virgin's parents, such as Book VI 104, a prayer to St Anne, the patron of married couples, which asks for a blessing on all marriages.[20]

Traditional Christian doctrine also taught that a main purpose of marriage was to contain sexual desire, and the function of the marital act was procreation. Sexual relations are nothing but lust (*concupisciencia*) if they are not undertaken for this purpose, within marriage and in moderation. Birgitta follows these arguments: a man who lusts after women or cannot remain chaste should find a wife and be faithful to her.[21] Outside marriage lust is to be abhorred, and licentious people are likened to a vessel filled with sperm which is so bitter that it cannot be tasted.[22] Within marriage excessive sexual appetite is viewed with revulsion, as with a knight who had been loyal to his wife but 'spilt his seed through unsuitable embraces in indecent gestures'.[23] Nevertheless, she shows a certain realism about sexual desire, provided it is undertaken without excessive lust and with the purpose of procreation, and in Book VI 27 Christ even sanctions a man 'to have moderate pleasure' – which is an attitude that was not formally adopted by theologians until the sixteenth century.[24]

In all her comments on marriage, which are strewn among her revelations, she shows an awareness of its practical sides. In Book I 26 she outlines reasons why people marry: for a beautiful face, extensive possessions, sexual desire, for celebration, fine clothes, excessive food and general merriment; to beget children for their own pleasure and reputation. Christ disapproves of any marriage that is exclusively pleasure-seeking and frivolous and says that a good marriage demands a body and soul that are unconcerned with sensual

18 Ex. 21.
19 For further illustration see Blamires 1992.
20 See too Books I 9, VI 49, 55. On the importance of St Anne to Birgitta see Lindgren 1990.
21 Books VI 27, I 47.
22 Book VI 36.
23 Book VI 39.
24 This point is made by Fogelqvist 1993, p. 235, note 269.

beauty, worldly and material things, and follows instead the virtues of sobriety and humility, and brings up children in a true Christian spirit. There are playful images of bridal couples used to draw a spiritual analogy, such as the allegory of the soul's love of God, describing how the devil tries to prevent the union of a betrothed couple by stratagems: he obstructs their exchange of letters, conversations and their bodily union together naked in bed.[25] Christ tells her to be 'like the bride who stands by the bed curtain, who is ready to obey at once the will of the bridegroom when he calls her'.[26] A good bride must have an appealing mouth, clean ears(!), chaste eyes and a steady heart.[27] The bridegroom who hides from his bride shall be the more ardently desired.[28] Birgitta also gives advice to the impoverished father of a bride and encourages his friends to lend financial support; and she describes an infatuated bride who does not care about her dowry, unlike her responsible bridegroom.[29] Elsewhere, she tells of a bride who absconds from her husband, and advises a betrothed woman on how to obtain as much as she can for her dowry.[30] She warns of seductive female power and concurs with the Pauline view that 'woman should be subordinate to man'.[31] Wifely obedience, modesty and the authority of the husband are taken for granted.[32] She also advocates mutual respect and companionship in marriage, comparing Christ's love to the love of a good husband for a faithful wife: 'My rest is your rest and my comfort is your comfort.' The wife answers: 'Since I have my sustenance from your work, warmth from your embrace, and sweetness from your words, I would rather die than be parted from you.'[33] She takes a realistic approach to marriage as a means of social or political expediency, stating that property and a male heir are the true fruits of a good marriage. In keeping with the law, however, she stresses that the consent of the bridal pair is also required, otherwise the marriage is merely 'child's play'.[34]

Birgitta and Ulf

Can Birgitta's views be seen in her own marriage? Her relationship with Ulf is touched on only fleetingly in the sources, but there are indications that it was a good match and an affectionate marriage, and that she came to love him 'like

25 Book IV 75.
26 Book IV 25.
27 Book IV 82.
28 Book VII 31.
29 Ex. 70.
30 Ex. 85, Book VI 13.
31 Book IV 84.
32 Books I 40, I 59.
33 Book IV 83.
34 Book VIII 9.

her own heart'.[35] We are told how at her request the couple lived chaste for one year after their marriage (possibly longer according to other accounts) and whenever they had sexual relations they always prayed for a child first.[36] She was apparently not repelled by her own sexual feelings, although how much she rewrites the past once she became widowed is unclear. After Ulf's death, she looks back on her physical happiness with distaste: human sexual pleasure is compared to a sulphurous mountain containing the boils of the soul, the stench of desire, and the glow of punishment; and elsewhere, Christ asks her whether she prefers her former physical to her present spiritual desire and she answers that she is ashamed of her former desire, which was like poison and now tastes as bitter as it originally was sweet.[37] In far more shocking terms, in a revelation which probably dates from her husband's lifetime, she expresses a repudiation of her conjugal life:

> She saw as it were a body covered in sperm and totally deformed. When she showed surprise and fear, the Spirit said to her: 'I created you from your parents' seed. I gave you limbs and a beautiful body, and in it I sent a soul which was not made of any other power but God's. When you came to church to be baptised I gave you my consent and made you my daughter, you who were the devil's daughter by the sin of Adam. Then I nourished you. My angels protected you, for otherwise none could have saved you from demons. I also gave you health and tokens of honour, and I permitted you to enter marriage and have all that you desired. Afterwards I led you to my Spirit, in order that you should come to know me and love nothing as much as me.'

The Spirit goes on to tell her that she has since her youth provoked God with her bodily desires, in food and clothing, and in her desire for social distinction at the expense of others, so that she now resembles the body before her:

> For your extravagance, you deserve all your limbs to be dismembered, your flesh consumed by putrefaction, your skin burst with boils, your eyes gouged out, your mouth distorted, your hands and feet chopped off, and all your limbs repeatedly mutilated. For your contempt of the poor and my friends and for your avarice you deserve to be consumed by such a great hunger, that you would willingly eat your own limbs, like a piece of meat, yes, even eat your own excrement and drink your urine, and still not have your hunger satisfied. For your comfort and ease you deserve never to have rest, but always have wretchedness and misery. For the favour of men, which you desired more than my favour, you deserve to be so despised by all that even your children and dear friends would flee from you as to their eyes and noses you smell like rotting flesh and human excrement, and they would prefer to hear you were dead a hundred times than see you alive.

35 AP p. 479.
36 AP p. 77.
37 Book V rev. 11, Book I 32.

> Since you caused your neighbour harm by taking and retaining alienated property in your pride and greed you deserve a sword to chop up your limbs and bones, and the sharpest saw to carve up your flesh, for although the unhappy man suffered and was tormented, you showed no mercy on him.

Yet because of God's mercy, he is prepared to forgive her if she renounces her former life and embraces an ascetic attitude:

> I command you eternally to hate all physical sexual contact, for if you wish to do my bidding, you shall henceforth become a mother to spiritual children, just as you have been a mother to fleshly children.[38]

Children

Birgitta and Ulf had eight children, four sons and four daughters.[39] The eldest, Märta, was born at the earliest in 1319 and married sometime between 1334

38 'Vidit quasi corpus respersum spermate et totum deforme. Cumque illa miraretur et contremisceret, ait ei spiritus: "Ego creaui te ex semine parentum tuorum. Dedi membra et corpus pulchrum, et in illud misi animam, non aliunde creatam sed ex sola deitatis mee potencia. Cumque venisses ad ecclesiam ad baptismum, consensi in te et feci te filiam meam, que propter peccatum Ade eras filia dyaboli. Inde enutriui te. Angeli mei custodiebant te, non enim aliter propter demones subsistere posses. Deinde dedi tibi sanitatem et honores, et feci te venire ad coniugium et omnia habere, que desiderasti. Inde adduxi te in spiritum meum, ad hoc solum, vt me cognosceres et nichil sicut me diligeres. . . . Pro luxuria tua digna esses, vt omnium membrorum tuorum compagines dissoluerentur, caro putredine consumeretur, cuitis pre tumore remperetur, oculi erurentur, os distorqueretur, manus et pedes absciderentur et omnia membra sine cessaciones mutilarentur. Pro contemptu pauperum et amicorum meorum et pro auaricia tua digna esses, vt tanta te inuaderet fames, quod membra tua, si essent vnum frustum carnis, libenter vorares et stercus tuum libencius comederes et vrinam tuam bibires, nec tamen fames extingui posset. Pro requie tua et accidia digna esses nullam omnino habere requiem sed vbique miseriam et tristiciam. Pro fauore hominum, quem querabas plus quam me, tantam mereris deireccionem omnium, vt eciam filii tui et amici carissimi fugerent te, et quasi fetida caro et stercus humanum feteres in oculis eorum et naribus, mallentque te in centuplum audire mortuam quam videre viuam. Pro eo autem, quod eciam proximo tuo intulisti dampnum et ad superbiam tuam dilatandam aliena habuisti et detinuisti, dignum esset, vt omnia membra tua et ossa gladius membratim diuideret et serra acutissima carnes sine cessacione laceraret, eo quod miser affligebatur et non compaciebaris ei. . . . Precipio tibi omnem carnis commixtionem in perpetuum odire, quia, si secundum voluntatem meam esse volueris, eris mater filiorum deinceps spiritualium, sicut hactenus fueras mater carnalium." ' Ex. 75. See Hollman 1956, p. 60, on this revelation. In one manuscript, MS Cod. Ups. C2, dating from the end of the fourteenth century, the text is more detailed, and is probably the unabridged original version, which retains much of the personal detail, including the last sentence (quoted here).

39 Their dates of birth are uncertain; but Klockars 1976, pp. 93–100, has suggested a

and 1341 to a knight named Sigvid Ribbing, in what was clearly a political match. The marriage negotiation sheds some light on the relationship between Birgitta and Ulf when there was a conflict of opinion. At the time of the betrothal Birgitta was pregnant with her youngest child Cecilia, and the story is told in the *Diarium Vadstenense* in 1399 (which is the year of Cecilia's death):

> when she [Cecilia] was still in her mother's womb, it happened that a very great tyrant became betrothed to one of St Birgitta's daughters against Birgitta's will, although it pleased her husband and the king and council. He had in fact previously caused the kingdom great harm. She therefore was overcome by constant weeping, and it happened once that as she was weeping bitterly the child in her womb cried out 'Dear mother, do not kill me!'[40]

Although Birgitta opposed the marriage, her opinion in the match was not taken into account, and Ulf proceeded with arrangements for the marriage without her approval. The clash of interests between husband and wife, Birgitta's concern for her eldest daughter, as well as her acute sense that morally Sigvid was an unfitting son-in-law, all demonstrate her close interest in family affairs. The cry of the unborn baby suggests that she may have been starving herself or suffering depression or anger at the prospect of the match. By neglecting her body during her pregnancy – in whatever way – she asserts her own views in protest against the marriage; and yet it is the unborn baby, and not Ulf or Märta, who makes her submit to her husband's decision.

Birgitta continues to disapprove of her son-in-law and later gives vent to her feelings in three revelations. Sigvid Ribbing was related to King Magnus's stepfather, Knut Porse, and both men were from the south-western province of Halland, which had been a pawn in political dealings between Sweden, Norway and Denmark.[41] Knut Porse established a political base in Halland from where he mounted plundering attacks on neighbouring lands, and set upon individuals like a Swedish cleric on his way to Paris, and ships from Newcastle, which provoked a protest from King Edward III of England in

convincing ordering, followed here, which is different from that suggested by earlier scholars.

40 'cum adhuc esset in utero matris, contigebat, quod unus maximus tyrannus desponsavit quandam filiam sancte Byrgitte, quasi contra voluntatem eiusdem sancte, quia sic placuit marito suo et regi et consiliariis regni; quia magnam dampnum antea inferebat regno. Que cum ob hoc continuis indicibiliter affligeretur fletibus, semel cum amarissime fleret, fertur infantem in utero clamasse: "Carissima", inquit, "mater, noli me interficere!" ' Gejrot 1988, p. 133. According to the embellished account in *Margareta Clausdotters krönika*, the story occurred during the betrothal ceremony, and Birgitta suddenly sees the futility of her anger and enters the betrothal feast with a light heart.

41 See further on Sigvid Ribbing, Klockars 1976, pp. 76–84, on which this account is based.

1329. After Knut's death Sigvid Ribbing took over the lordship of southern Halland, acting as an independent leader of the border province between Sweden and Denmark, and adopting aggressive piratical policies, thus earning himself the nickname from his mother-in-law of *latro* ('the robber'). In Book VI 23, she accuses him of setting a bad example, killing innocent people in his anger, imposing high taxes on the poor, and of greed, immorality and pride. Nevertheless, Birgitta finds excuses for him saying that he was born 'to do the devil's work' and without a chance of redeeming himself. In the following two revelations, further advice is given to him which he allegedly ignores. The last mention of him is in May 1345; and Märta afterwards married a man named Knut Algotsson (brother of King Magnus's favourite, Bengt), with whom she went into exile in 1357 to Norway where she became lady-in-waiting to the queen.

The next daughter after Märta was Ingeborg, named after her maternal grandmother. She entered the Cistercian convent at Riseberga in Närke in 1341, probably at the minimum age of twelve, but died some years later and after she had taken her vows.[42] On hearing of her death we are told in a revelation how her mother wept and sighed loudly, not because she mourned her but because she had failed to discipline her properly and curb her vanity. Christ reassures her that a mother who brings up a daughter to the best of her ability is a true mother, but one who is indifferent to her daughter's worldly ways is but a stepmother.[43]

The most famous daughter was Katarina, the fourth child to be born, probably around 1331; she was married sometime before 1344 to a knight named Eggard van Kyren, whose family was from Holstein, and also intricately involved in Swedish political affairs. Before her marriage was consummated, Katarina left Sweden to visit her mother in Rome, and while she was away her husband died. She became her mother's companion for the rest of her life and played a central role in the canonisation application. She became the first abbess at Vadstena; and died there on 24 March 1381. Later she was revered as a saint in Sweden and in 1489 her relics were translated. The presentation of Katarina throughout her life shows how she achieved a double ideal of womanhood, symbolising on the one hand the worldly experience of the widow, and on the other, the purity of the virgin. As such, she is the exemplary first abbess of Vadstena, demonstrating both practical experience and a chaste existence.[44]

Birgitta was in danger of her life at the birth of her youngest daughter, Cecilia, and the women who attended her saw a woman dressed in white enter the room and touch each of her limbs so that she gave birth quite

42 DS no. 3558 tells that Sigvid and Märta put their seal on Ulf's deed of gift to the monastery in 1341.
43 Ex. 98. AP p. 494.
44 On Katarina see further Chapter IV, pp. 109–13.

painlessly.[45] Cecilia received an early convent training in the Dominican house in Skänninge, but was not suited to monastic life, and her brother Karl at her request removed her, to marry a magnate named Bengt Filipsson who was involved in the political turmoil of the 1350s. A marriage is discussed in Book IV 71, which might relate to Cecilia's. It is one of the central revelations in which the states of virginity and marriage are treated and takes the form of a dialogue between Christ and Birgitta. Four questions are asked. First: if a vine branch given by one friend to another was planted where it gave pleasure, but the giver asked his friend to move it further away to where it would bear more fruit, how should the friend respond? Second (and here the formulation is sophistic and legalistic): if a father and mother gave their daughter to a young man with the daughter's consent but the man did not say whether or not he wished to marry her, would the daughter be betrothed or not? The third question contains a courtly image: three young ladies stood before a nobleman who informed them that the one who could awaken his true love would win his affection. The first said she would rather die than be defiled by another man, the second said she would suffer any torment rather than offend or hurt him and the third said she would suffer all torments on his behalf; surely, Birgitta answers, all three ladies deserve his love. The last question asks: if corn is given and a man is hungry, should he eat it at once or plant it to produce more food? Christ then explains that he wishes Birgitta's daughter, who had been placed in a convent, to be 'replanted' elsewhere. Birgitta had previously not received clear answers as to which path to choose for the girl, virginity or marriage, but now an unequivocal response is given, which endorses the state of marriage:

> Virginity is good and highest . . . but if virginity of the body is observed without virginity of the mind, then virginity is compromised. For a humble and devout wife is more pleasing to me than a proud and shameless virgin.[46]

Judging by contemporary naming conventions, the oldest son was Gudmar, after his paternal grandfather, who according to later sources, died as a schoolboy in Stockholm. Nothing else is known of him. Another son who died while a child was Bengt, who was buried at Alvastra monastery. Birgitta weeps at his lingering illness and is assured by Christ that his death was not the result of parental sin.[47] Only two sons lived to adulthood. The first was Karl, allegedly Birgitta's favourite.[48] He was probably born at the end of the

45 AP p. 79.
46 'Virginitas bona est et summa . . . Si vero unum sine alia defuerit, scilicet virginitas carnis et non virginitas mentis, deformata est virginitas. Nam accepcior est michi conuigata deuota et humilis quam virgo superba et impudica . . .'. Aili 1992, p. 214.
47 AP p. 91.
48 AP p. 264.

1320s and is first mentioned in 1348, where he is described as a knight and lawman. During the 1350s and 1360s he was embroiled in political affairs in Sweden, which included a period of forced exile in Germany in 1362. The scattered references to him in the sources suggest he was a worldly, pleasure-seeking man, and Birgitta expresses her concern for his rash and excessive behaviour in her revelations. When he neglected to fast on the vigil of St John the Baptist, for instance, John appeared to Birgitta promising to help Karl and to equip him with necessary weapons to fit his knightly status.[49] Another episode concerns his stubborn refusal to confess a sin, which his mother insisted he had committed.[50] He married three times. His first wife, Katarina Gisladotter, was so impressed by her sister-in-law Katarina's asceticism that she began to wear the plain beguine's dress, much to her husband's annoyance, which he takes out on his sister: 'Isn't it enough that you turn yourself into a beguine? Will you also make my wife into a beguine and an object of ridicule for the people?'[51] His second wife was a Norwegian noblewoman, Gyda, who bequeathed a valuable crown to Birgitta which provided sufficient financial support for her household in Rome for a whole year. His third wife was Katarina Glysingsdotter, whose mother lived in Birgitta's household in Rome for five years, and was a witness in the canonisation proceedings. Karl died while accompanying his mother on her pilgrimage to the Holy Land in 1372.[52]

Karl's younger brother, Birger, was born some time in the 1330s, probably after Birgitta's father's death, as he is given his name. He is first mentioned in 1354, but little is known about him until after his mother's death, when he was lawman and councillor, first in Tiohärad, Småland, and then in Närke. In a letter to Birger, written from Rome, Birgitta outlines the ideals of knighthood and addresses him as a young nobleman with estates and legal standing:

> Praise, honour and glory be to Lord Jesus Christ especially for the bitter pains he suffered on the gallows of the cross for our sake. Dearest son, if you ask for proper love from your God, Creator and Saviour, then bear his suffering always in your heart and prepare yourself often to partake of his holy body in accordance with the advice of your confessor. Further, wherever you are, ask for the house of the poor and help them according to your means. God will reward you well. Again, pay those who have worked for your sake well, and chastise those under your authority reasonably and gently and have none who is ill-disposed towards God in your service. Next, when you get up in the morning submit your soul and life to God and bid him protect your thoughts, words and deeds, make the sign of the cross on your face and on your heart and say 'Jesus Christ the Nazarene, king of the Jews, have

49 AP p. 79, Book IV 74.
50 AP p. 323.
51 Annerstedt 1876.
52 See further pp. 124–6 below.

> mercy on me.' When you hear mass then think of our Lord Almighty's hard pains and your own sins. Again, when you sit at table, have godly and courteous conversation, and beware of Sweden's sinful ways. Many seldom leave the table before they have become like grunting pigs in a common house. Do not use the name of the devil. When you are about to speak or answer, make the sign of the cross on your heart and say 'Jesus Christ, Jesus Christ, Jesus Christ.' So you will receive prudent words with which to speak and answer. Fear God in all your doings; when you sit in judgement consider your words before you express them. Judge also your fellow Christian as you would answer before God's harsh judgement; if anyone does you an injustice, take refuge in Sweden's law and do not take revenge in your anger; even if it happens that justice is not done to you by your company; bow to reconciliation and hand the matter to our Lord Jesus Christ. Do not doubt that he will help you better for righteousness than you ever thought possible; herewith I commend to you with life and soul the Holy Trinity, Virgin Mary and all the saints in heaven.[53]

Her maternal advice for Birger to follow the code of conduct which befits his status emphasises godly behaviour as well as courteous manners and restraint. It also gives guidance in political matters, advising him to observe Swedish law, and on how to deal with his fellow knights. He travelled several times to Rome to visit his mother and accompanied her to the Holy Land where he was knighted in 1372. He accompanied his mother's body back to

53 'Loff heeder oc äre ware herranom ihesu cristo enkanneliga fore the bittara pyna han ledh vppo korssens galga för wara skuld Alle kierista sön begerer thw foo retthen kierligh tiil thin gud skappere oc aatherlössöre tha bär hans pina all tiidh i tiith hierta oc reedh tegh tiil offte gudeliga anamme hans helliga likama epther thin skriffefaders raad Framdelis ehwar thw esth spör thw hws armath folk hielpp them epther thin empne gud löner tegh well Item bettalle well them som haffue arbeidet foor thina skuld oc neps thinom wnderssaathe skellige mz mildhedh oc haff engen ilhärdhoghan mothe gud i thina tyänisth Item tha thw stonder opp oom morgenen anthworde gwdhi syell oc liiff oc bedh hanum beskerma thina tancke ordh oc gerninga, gör korss i tiith antlede oc vppo tiith hiertha oc sigh Ihesus christus nazarenus iwdhena koningh forbarme tegh öffwer migh Tha thw hörer messa tha tenck vppo wors herre alzwollige macth hordhe pina oc thina eghna syndher Item tha tw sitther wedh bordh haff gwdeligth oc höwiskt snack wacthe tegh för Swärigis sydhwänia, Manghe goo syellan fraa bordh för en the äre som grymthande swin i menoghe hws Item nepn icke gerna diefwuleen Item naar thw skalth talle eller swara gör korss vppo thit herta oc sigh Ihesus christus Ihesus christus Ihesus christus Swo ffar thw skelligeen ordh bodhe tiil talle oc swara, rädhz gud i alle thina gerningha tha thw sitther i doom betenck granth thin ordh för en thw them fraam föör Dööm swo thin iamcristen som tw wilth swaare fore gudz strenge dom gör tegh nogen oreth fly tiil Swerigis lagh hemps icke i thina wredhe, er thz oc swo ath tegh skeer icke reeth aff tiith herskab giff tegh tiil fredz oc anthwordhe thina sagh warom herra ihesu christo tweka encthe han hielpper tegh bäther tiil reth en thw nogen tiidh tencke kan her mz befaller iagh tegh mz liiff oc siell the helligee treffollighedh iomffrw maria oc allom helganom i himmerike'. The letter, for which there is no Latin version, survives in a late fifteenth-century copy. Klemming 1857–84, vol. V, pp. 140–1.

Sweden in 1373, and later assisted in the building work at Vadstena monastery. He himself died in 1391, only weeks before Birgitta's canonisation was pronounced. He was married to a sister of Karl's third wife, and for a second time in 1378 to one Margareta Siggadotter. The image of Birger as an honourable knight is reinforced in *Margareta Clausdotters krönika* in which he is juxtaposed with his brother Karl at their meeting with the pope and portrayed as the epitome of the restrained, modest man about whom the pope comments 'You are truly your mother's son.'[54]

It was a necessary part of the depiction of the future saint that she should be seen as fulfilling her role as a parent completely, and of doing her utmost for her children's salvation. In her utterances to and about her children, Birgitta comes over as a stern mother who frequently upbraids and admonishes her offspring, and is always closely involved in their upbringing. That she nursed her own children, as other members of the upper classes clearly did in Scandinavia, is suggested on one occasion when she sees the relics of the Virgin's milk in a monastery and at vespers the Virgin authenticates the relics, saying that just as Birgitta had nursed her own children, so this relic had been in the Virgin's breast.[55] Her conflict of maternal love and duty is powerfully and poignantly expressed in a vision which takes place as she prepares to go to Rome in 1349, leaving behind her children who were young, rich and powerful and in danger of worldly temptation. She sees a young boy blowing on a fire to heat a cooking pot, who tells her that he is fanning the flames of her maternal love. After this, she vows to place her love of God above everything.[56] When she later makes the transition into a spiritual life, her first-hand understanding of maternal devotion and suffering is translated into a deep sense of compassion that leads to a strong identification with the maternal joys and sorrows of the Virgin in particular.[57]

Piety in marriage

What is known of Birgitta's daily life at Ulvåsa is little, although a number of female witnesses in the canonisation proceedings provide occasional insights into her life during her marriage. Her revelations assume that a life of conspicuous consumption was proper for a woman of her class, but that high breeding carried with it a correspondingly high, and therefore demanding, expectation of exemplary behaviour.

Her religious fervour deepened during her married life, and she adopted ascetic practices, which again follow standard hagiographical typology. The *vita* describes her as a sober and conscientious mistress of her home, who

54 Annerstedt 1876.
55 Westman 1911, p. 301. On breast-feeding see further Krötzl 1989, p. 29.
56 Ex. 95.
57 On Birgitta as mother see further Atkinson 1991, pp. 170–87.

spent time in fervent prayer, confessed every day, fasted, read devotional writings, and performed almsdeeds.[58] Her fasting was strictly and unostentatiously observed, and she would sit at table with her husband joining in the feasting and drinking from a silver chalice, but in reality drinking only water and eating bread.[59] These plain statements are further illustrated by a number of homely witness accounts and revelations, which help to suggest their veracity. We are told for instance how she had had a luxurious bed made at her home at Ulvåsa, and when it was ready, she felt as if she had been dealt a hard blow on her head and she heard a voice through the wall reproaching her for her vanity when Christ had hung unsupported on the cross: after this she preferred to sleep on straw and bearskins.[60] Her practical care and concern for others is reflected in the hospital she founded near her home, a building where the poor and needy from surrounding areas could come, and where she had nurses to tend them, aided by herself and her daughters.[61]

She also spent much time in prayer as is suggested by a Swedish noblewoman named Kristina Bosdotter, who relates that she shared a chamber with her for a year and watched her get up many times at night to pray, sometimes even all night.[62] By the later middle ages private devotion had become a central part of lay piety, and prayers and meditations were read quietly, in the privacy of the home. Birgitta is known to have composed a number of prayers and meditations herself, and it is likely that some of them date from the years of her marriage. There are seven extant meditations which are personal, reflective pieces, sometimes inscrutable and obscurely articulated, with idiosyncratic imagery (such as of God's ineffability as a burst of gunpowder, Christ's heart as 'a little piece of flesh', or the juxtaposition of a heel with an eye to compare the magnitude of Christ's suffering and pain).[63] They are soliloquies in which she reflects aloud on the earthly life of Christ and the Virgin, and they contain themes and images to which she later returns in her revelations. In one, she says she has more difficulty in understanding non-material than material things and she meditates over the paths man has to choose between, guiding him away from excessive eating, sleeping and drinking. Another is a

58 Specific examples of her asceticism described in the *vita* cannot be dated specifically to the years of her marriage: on Fridays she tasted gentian in her mouth as a reminder of the bitterness of the drink of gall that had been offered to Christ on the cross, she poured hot wax over her bare flesh on Fridays, always keeping the wounds open on her body, and she wore a knotted girdle against her skin at all times. AP pp. 99–100.

59 AP p. 581. In Book VI 94 (which cannot be dated) she is taught to pray for moderation in her dress, food and sleep.

60 Ex. 53.

61 AP p. 78. Other witnesses say she helped hospitals to be repaired in many parts of the kingdom. Her care of the poor is dealt with in article 20 of the canonisation process.

62 AP p. 66.

63 See further Morris 1996.

fragment of a letter to her confessor about the state of her soul, which has not improved since the last time she made confession; and another starts with a quotation from St Bernard, that 'many know much yet know not themselves', which she then goes on to relate to her own experience, developing a simple theology on the faculties of understanding which are given to man and which distinguish him from animals. Another takes the form of a litany, in the first person, and in the petitions she asks for her heart to be filled with burning love, and at the end she asks for the gift of grace to 'receive words and deeds and do and speak according to his blessed will'. Ready to receive God in her heart, she appears to be expressing a wish to be given the charisma to receive and publish divine words, and to become a medium of communication between God and man. Another personal meditation echoes the popular devotion to the Sacred Heart and speaks of her own heart which contains a boil pierced with a thorn; and this image she associates with her husband and loved ones:

> My Lord, I bewail to you how my heart seems to be inclined. It seems as if there is a boil in my heart; there are also through my heart two thorns and around the outside of it is drawn a membrane which constricts it and oppresses me very severely. My dear Lord God, this is impossible for me to do myself without your help; therefore I ask you for the sake of all the humility which you revealed in the world: tear out the membrane which I associate with pride, and weave about it the humility which without beginning has been in the virtue of your divinity. My Lord God I pray to you because your head was crowned with thorns; rip the thorn which is in my heart, which is bodily love for my husband or children or friends or relatives, and place there instead divine love for the gain of my fellow Christians. I ask you my dear Lord because your blessed hands and feet were torn asunder by the nails. Rip out of my heart that thorn which is wordly lust and place there instead desire and lust for your service and for your eternal kingdom.[64]

[64] 'Herra min iak käre mik for thik huru mik thykkir mit hiärta vara skipat mik thykke som j hiärtano är een etirblema, Ther standa ok gönom hiärtat twe thorna ok vtan vm thz är draghin en hinna som thz thrängir ok quäl mik mykyt vadhelica, min käre herra gudh thetta är mik omöghelikit at göra siälue vtan mz thine hiälp thy bidhir jak thik for alla the ödhmiukt som thu oppinbaradhe j världinne, Riiff vt aff the hinnona ther jak mener mz höghfärdh oc weff ther vm the ödhmiukt ther vtan ophoff hawir varit j thins guddoms dygdh Min herra gudh jak bidhir thik for thz at thit hofwodh kronadhis mz thorne riiff vt then thornin som star j mino hiärta som är kötlikin kärlekir til bonda älla til barna vini älla frändir ok sät ther atir j före gudhelikin kärlekir til mins jamcristins siäla gagn Jak bidhir thik min käre herra fore thy at thina signadha händir oc fötir rifnadho sundir for naglomen riff vt aff mino hiärta thän thornin som är världina giri ok sät ther j fore astundan oc giri til thina thiänist ok til thit äuärdhelica rike.' Klemming 1857–84, vol. 2 p. 266.

These meditations are important since they are a repository of Birgitta's rich images gathered early in her life, from iconography, doctrine, Bible and liturgy. The germ of ideas and insights which she has gained from her observation of the world around her is spontaneously allowed to meander and develop into a personal reflection which in itself may be of little intrinsic value or literary or theological merit, but which allows a glimpse into the way ideas and images become associated together in her mind and find their verbal expression. We see her at a formative stage of her devotional life, expressing herself unselfconsciously in her native tongue in texts that were not, it appears, subject to reworking by her confessors. We see her, further, as the author of her own spiritual thoughts and private prayers. They are not 'revelations', containing revealed knowledge, but they are autobiographical commentaries on her immediate spiritual concerns, and provide evidence that her gift of the spirit was already manifesting itself during her married years.

The Swedish meditations do not become part of the official Birgittine canon, and indeed never appear in a Latin version; but there are four longer and stylistically more sophisticated prayers, known as the *Quattuor Oraciones*, that do form part of the official text corpus.[65] In structure these prayers, unlike the meditations, comprise polished, impersonal and visual pieces, with repetitive, if somewhat pedantic and inelegant formulae, and they adopt the standard imagery of affective mysticism. They probably date from the years of her marriage, as is suggested in the opening of their Swedish translation where it is stated that while her husband was away she asked constantly for a suitable manner of praying to be shown to her.[66] Two prayers concern the life of Christ whom she depicts as a crowned king, but also as knightly ruler and secular lord, an image seen also in the meditations and again in the revelations. The two other prayers concern the Virgin's life and stress her maternal sorrow in language that verges on the sensational, and they praise her body in rich imagery which is reminiscent of the Song of Songs. The following extract is from the Old Swedish text, which (in fragments at least) has priority over the Latin text and goes back to a very early stage in the writing down of the Revelations.

> My Lord Jesus Christ, may your feet be praised above those of learned masters, for they walked a harder road than they taught others to walk. My Lord Jesus Christ, joy and praise and honour be to all your holy limbs, from the crown of your head to the soles of your feet, because you appear to men in the likeness of bread, although you appear with all your limbs living

65 See Eklund 1991. For an English translation and notes see Tjader Harris 1990. There are also about thirty shorter prayers attributed to her (some extracted from her revelations) found in fifteenth-century collections of prayer books, but it is difficult to determine exactly how many there were or the authenticity of them. See Geete 1907–09, and Klemming 1857–84, vol. 4 pp. 132–76.

66 MS A36, Stockholm Royal Library. Klemming 1857–84, vol. 4 p. 132.

before the company of heaven. Blessed be you, my Virgin Mary, Holy Mother of God, for none has loved the Creator as much as you, because you are the best Creature which God created. Honoured be you my Virgin Mary, Holy Mother of God, because of the annunciation of the angel to your father and mother. And from that most precious union that there ever was, your body was conceived, and like other children, was born from its mother's womb.[67]

The way into states of prayer was by meditating on the scriptures, reciting the Office or by contemplating liturgical texts or psalms in private. Much of Birgitta's meditation and prayer was no doubt provoked by her reading and listening to reading aloud, and involved a complete immersion in the words of the scriptures, combined with the powerful effect of reminiscence.[68] With her background she was probably better placed than any other Swedish woman to have books at her disposal in the vernacular language. She also became familiar with liturgical Latin, as well as basic Latin grammar, as is suggested by the fact that she joined her sons' Latin studies with Nikolaus Hermansson (c.1326–91), who was later bishop of Linköping and a close friend of Birger and Katarina, and who eventually became one of the chief promotors of the Birgittine cause.[69]

67 'Min hærre ihesus christus thyne føter lofuins ofuer alla the thær mæstere snille fingo thy at the gingo hardhare væg æn the androm kændo. Min hærra ihesus christus glædhi hether ok æra vordhe allom thynom hælgha likama fran thynom jæssa oc under thyna ylia thær fore mænniskiom synis j brøtz liknilse. Oc synis mz allom lymmom lifuande for allo hymmerikis hærskapi. Signadh vordhe thw myn jomfrw sancta maria gudhz modher thy at ingen som thu sin skapara swa møket ælskade for thy æst thu the bæste Creatwre thær gudh skapade. Hedher hafue thu myn jomfrw sancta maria gudhz modher thær mædh ængle fadher ok modher budhadis Oc af thy dyrasta hionalaghi thær nokon thyma vordh thin likame afladhis Oc som annor barn af modher lifue føddis.' Eklund 1983–84, pp. 22–3. The reworked, far more polished version of the same passage in Latin reads as follows: 'Domine mi Ihesu Christe, magister bone, benedicantur et perhenniter adorentur pedes tui beatissimi, quia sum magno dolore tuo per asperiorem viam, quam alios docuisti, tu in hoc mundo discalciatis pedibus ambulasti et in fine pro nobis eos duris clauis cruci affigi permisisti, qui viuis et regnas cum Deo patre in vnitate Spiritus Sancti per omnia secula seculorum, Amen.' Benedicta et venerabilis sis tu, domina mea Virgo Maria, Dei mater sanctissima, cuius tu vere es optima creatura et nullus vmquam tam intime eum dilexit sicut tu, domina gloriosa. Gloria tibi sit, domina mea Virgo Maria, mater Dei, que ab illo angelo, quo Christus tibi nunciatus fuit, ab eodem eciam tu patri et matri tue nunciata fuisti et de eorum coniugio honestissimo concepta et genita extitisti.' This extract provides an illustration of the complexities of the textual transmission of all the Birgittine texts.

68 See further Leclercq 1974, p. 91.

69 He was revered as a saint in the diocese of Linköping and the official deposition of his relics took place in 1515. He was author of a number of rhymed offices, to St Anne and St Ansgar, whose cult was revived in the later middle ages. His Office to Birgitta was composed sometime before her canonisation, and the opening lines of

She is known to have read the saints' lives, which may be the text known as the *Fornsvenska Legendariet* (*Old Swedish Legendary*), compiled between 1276 and 1307 by a Dominican friar from Östergötland, and is a collection of saints' lives, chronologically ordered, based on Jacob of Voragine's *Legenda aurea.*[70] She also commissioned part of the Bible to be translated into Swedish, and this may be the extant paraphrase of the Pentateuch, about two thirds of which are straight translation and the other part is an exposition which derives from Thomas Aquinas's *Summa theologiae.*[71] Who was responsible for the translation is unknown although a number of candidates have been put forward, including Nikolaus Hermansson and Birgitta's confessor Magister Mathias. Another book that is specifically referred to is the *Speculum Virginum*, which she had read to her and became rapt in spirit and heard a voice telling her that virginity merited a crown, widowhood approached God and states of marriage were not excluded from heaven, but obedience brings all to glory.[72] Birgitta shared her interest in books with her husband, and the *vita* presents an unconventional picture of a wife instructing her husband to study and read, and tells how Birgitta influenced Ulf to lead a more devout life 'for even though he was a vigorous man and an important member of the king of Sweden's council, he occupied himself – at his wife's advice and admonishment – in learning to read the Hours of the Most Blessed Virgin Mary and the books containing the laws and legal judgements; and he studied to fulfil what belongs to justice and law'.[73]

Life at court

In the mid-1330s Birgitta was appointed *magistra* to the new queen, Blanche of Namur, a Flemish princess whom Magnus Eriksson had married in 1335, in Bohus castle, a year before his coronation in Storkyrkan, Stockholm.[74] Blanche was the daughter of Count Jean I of Namur, who played a prominent role in

the antiphon for the first vespers are among the most celebrated lines in medieval Swedish poetry:

Rosa rorans bonitatem
stella stillans claritatem.
Birgitta, vas gratiae,
rora celi pietatem,
stilla vite puritatem
in vallem miseriae.

(Rose, distilling dew of goodness/ Star, pouring out brightness/ Birgitta, vessel of grace,/ Bedew the pity of heaven/ Pour purity of Life/ Into the vale of tears.) See Schück 1893 and Lundén 1971.

70 AP pp. 66, 78. See further on Birgitta's literary influences Klockars 1966.
71 See Thorell 1959.
72 Ex. 96.
73 AP pp. 64, 79.
74 AP p. 528. See further on Blanche, Imsen 1997.

the struggle for the wealthy Low Countries at the beginning of the Hundred Years War and was connected to one of the foremost princely houses of Europe. Not only was he a vassal to the French king and German emperor but he also had strong economic allegiances with the king of England and his family took a part in the English campaigns in the Hundred Years War. Blanche's mother, Marie of Artois, was an enterprising woman and wealthy landowner who largely ruled Namur while her husband and sons were on campaigns. They had eleven children, and two of their sons, Robert, who was described by the fourteenth-century French chronicler Froissart as a 'gentil et vaillant chevalier', and Louis, did service for Magnus Eriksson for which they received payments in 1345 and 1353.[75] In June 1334, Magnus had safe conduct letters to travel through Flanders, presumably on his way to France, and it is likely that it was on this journey that he was betrothed to Blanche. In August 1335 she travelled north with great ceremony for her wedding, with a splendid wedding attire apparently bought in Paris, and a significant dowry. The marriage alliance must have opened up new economic and political links in Sweden, and also introduced new cultural impulses, which are seen in new courtly traditions and works of literature based on German and French models, in particular rhymed chronicles and courtly romances. (On one occasion, indeed, Birgitta is chastised for enjoying such unedifying stories of heroic worldly deeds.[76])

Birgitta's role in the royal entourage was probably as mentor to the new queen, giving guidance on court customs, and instructing her in Swedish, although French and German were probably also court languages. Although little is known of her role at court, she presumably had a position of great influence. One story tells how Blanche had brought an ebony reliquary with her from France which contained the relics of several saints, including St Louis. Birgitta noticed that the box had been put in an unfitting place by the servants and that a splendid light shone from it, and she heard a voice saying 'Behold the treasure of God, who is honoured in heaven, and scorned in earth.' She then placed the reliquary on an altar.[77]

Later in her revelations, however, she develops an ambiguous attitude to the queen, but one that is part of a discernible pattern when there is a cycle of revelations directed at particular individuals: she describes, criticises and upbraids the person in question in one revelation, in another she gives practical advice as to how people should mend their ways, and if there are any further ones they contain reprimands and condemnations for not taking her guidance. In Book VIII 10 Blanche is compared to a gnawed apple which has been planted in another land so that it would bear flowers and fruit and learn from God's word, but instead the queen speaks indecently and acts vainly.

75 Koht 1924, p. 576. See too Paravicini 1992.
76 Book VI 27.
77 AP pp. 528, 632, Ex. 59.

According to Book VIII 11, the king and queen had become celibate after the birth of their second son. They are reproached for abandoning their conjugal relations for the wrong reasons; Magnus is accused of sinful concupiscence, fickleness and unsteadiness of mind, and Blanche of a desire to please others and to escape birth pains with another child. In Book VIII 12 there is advice on how a king should treat his wife: a woman must be loved if she is good, but she can be an obstacle for a man seeking perfection. Therefore a husband must guide her sometimes with gentle words, like a counsellor, sometimes by stern words, like a teacher, and sometimes with painful treatment, like a doctor. A woman must be listened to carefully, reprimanded in private and educated in modesty; if necessary her husband should ignore her. The following chapter tells how Blanche struggles in her mind between good and evil thoughts, between pursuing her worldly life of luxury or adopting a life of renunciation and poverty.[78] She is given the examples (probably following the *Legenda aurea*) of St Elisabeth of Hungary who renounced riches, and of St Lucy, who on entering a brothel argued that her crown of virginity would be increased for every time her body was violated there. The last revelation in the cycle tells of Christ's increased impatience with Blanche when she opts for a life of leisure.

Santiago de Compostela

A characteristic feature in the life of the pious nobility in the middle ages was pilgrimage; and in the summer of 1341, Birgitta, accompanied by Ulf, set out to Santiago de Compostela on the first of the three major pilgrimages she was to undertake in her life.[79] The pilgrimage to Santiago was a journey that many of her forebears, including her father, had undertaken. The Swedish entourage must have included a number of clerics and laymen, but apart from Birgitta and Ulf, the only named person was their confessor, a Cistercian named Svennung, who was later abbot of the monastery at Varnhem in Skara diocese.[80]

Which of the main pilgrim routes across Europe they took is unknown, but they probably travelled over the Baltic to Lübeck or Stralsund and then to Cologne. Nor is anything known of their visit to the shrines in Spain, but during their return from the pilgrimage, in Arras in Flanders, Ulf fell ill. Birgitta, fearing he would not survive, received a vision of St Denis, who tells her she is chosen by God to do his will and as a sign he reassures her that Ulf will recover from his illness.[81] In Arras she also received a prophetic

78 The full text is given in Book IV 4.

79 AP pp. 482, 309. She is frequently represented as a pilgrim in the iconography; see for example the illustrations in Lundén 1957–59. In general on pilgrimage to Compostela see Davies 1982, and on pilgrimage from Scandinavia Krötzl 1987.

80 Book VI 36.

81 AP p. 80, Ex. 92. St Denis also appeared to her in Book IV 103–4.

revelation in which she was told by a handsome youth that she would visit Rome and Jerusalem, and describing how she would depart this life. When Ulf recovered the pilgrim party continued its journey back to Sweden. On their return, the *vita* records that:

> between them, they maintained a mutual continence and decided to enter a monastery. And after all their affairs and goods had been set in order to this end, her husband – still having the same purpose – died in the year of our Lord, 1344.[82]

The suggestion that with renewed spiritual devotion they took a vow of chastity and resolved to enter into holy orders raises many questions as to their plans, the extent of Ulf's resolve, and the type of order they planned to enter. How far was it a joint ambition shared by them both? Was Ulf already mortally ill and in need of a place where he could be cared for and eventually buried? Had they the Cistercian house at Alvastra in mind, where Ulf was buried and Birgitta lived after his death? Or did they plan to become Franciscan tertiaries, members of the lay branch of the Franciscan order? Or did Birgitta intend to become a vowess without monastic affiliation, and to live an active holy life rather than live as a sequestered nun?

There is no unequivocal answer to these questions. It is likely that their piety increased after both their pilgrimage and Ulf's illness, and it was certainly by no means uncommon for devout married couples to decide on chastity and a tertiary affiliation, provided both partners were in agreement.[83] However, in spite of the suggestion that she or both of them became tertiaries, it is doubtful whether she had any formal Franciscan connection in the 1340s.[84]

Although the date 1344 given for Ulf's death occurs in the *vita* and is the date recorded on Ulf's tombstone at Alvastra, an alternative date of 1346 has also gained currency in recent years on the grounds that some manuscripts give 1346 for the year of her calling to the spiritual life, which is alleged to have happened a few days after Ulf's death.[85] The later date of 1346 is also supported by the statements recording the number of years of her active calling, which is given in the *vita* as the twenty-eighth year before her death

82 '. . . qui mutuam inter se tenentes continenciam statuerunt intrare monasterium, et ordinatis ad hoc rebus suis et bonis, vir in eodem proposito est defunctus anno Domini mccexliiij.' AP p. 80.

83 For example, Caterina of Genoa and Marie of Oignies; see Bynum 1987, pp. 221, 227. See also Elliott 1993, pp. 196–205.

84 The tradition that she became a tertiary may instead have been promoted in the seventeenth century by Franciscan scholars attempting to explain the strong appeal she had always had within the Order. See Roelvink 1993. Ex. 67 and 90 clarify her Franciscan disposition. See too Morris 1999 (forthcoming).

85 The debate is summarised in Tjader Harris 1990, p. 240 note 32. See too Ekwall 1973, Liedgren 1974, Ekwall 1976 and Jönsson 1992, p. 36.

(i.e. twenty-seven years before her death in 1373). While these arguments seem plausible, they need to be considered in the context of the vast output of revelations. It is clear from their subject matter that at least half of all her visions belonged to 'the Sweden years', that is, the few years between her calling and her departure for Rome. The question remains whether she indeed produced so many of her most important visions in so short a space of time.

Ulf appears to his wife after his death, when he is in purgatory. He tells her he has felt judgement upon him, and now he is approaching mercy. For five misdemeanours he had been punished. He had poked fun at the 'mad boy whom you know, taking delight and pleasure in his foolish gestures'; probably a member of their household, perhaps a mentally handicapped boy whom Birgitta had taken in. Second, out of negligence, he had failed to pay a debt to a widow whose estate he had bought; the widow would come to Birgitta the next day for the money she was owed. Third, without due seriousness, he had promised support to a man in difficulty, who subsequently rose against the king. Fourth, he had participated in tournaments and other public ceremonies with excessive pride and vanity. And fifth, he had been exceptionally harsh on a knight who was condemned to exile. Birgitta then asks what mitigating deeds might save him from the pains of purgatory, and he lists six. First, he had confessed every Friday; second, as judge, he judged according to his conscience and not for worldly profit, and was willing to rectify his mistakes; third, he had kept from his wife's bed once he learned that she was pregnant; fourth, he was generous in his hospitality towards the poor, and avoided incurring debts; fifth, he showed abstinence when he was on his pilgrimage to Spain by not taking any refreshment between resting places, thereby atoning for his previous excesses at the dinner table – and 'now I am certain of my salvation, but yet I am not certain when I shall be saved'; and sixth, he gave his judgements into the care of those he knew to be just, so that they would pay his debts, and for fear of being in debt he returned 'a district' to the king, in order also that God's judgement would not be severe. He then addresses his wife:

> Now, however, since it has been granted to me to ask for help, I ask you to have masses celebrated for a whole year to honour our Salvatrix, the most blessed Lady Mary, the angels, all the saints and the dead; especially the Passion of Christ, our Saviour. For thereby I hope to gain salvation quicker. You should above all be considerate towards the poor, not refraining from distributing vessels, horses and other items in which I took pleasure, and which caused me to sin. If you can, you should not neglect to offer chalices as sacrifice to God, for by such things the salvation of souls is hastened. But the immovable property you should give to the children, for my conscience does not chastise me for unjustly acquiring, retaining or wishing to keep anything.[86]

86 'Nunc igitur, quia datum est michi auxilium petere, rogo te, vt per annum integrum

Ulf's will is not extant, but this vision may be a rewriting in more intimate terms of a will which was framed legally before his death, perhaps before the pilgrimage, which was customary practice.[87] Its echoes of testamentary settlements and letters of indulgence are mixed with personal details of his failings. According to the formulae of medieval wills, the deceased had to acquit himself of all debts, spiritual and temporal (here reflected in specific mention of a widow, the king, his debts of conscience, and in judgements he had made which were insincere, or unjust). To die in charity he had to be discharged from all his debts, to have shown mercy towards the poor, and to have indulged in pious deeds, such as fasting and pilgrimage (all of which are included in Ulf's list of mitigating deeds). The vision also outlines details of the penances, prayers, supplications and meritorious deeds which he asked to be performed on his behalf by those in charge of the disposal of his property.

All Christians but the most saintly might expect to spend some time in purgatory, and although by modern standards this vision appears a harsh and severe judgement by a wife on the man to whom she had been married for almost thirty years, Ulf may in fact have got off lightly. Elsewhere, Birgitta was to describe the pains and torments of purgatory in ghastly physical detail, in terms more suggestive of depictions of hell than purgatory.[88] Ulf had come a long way towards salvation and is treated with generosity by his wife, who addresses him affectionately as a *felix anima* ('blessed soul').

In this revelation about her husband she shows the same firmness of judgement that she had shown towards herself in Ex. 75 and in her letter to her son Birger which were quoted above. She demonstrates the moral imperatives that were to dominate all of her spiritual life and her dealings with others. In many ways Ulf's death came as a relief to Birgitta, as a release from earthly pressures and pleasures towards which she was always tempted, either by natural instinct or conjugal duty. She had been a loyal and obedient wife, but now she was ready for the new life that lay ahead of her. She broke her former earthly ties in a symbolic gesture: the ring Ulf had given to her on his deathbed, bidding her to pray for his soul, she now discarded, declaring that it reminded her too much of her earthly ties:

When I buried my husband, I buried with him all bodily love, and although

facias continue celebrari missas de saluatrice nostra sanctissima Maria, de angelis, de omnibus sanctis et pro defunctis. Insuper de passione Christi, saluatoris nostri, quia spero me liberari cicius. Insuper et precipue sollicita sis circa pauperes, non parcendo distribuere vasa et equos et alia, in quibus delectando maxime peccabam. Calices quoque aliquos, si poteris, pro sacrificio Dei non negligas offerre, quia citissime proficiunt anime ad salutem. Immobilia vero relinque filiis, non enim remordet consciencia mea aliqua vel male acquisiuisse vel tenuisse vel tenere voluisse.' Ex. 56. Hollman 1956, p. 179.

87 See for example Rosenthal 1972.

88 Duffy 1992, p. 338, for example, cites her revelations as the best-known descriptions of purgatory in fifteenth-century England.

> I loved him with all my heart, I should not wish to buy back his life, not with the least money. But as long as I wore the ring on my hand it was to me like a burden, since in seeing it I was reminded of my former love . . .[89]

Inasmuch as marriage was a public confirmation of her status and marked the boundaries of a woman's exercise of power, for Birgitta it was a vital first step on her way to sainthood, as it confirmed, sanctioned and extended her role and authority within the social and political sphere. She had shown that she remained always well-intentioned and devout in her material life as a wife and mother; but as a widow she would be able to channel her philanthropic, pastoral piety into a purer form of asceticism. The framework provided by the sources is constructed according to hagiographic conventions documenting the particular stages in her life: Ulf is paid scant attention, Birgitta is seen as the exemplary wife and caring mother; and in her life everything is subordinated to the praise of God. Underneath the stereotypical surface, there is, however, much detail which exposes her character as a powerful, prayerful and practical woman.

89 'Quando sepeliui virum meum, sepeliui cum eo omnem amorem carnalem, et licet dilexerim eum sicud cor meum, nollem tamen cum vno denario contra velle Dei redimere vitam eius, sed quando habui anulum in manu mea, erat michi quasi onus, quia jnspiciendo eum animus meus recordabatur priorum dileccionum, . . .'. AP p. 479.

III

Widowhood at Alvastra

> Tu autem, sponsa mea, si nichil nisi me desideraueris, si omnia pro me contempseris, non solum filios et parentes, sed eciam honores et diuicias, ego dabo tibi stipendium preciosissimum et dulcissimum.
>
> But if you, my Bride, desire nothing but me, if you reject everything for my sake, not only your children and relatives, but also titles and riches, I will give you the sweetest and most precious reward.
>
> (Book I 2)

THE FIVE YEARS that now followed mark the beginning of Birgitta's active religious calling and were the most formative and productive years of her life. As a wealthy widow in her early forties, she was in a position to choose the course of her future life. Her choice to remain in society but under the protection of a monastic house no doubt reflects a mixture of secular and religious considerations and it highlights a conflict between her worldly obligations and her personal desire to dedicate herself wholly to a spiritual life. The sources tell how in her private devotions she learned to struggle against her worldly instincts and to nurture humility and obedience. They tell too how she became more closely involved in secular affairs and showed an increasing confidence in expressing forthright opinion in political matters when she gave advice in matters of state.

The calling vision

Within a few days of Ulf's death, Birgitta was summoned to the religious life in a vision known as the 'calling vision':

> After some days, when the bride of Christ was worried about the change in her status and its bearing on her service of God, and while she was praying about this in her chapel, she became rapt in spirit; and while she was in ecstasy, she saw a bright cloud from which she heard a voice saying to her: 'Woman, hear me.' Completely terrified, and fearing that it was an illusion, she fled to her chamber; and at once she confessed and received the Body of Christ. When at last, after some days, she was at prayer in the same chapel, again that bright cloud appeared to her; and from it, she heard again a voice uttering words like those before, namely 'Woman, hear me.' Then the lady,

> again thoroughly terrified, fled to her chamber; and having confessed she communicated as before, fearing that the voice was an illusion. Finally, after some days, when she was praying again in the same place, she was indeed rapt in spirit, and again saw the bright cloud and in it, the likeness of a human being, who said this: 'Woman, hear me; I am your God, who wishes to speak with you.' Terrified, therefore, and thinking it was an illusion, she heard again: 'Fear not', he said, 'for I am the Creator of all, and not a deceiver. I do not speak to you for your sake alone, but for the sake of the salvation of others. Hear the things that I speak; and go to master Mathias, your confessor, who has the experience of discerning the two types of spirit. Say to him on my behalf what I now say to you: you shall be my bride and my channel, and you shall hear and see spiritual things, and my Spirit shall remain with you even until your death.'[1]

The central message of the revelation, which is reminiscent of the calling of some of the Old Testament prophets, is that Birgitta is summoned not for her own sake, but 'propter salutem aliorum' for the salvation of others. She was not to experience a mystical *unio* with God, in the manner of many of her predecessors, who sensed the ineffable and intense feeling of God entering their soul and revealing himself in a mysticism of transcendent love.[2] Nor was she to teach the method of the developed spiritual life, which began with the purgation of the self, and progressed though an interest in the spiritual welfare of others, an exploration of doctrinal solutions to real problems, an experience of devotional visions of Christ and the Virgin, and finally reached the unitive, and even erotic, stage in which the divine figure wooed the visionary.[3] Although Birgitta shares features in common with some of the stages of this spiritual journey, only rarely does she achieve a state in which she is united

1 'Post aliquos dies cum sponsa Christi solicita esset de mutacione status sui ad seruiendum Deo et super hoc stabat orando in capella sua, tunc rapta fuit in spiritu, et cum esset in extasi vidit nubem lucidam et de nube audiuit vocem dicentem sibi: "Mulier, audi me." Et ipsa perterrita timens, quod esset illusio, auffigit ad cameram suam, et statim confessa accepit postmodum corpus Christi. Demum cum post aliquos dies staret in oracione in eadem capella, iterum apparuit ei illa nubes lucida, et de nube audiuit iterum vocem, similia verba proferentem sicut prius, scilicet: "Mulier, audi me." Et tunc ipsa domina perterrita iterum fugit ad cameram et confessa et communicata fuit sicut prius timens illam vocem esse illusionem, deinde cum post aliquos dies iterum oraret, et rapta est in spiritu et iterum vidit nubem lucidam et in ea similitudinem hominis sic dicentem: "Mulier, audi me, ego sum Deus tuus, qui tecum loqui volo." Conterrita igitur illa putans illusionem, audiuit iterum: "Noli" inquit, "timere, quia ego sum omnium conditor, non deceptor, non enim loquor tecum propter te solam, sed propter salutem aliorum. Audi loquor et vade ad magistrum Mathiam, confessorem tuum, qui expertus est duorum spirituum secundum discrecionem, dic ei ex parte mea, que dico tibi, quia tu eris sponsa mea et canale meum et audies et videbis spiritualia, et spiritus meus permanebit tecum vsque ad mortem." ' AP pp. 80–1.

2 See on the nature of mysticism and Birgitta's place in its history Dinzelbacher 1991.

3 These stages are identified and examined by Petroff 1986, pp. 6–20.

with God in a boundless union of reciprocal mystical love.[4] Her role was essentially as a conduit of moral guidance to other people and actively to participate in their salvation. The word 'mystic' is therefore less applicable to her than 'visionary' or 'prophet'.[5]

Propheticism was traditionally recognised as one of the *charismata* of the Holy Spirit. The prophet was charged with communicating the divine message to the people, and he (or she) became the receptacle of divine wisdom and the means of making God's word known. Gregory the Great provides a rationale of prophecy in his homilies on the Book of Ezekiel, which became central to later discussions of prophecy. He argues that prophecy can speak about the past and present as well as the future, and he describes it as dealing with the disclosure of hidden things, and the revealing of a secret knowledge which has an unchallengeable truth.[6] The prophet sees things spiritually where others see them corporeally, and in his (or her) mind internal things are so linked with external things that they both together seem indistinguishable.

In the general understanding of the concept of prophecy as it had been developed by the later middle ages, Birgitta is deemed a prophet who was given privileged knowledge about the past, present and future. Her confessors' *vita* accordingly describes her as having had 'the true spirit of prophecy and intellectual vision', and they say they had witnessed things which she had prophetically foretold many years before: 'Indeed, after this lady had been called into the Spirit of God, she prophesied not only about the future – as did the prophets – but also about the present and past.'[7] More specifically, this type of religious prophecy, as Robert Lerner has suggested, is an expression of dissatisfaction with prevailing attitudes and a hope for the future; and therefore to be heard, the words of the prophet had to be in accordance with the general mood of the time.[8]

The phrase in the 'calling vision' that she would become the 'bride and channel' ('sponsa et canale') of Christ confirms her role as the communicator of divine knowledge.[9] Again, despite the frequency of the references to her as 'bride' throughout the revelations, the bridal imagery and her bridal role are played down, and she is called simply to obedience and to fulfil God's will in the world. Her spiritual union with Christ was to produce spiritual children who would do God's will in the world, and to contribute towards the work of

4 Dinzelbacher 1991, p. 363, identifies Ex. 116 (wrongly given as 166) as the only unequivocal record of a unitive experience.

5 She never uses the term 'prophet' of herself, however. On Birgitta as prophet, see the discussions by Lindblom 1963, pp. 18–26; Piltz 1991; Piltz 1993; Sahlin 1996.

6 See Evans 1986, pp. 42–5.

7 AP p. 86.

8 Lerner 1976, especially p. 17.

9 The phrase is often translated as 'bride and mouthpiece'; see for discussions Piltz 1993, Børresen 1991, and Sahlin 1996, 'Birgitta of Sweden . . .', pp. 67–82.

salvation. To achieve this, she is designated as a *canale*, which strictly means a 'pipe', 'channel', or 'conduit of liquids' and she is called to an active role, to be the means by which God makes his will known to man, and to work tirelessly towards the salvation of the world.[10]

Self-doubt and support

Birgitta's new status as a widow gave her an independence she had previously not had: jurisdiction over economic matters, freedom to dispose of her goods and property and to make provisions for her children.

In the main, the sources are silent on the disposal of her estates, as they are about the provisions of Ulf's will.[11] She divided her possessions among her children and the poor, but kept some aside for her journey to Rome, which had already been foretold to her.[12] Several episodes, presumably dating from the years around Ulf's death, are recorded in Book VI in connection with visits to her estates, and provide glimpses into her changed life and the gradual development of her spirituality at this time. Book VI 76 tells of a fire which burned up all her belongings and those of her servants while she was staying at the farm of a man in her employment, who was a wizard (*incantator*) from Hjo in Skara diocese.[13] Christ first chides her for employing people with good looks and attractive clothes, whose moral laxity she does not restrain for fear of appearing too severe with them and for wishing to ingratiate herself with them. Secondly, Christ says that the wizard has false beliefs and swears oaths and invokes demonic formulas to ensure a good catch when he is fishing. He ignored Birgitta's admonishments and was afterwards found dead in his bed 'with his neck bent backwards'. This local incident suggests an unwillingness on Birgitta's part to be harsh and judgemental on her servantfolk and subordinates during the early days of her widowhood at least; later, her attitude was less conciliatory. Other revelations in the same section of Book VI deal with pagan practices which probably shed light on local custom and folklore in Sweden at the time. One concerns a house she stayed at, where the devil's

10 The term *canale* is used of Birgitta by St Agnes in Book III 30, and elsewhere the receipt of God's word is described by means of a tube conducting wine (Book VII 31 *fistulam*), a drink which sustains and fortifies her (Book V int. 11), a musical instrument (Book IV 100), a vessel of wine (Book II 16), a servant carrying precious gold for his master (Book II 14), a bride who obeys her husband (Book I 59), a daughter-in-law who carries out the wishes of her husband's ageing parents (Book VI 88) and a furnace (Book VII 12). In Book V int. 11.10 the idea is used in a metaphor describing God's words as a thirst-quenching drink.

11 Later sources and the Vadstena land records reveal that by the end of the medieval period most of her and Ulf's estates had come into the possession of Vadstena monastery. See Klockars 1976, pp. 101–08.

12 AP p. 88.

13 AP p. 514.

voice could be heard from inside the oven, giving responses and prophecies, except when she was nearby.[14] She heard a divine voice telling her that the inhabitants of the house revered household gods (*penates*) and did not go to church, and the voice instructed her confessor to teach them the true faith and exhort them to cease putting out milk for snakes, and stop making offerings of their cattle, swine, bread, wine and other things.[15] The following revelation describes a charlatan priest who administered the mass, but was forgiven when Birgitta prayed for him; and in this revelation she addresses the philosophical question of whether the congregation to whom he had administered the sacrament or the children he had baptised would be damned. The next revelation concerns a woman who was possessed by the devil so that in turns she swelled up as if pregnant and then became emaciated, and when her mistress asked Birgitta's advice, the woman was instructed through Christ to repent of a longstanding sin and accused of having received communion without full confession. In Book VI 81 a three-year-old boy became distraught unless water was sprinkled on him, and his mother was possessed by a devil; she had given the child a 'baptism as women do who do not recognise the words of the Holy Trinity'. In the last revelation in the sequence a knight asked a sybil (*phiton*) whether a revolt against the king of Sweden should be undertaken, and the old woman prophesied that peace would prevail; the knight then related this to the king in Birgitta's presence, and she immediately heard Christ tell her that the old woman was an instrument of the devil and that all people who rely on sorcery should be dealt with severely.

Through outright condemnation of sorcery like this Birgitta distances herself from those who engage in superstitious practice. The divide between prophetic calling and witchcraft was of course a delicate one, but by adducing demonstrations of her own hostility to supernatural practices, Birgitta's supporters were able to show that she herself could be completely dissociated from sorcery.[16] For a woman – even a highly placed noblewoman – to act in a way that ran counter to convention and custom and to interfere in other people's moral behaviour, as Birgitta does in some of these instances, and for her to assume an authority which exceeded social expectations, was to run the risk of being accused of witchcraft herself. Indeed, there were occasions when she was accused of being a pythoness or sorceress. A certain Juliana Nilsdotter's testimony tells how a number of Swedish noblemen had become concerned that the king was relying on Birgitta's counsel; and Birgitta's daughter, Katarina Ulfsdotter, also remarks on the hostility of the Swedish nobility towards Birgitta, who, she says, did not believe that she spoke on behalf of God and would have killed her had they not feared retribution from her

14 Book VI 78. According to AP p. 540 this event took place near Lödöse.

15 Birgitta uses here the same motif as her confessor Mathias, in his *Homo Conditus*, on putting out porridge for the trolls. See Piltz 1986, p. 146.

16 See further Sahlin 1996, 'Gender and Prophetic Authority . . .'.

relatives.[17] A knight called Knut, seeing that the king had been converted to a devout life by Birgitta, tipped water on her from a window as she crossed a narrow street; a knight named Karl deliberately pushed into her in the court; and one of the king's advisers persuaded a man to feign drunkenness and accuse her of too much dreaming:

> '. . . you dream too much and keep vigil too much, it would do you good to drink more and sleep more. Surely God does not abandon monastic people and speak with proud people of the world. It's folly to trust your words.'[18]

Such incidents are suggestive of Birgitta's vulnerability at the time of her calling and of her need for support from members of the Church establishment who recognised her special visionary gift. The man to whom she was instructed to turn in the 'calling' revelation was Mathias Övidsson, canon of Linköping cathedral, who was said to have been expert in the 'discernment of spirits', the ability to distinguish between good and evil spirits.[19] The undisputed facts about his life are few.[20] He was probably born about the same time as Birgitta; and his name is first mentioned in diocesan documents from Linköping in 1333. He studied almost certainly in Paris, and held the title *magister in artibus* when he returned to Sweden and became canon and prebendary at Linköping. Between 1333 and 1342 there is no record of him, and during these years he was probably engaged in further studies in Paris, now in theology. When he returned to Sweden he must have been qualified as *magister in theologia* or *magister in sacra pagina*, as the Birgittine documents refer to him.

Mathias was a prolific writer with something of a reputation as a theologian in Europe. Two handbooks on the art of poetry, the *Poetria* and *Testa nucis*, demonstrate his breadth of learning in the humanist tradition.[21] His most substantial work, preserved only in fragments, is the alphabetical concordance of the Bible, known as the *Alphabetum distinccionum*, which contains literal, allegorical and moral discussions of the main nouns, verbs, names and natural objects mentioned in the Scripture; this is probably the work the Birgittine sources refer to as his glossary of the Bible. He places special emphasis on the moral interpretations and many of the entries resemble theological excurses

17 AP pp. 66, 313.

18 'nimis sompnias, nimis vigilas, expedit tibi plus bibere et plus dormire, numquit Deus relinquit religiosas personas et cum superbis personis mundi loquitur? Vanum enim est verbis tuis dare fidem.' AP p. 493.

19 See *Dictionnaire de spiritualité ascétique et mystique* s.v. 'Discernement des esprits'. During the fourteenth century the discernment of spirits was keenly debated, and its traditional interpretation as a special gift – like prophecy – was called into question by the theologian and academic Jean Gerson who was later to be one of Birgitta's main opponents. See further Chapter VI, p. 153.

20 On Mathias see especially Strömberg 1943, Strömberg 1944, Piltz 1974.

21 See Bergh 1996.

on particular doctrinal issues.[22] Another work is the *Homo conditus*, a theological handbook intended for preachers, written in a direct, popular style and steeped in scriptural language. The *Copia exemplorum* complements the *Homo conditus*, and is a pastoral manual containing homiletic *exempla*, many of them deriving from French mendicant tradition and providing guidance for the conversion and confession of ordinary laymen.[23]

Probably his most original and important work is the *Exposicio super apocalypsim*, which gives a literal and spiritual exposition of the Book of the Apocalypse.[24] This is the work which Bernadino of Siena (1380–1444), the great Italian preacher, copied and used as a major source for his sermons, and which Nicholas of Cusa (1401–46) ordered to be copied, after hearing Bernadino draw on the Swedish theologian's work. It describes the deep-rooted theological truths as they are realised in the three ages, past, present and future. The seven churches signify the seven virtues of the active man. The seven seals are the seven afflictions: the suffering of the just, the well-being of the wicked, the struggles against heretics, false brethren and hypocrites, the prosperity of the wicked and the sins of the good. The seven trumpets represent the sevenfold corruption of the Church. The punishment for everything will be undertaken by evil princes, who are symbolised by grasshoppers and scorpions. True Christians will decrease in number, and their influence will wane. The end will be at hand, and Antichrist will deceive the world with all kinds of stratagems. Yet Christ will watch over his Church and ensure that it does not perish. He makes the Scripture plainer and more comprehensible by means of his good shepherds, although their efforts will remain largely unheeded. Mathias presents a gloomy picture of the state of Christendom, and urges a thorough reform of the Church by savage attacks on priests and clerics, who are more corrupt, ambitious and greedy than any pagan, and attacks on the Roman curia, which he considers is more degenerate than any local church.

Mathias's writings are estimated to have run to some 1600 pages in folio, and many of them are still unedited. Nor has his theology been studied in any depth, which makes it difficult to assess his impact on Swedish theological discourse, and more particularly, on Birgitta's spiritual development.[25] In most respects he is a traditionalist, who belongs more naturally to the thirteenth than the fourteenth century, and to the great tradition of Bible commentators. He presses for a return to biblical study as a basis of theology, using always holy Scripture as the starting point of his teaching. In his emphasis on

22 Piltz discusses, for example, his entry on *posse*, which reflects the contemporary scholastic debate on God's *potentia absoluta* and *potentia ordinata*, and on *fomes*, which makes plain his defence, in line with Franciscan doctrine, of the immaculate conception of the Virgin. Piltz 1986, pp. 140–1.

23 Piltz 1984, Wåhlin 1990.

24 It has not been edited in full, but see Billing-Ottosson 1960. The following summary and discussion is based on Piltz 1986.

25 But see Piltz 1986.

biblical study there is a strong Franciscan echo, and he frequently cites St Bonaventure (d.1274), who saw theology not as a dry and distant discipline, but one which touched the ordinary lives of people in their moral as well as intellectual affairs. The Bible, for Bonaventure as for Mathias, was always to be at the centre of religious study, and theology must be a pastoral, not purely an academic pursuit. Furthermore, he is a learned preacher who has a mistrust of logic-chopping scholastic argument, which was characteristic of fourteenth-century debate; and he was also concerned over the lamentable state of the Church of his time and the lax moral standards around him. He must also have been familiar with a number of individual heresies, such as the doctrine of the beatific vision, and with theological debates within the Church, such as Averroism, which argued that reason and philosophy were superior to faith and knowledge, and which was was banned repeatedly by the Paris bishops. He must also have confronted the tide of Nominalism that was sweeping the schools of Europe. Birgitta suggests that he battled intellectually with some of these new doctrines and underwent a personal struggle of faith at some stage in his life, when he was confronted by heretical demons asserting 'We are the truth.' Her advice to him, when he is faced with doubt, is to 'Preach firmly.'[26] Strewn across the entire body of Revelations there are several references to his intellectual struggles and stand against heresy; and indeed, their frequent repetition and insistent wording may suggest that he had in fact acquired a reputation for heresy from which the Birgittine editors later wished to dissociate themselves.[27]

It is unknown exactly when Birgitta and Mathias became acquainted, but he may have been her confessor during her marriage, and he is referred to as her confessor in her calling vision. Mathias's influence on Birgitta must have developed considerably at the beginning of her mystical life: her visions and his writings were being produced more or less at the same time, and their close confessor–confessant relationship must have led to the exchange of thoughts and wide-ranging discussions on similar topics, even if her approach was from the perspective of revealed knowledge, and his from that of reasoned knowledge. One revelation tells how Mathias asked her while he was writing his commentary on the Apocalypse, 'to pray for spiritual knowledge of when the Antichrist would come and whether the Book of Revelation was indeed written by St John, for many claimed the opposite'; and in another revelation Christ acknowledges that the words of the Book of the Apocalypse

26 E.g. Book VI 75. AP pp. 530, 620.

27 An example is Book V int. 16.3. (Here his success in withstanding temptations is compared to the intellectual arrogance of the cleric of the vision. Mathias has otherwise nothing to do with the vision, and the introduction of his name appears like an editorial addition.) See too AP pp. 530, 620, Book VI 75. The suggestion that Mathias may have been connected with new intellectual ideas, such as Nominalism, cannot however be upheld until more work is done on his theology.

are obscure, but would be made clear when it pleased him.[28] Her revelations frequently contain echoes of the motifs and images employed by preachers, and here again she must have adopted many of Mathias's methods. Proverbs, *exempla* and realistic details are drawn from everyday life, as well as the Bible, from which allegories are developed, using the traditional fourfold division of scriptural exegesis (i.e. the literal, the allegorical, the anagogic and the tropological interpretations of the biblical text); although in Birgitta's exegeses these divisions are frequently blurred. In addition to their shared interest in preaching, Birgitta and Mathias also have a similar view of the state of the Church and the importance of the Bible as a foundation for faith, and all of these major themes came to dominate her subsequent visionary life.

Cistercian milieu

After settling Ulf's estate Birgitta moved to the Cistercian monastery of Alvastra, where he had been buried.[29] Alvastra, which was founded in 1143, was situated in a secluded site close to the eastern shore of Lake Vättern, at the foot of the Omberg hills, and near to the power base of the twelfth-century Sverker kings. King Sverker the Elder's wife, Ulfhild, had been given the site of the monastery and village of Alvastra on her marriage, and it appears that it was she who was instrumental in inviting the Cistercians to establish their order in Sweden: according to the *Exordium Magnum,* St Bernard had sent a group of monks from Clairvaux 'at the request of a pious lady, the Queen of Sweden'.[30]

It is not clear what Birgitta's relations with the monastery were: a male house of one of the strictest monastic orders seemed an unlikely place for a high-ranking noblewoman to take up residence. Perhaps it is significant that she chose not to enter one of the Cistercian nunneries, such as the royal foundation at nearby Vreta, the oldest and most distinguished nunnery in Sweden which served a clear purpose in providing unmarried women and widows from the higher nobility and even royalty with a place, including those that did not feel a religious vocation. She may have moved to Alvastra at the instigation of Mathias, who was a friend of Peter Olofsson, then sub-prior, and she is likely to have made an endowment to the monastery in exchange for permission to live there.[31] Peter became her confessor at the monastery around

28 Book VI 89, I 56. Apocalyptic images and their typology are a key part of Birgitta's visions. See further Piltz 1991 and Piltz 1993, who argues that she uses the Bible, and especially the Book of the Apocalypse and the Old Testament, as a frame and structure, rather like a stage, into which she sets herself physically and takes part in biblical narratives.

29 AP pp. 479, 499. Ulf's grave was discovered in 1828, and is now in the Historiska Museet, Stockholm.

30 France 1992, p. 164, and pp. 29–32.

31 France 1992, p. 396. Born around 1307, Peter was well acquainted with Birgitta's close family, but little else is known about him until the late 1340s, when he was

1345, and was present when her husband Ulf died. He remained at her side for the remainder of her life, as the main transcriber of her revelations.

Even at this early stage in her life as a visionary, she is more secure in a male domain. Nevertheless, her supporters had to ensure that she gained acceptance by the suspicious male community at the monastery. Decrees from the General Chapter had expressly forbidden the entry of laymen into enclosures; and women were not allowed to stay overnight without a special dispensation.[32] Although Birgitta is unlikely to have lived within the enclosure itself at Alvastra she may have been allowed into the part of the church which was used by the monastic laypeople. Certainly she had easy access to the church, as is testified by Juliana Nilsdotter, one of her companions at the time, who provides a valuable glimpse into her life in these years:

> At night she got up several times to pray, and when the cock crowed, she got up for good and remained in the church until the singing of prime. And then in order to get warm from the icy cold, she went to a heated room and there read part of the psalter, as long as she was staying there, and returned to the church until the main meal, praying and hearing the canonical hours. When she had eaten, she went back to prayer straightway for a while and spent time on pious works for decorating altars and the priests' garments; and she had chalices made and gave them to the churches and she never ceased from her labour until at the hour of vespers she returned to the church until supper. Afterwards she took care of business with her servants and then went to compline. Afterwards she refused to speak; indeed she spoke with no one until the first hour of the next day.[33]

But her presence at the monastery was not generally welcome. One longstanding resident of some forty years – a devout man by the name of Gerekinus, who was prone to seeing heavenly apparitions when he spent his nights in prayer, and who saw the boy Jesus when the host was elevated during the mass – objected to the presence of a woman there: 'Why does that lady reside here in a monastery of monks, introducing a new custom against

called to become a transcriber of the revelations, a role, we are told, that he felt unfit for, and fell into a bodily paralysis until he accepted. For a brief biography see Aili 1995. See Ex. 48.

32 Ortved 1927, p. 93; McGuire 1990, p. 302 note 43.

33 'Jtem in noctibus pluries surrexit ad orandum, sed in gallicantu surrexit ex toto et remansit in ecclesia, quousque prima fuit cantata, et tunc propter refocillacionem frigoris adiuit estiuarium et ibi legit partem psalterij, quamdiu traxit ibi moram, et reuertebatur ad ecclesiam vsque a ad prandium orando et audiendo horas canonicas, post prandium morabatur statim in oracione ad tempus et deinde vacabat operi pio pro ornatu altarium et vestium sacerdotum, et calices fieri fecit et ecclesijs dedit et numquam alij vacabat operi, deinde hora vesperorum ad ecclesiam reuertebatur vsque ad cenam, facta cena et expeditis negocijs cum familiaribus legit completorium suum et postea negabat loqui, ymo neminj loquebatur vsque ad horam primam sequentis diei.' AP p. 65. Translation from McGuire 1990, p. 302.

our rule?' He heard a voice telling him that she had come in order that at the foot of this mountain (that is, Omberg) 'she may gather flowers from which all people, even beyond the world's end, shall receive medicine'.[34] With her special mystical gift, by which she was directly commanded by God, she had an authority which absolved her (and the abbot of the monastery who gave her special privileges) of all responsibility for contravening the monastic rule. Her presence at the monastery enabled her to bring about a renewal of the spiritual life there; for some brethren, like Gerekinus, and one named Paulus who doubted her sanity, experienced a deepening of their personal faith through her influence there, and Alvastra as a community gained a fresh impetus in its devotional life.[35]

Books I and II

During this period of growing spirituality Birgitta received a substantial number of visions. Some of her earliest ones are recorded in Book I, a collection of sixty revelations on disparate subjects. In their present form they extend from one to four printed pages and are written either in dialogue or meditation form, or they follow the pattern of homiletic discourses which use *exempla* and likenesses to introduce spiritual material. Usually, Birgitta is addressed by Christ, although in about a fifth of the revelations in Book I it is the Virgin who speaks; and an Angel and John the Baptist are also the mouthpieces in two revelations.

The way in which she experienced her visions varied.[36] Sometimes she appeared to be half-dead and sometimes she would fall into ecstasy while in prayer, or while reading.[37] On other occasions she would feel the movement of God in her heart, like the stirring of a child in the womb, as was experienced by Magister Mathias and Prior Peter at Alvastra who both saw and touched her body for themselves one Christmas Eve.[38] It is clear that she had little difficulty in becoming rapt in spirit, and the sources repeatedly tell that she received her visions while awake and not in sleep, although they are not received in a state of delerium, but are intellectually apprehended and stated.

The subjects of the revelations in Book I are typical of the themes and preoccupations that occur in later Books. Several revelations relate to Birgitta's visionary calling, and list the duties of the bride, her need for abstinence, continence, humility and obedience. She is taught how to develop an exemplary life in the imitation of Christ and she is given encouragement in her private

34 Ex. 55. See too Book IV 121, AP pp. 82, 619–20, 545.
35 AP p. 488. See further on her relations with the monks at Alvastra, McGuire 1990.
36 On the description of the various ways in which she received visions by Prior Peter, see AP p. 484.
37 E.g. Ex. 96.
38 Book VI 88.

devotions. Recommendations are made for Mathias of Linköping: because he can discern good from evil influence and genuine from fraudulent vision he should be entrusted with her spiritual guidance, teaching her more of Christian doctrine, and protecting her from misguided thoughts and from the suspicion and scorn of the sceptics around her. Some revelations outline her devotion to the Virgin.[39] Other revelations deal with clerics, like the lapsed prior of a Cistercian monastery in Book I 13 who is attacked for having buried an excommunicate.[40] Some criticise the pride and rapacity of the nobility, such as Book I 17, which is the first of many judgement scenes to occur in all the Revelation Books. Some visions in Book I attack people in general for their disdain of Christian virtues and insufficient love of God, and in particular there is a critique of degenerate clergy. Two revelations are directed at Pope Clement VI; and there are passionate calls for the reform of the Church.[41] Other revelations attack intellectual arrogance and the pursuit of knowledge for its own sake; and there is also advice on her intended monastery.[42]

A vigorous defence of the visions is given by Mathias in his celebrated Prologue to Book I, in which he becomes the guarantor of their authenticity, and declares publicly his recognition of her newly acquired role as prophet and visionary.[43] He opens with the statement, echoing Jeremiah 5.30, that wondrous and astonishing things were reported happening in his country: 'Stupor et mirabilia audita sunt in terra nostra.' He implies that the response to Birgitta's new role as the bride of Christ was being expressed by dismissive hostility, scorn and incredulity. He defends her special gifts with such vehemence, indeed, that he makes the remarkably bold statement that the fact of Christ revealing himself to Birgitta and choosing to make an earthly woman, and moreover one who had been married, into an instrument of divine grace, is more extraordinary than the Incarnation itself.[44]

The Prologue includes the revelation Birgitta received immediately after her 'calling vision', which contains an attack on the nobles of Sweden, many of them no doubt personally known to Birgitta.[45] After a preamble about devilish pride, it is said in this revelation that the courtiers and knights of Sweden

39 E.g. Book I 19.

40 Some have identified him with Prior Ragnvald of Alvastra, who was abbot while Birgitta was connected with the house. See Undhagen 1978, p. 275.

41 Book I 23–4, 6, 59.

42 E.g. Book I 33, 18.

43 See further Undhagen 1978, pp. 38–50.

44 This reference to the Incarnation (Prol. §§ 21–3) has led some scholars to see influence of the apocalyptic ideas of Joachim of Fiore (d.1202) and an expectation in Mathias of the dawning of a new, third, age for Christendom: Jørgensen 1954, II p. 23; Sundén 1973, p. 11; Undhagen 1978, p. 45 note 52. However, others argue that such influence remains to be more clearly demonstrated: Reeves 1969, p. 338 note 4; Fogelqvist 1993, p. 32 note 19. On the Prologue Revelation, see also Børresen 1991.

45 This revelation exists in Swedish translation, and was probably intended as a broadsheet aimed at 'swerikes mæn' 'Sweden's men'; see Liedgren 1961, Moberg 1980.

have sinned in pride and greed, and now they must be put to death, their limbs fed to wild animals and their chattels confiscated. The place of the high and mighty in society who have not heeded God's word will be taken by the meek and helpless, children and the destitute, in order that God's multitude will not be decreased; here again, Birgitta's calling as the vehicle of moral reform and the salvation of Sweden is reiterated.

Mathias implies, however, that an unconditional acceptance of Birgitta's new role is difficult even for the most devout believers, and he presents a number of arguments for demonstrating the authenticity of the revelations: evil spirits cannot deceive truly righteous people; Birgitta did not seek personal honour; witnesses could be found to confirm her alleged good deeds; the revelations are full of the 'power of truth' and therefore had to come from the 'spirit of truth'. He argues that her revelations are authentic because she is unlearned, and therefore could not fabricate her utterances, and that there was evidence of a miracle having taken place, exorcism of an evil spirit, and conversion to a devout life, which proved further the authenticity of her experiences.

Many of the themes in Book I are taken further in Book II. There is continued confirmation of the authenticity of the visions against the doubts of sceptics and several times it is stressed that the visions are indeed divinely inspired.[46] In Book II 1, her 'magister' is quoted in passing as having given her good instruction, thus confirming his supporting role of her. Book II 17 contains a plea to a preacher to disseminate her visions. In Book II 16 Christ says she should love all, including those who appear to hate and slander her. He advises her to beware of all pride, arrogance and fleshly desires, and to avoid vanity and worldly excesses and pleasures, and he tells her that she will be granted moderation in sleep and food for the well-being of her body. In Book II 18 she asks why she, 'a simple widow', has been chosen and she is compared to the phoenix which rose from the ashes when it had shed the skin of concupiscence.

The majority of the visions of Book II, however, concern her interest in public affairs and matters of state, and deal in particular with the role and function of those who perform the public ministry of Christian service, especially knights and preachers. The significant body of revelations on knighthood, across her whole output of visions, could be pieced together into a 'mirror of knights' which sheds light on her understanding of this social class.[47] She herself had close ties with this class and in her revelations she made many personal attacks on individuals who must have been well-known

46 E.g. Book II 10, 28.

47 Her attitude to knighthood has as not yet been examined in detail, either in the historical context of the Swedish knights amongst whom she lived, or as a metaphorical ideal of which the supreme embodiment was Christ, whom she depicts in full battle dress as a knight militant. See KLNM 'riddare', Löfqvist 1935.

to her; it is scarcely surprising, therefore, that she is sometimes denounced by them. Like St Bernard, who sought a unification between spiritual and earthly concerns in warfare, and a crusading ideal for knights in all they undertook, Birgitta saw the function and role of knights as inextricably bound up with their duty of service to God. The qualities they should pursue are similar to those necessary for joining religious orders: humility, obedience, patience and faith. Furthermore, she observes a deterioration of standards in the ideal of the chivalric as well as the monastic life, which has led to a weakening of both institutions.[48] One of the most important visions on knighthood is Book II 13, which contains an elaborate description of a dubbing ritual:

> Say then to the man who wishes to make his knighthood mine that he can please me again in this way. The man who wants to become a knight should proceed to the churchyard with his horse and equipment, and there leave his horse; for the horse is not created for man's pride but for use and defence in life and for combatting God's enemies. Then he shall put on his cloak, the band of which is placed over his forehead, so that in the same way as the deacon puts on a stole as a sign of obedience and divine patience, so the knight may put on the cloak and place the band over his forehead as a sign of promised knighthood and the obedience which he should adopt to defend my cross. The banner of worldly power shall go before him, so that he should know that he should obey worldly power in everything which is not against God. When he has come into the churchyard, the priests may receive him with the Church's banner, on which my suffering and my wounds must be displayed, as a sign that he should defend God's Church and faith and also obey the Church's leaders. But when he goes into the church the worldly banner must stay outside and my banner should precede him into the church, as a sign that divine power precedes worldly power and that man should care more for spiritual than temporal things. When the mass has been read as far as the 'Agnus Dei', the worldly lord – the king or another – shall go to the knight around the altar and say: 'Do you wish to become a knight?' When he answers 'I do' the king shall add: 'Do you promise God and me that you wish to defend the faith of the Holy Church and obey its representatives in everything which reflects God's honour?' When the knight says 'I do' he shall hand him a sword and say: 'See, I hand you the sword, so that you should not spare your life for the faith and God's Church, and so that you should subjugate God's enemies and defend God's friends.' Then he should give him a shield and say: 'See, I give to you a shield, so that you may defend yourself against God's enemies and give widows and orphans help and in everything increase God's honour.' Thereafter he shall place his hand on the knight's neck and say: 'See, now you are subordinate to the obedience and power of the Church. Ensure that just as you have bound yourself by a promise, that you also fulfil it in deeds.' After this he shall place the cloak and its band over him, so that he may daily have

48 Book II 7–10.

in mind what he had promised God and that through a pronouncement in the Church's presence he promised more than others to defend God's Church.[49]

Dubbing rituals which took place in the context of a mass, in church, were common practice in Europe at this time; but it has been suggested that the fact that Birgitta outlines the ritual in such a prescriptive fashion may suggest that it was new in Sweden and that she was advocating the introduction of the European ritual there.[50] Her view of the knight describes him first and foremost as a loyal servant of Christ (rather than of his secular ruler), for whom he should be prepared to lay down his life, to protect the Church and the faith. Although she reproduces the traditional spiritual and temporal objectives of the knight class she always places greatest emphasis on the spiritual role of knighthood.

49 'Dic ergo illi, qui miliciam suam ad me conuertere vellet, quod sub hac forma michi denuo placere posset. Quicumque enim miles fieri vellet, deberet cum equo suo et apparatu ad cimiterium ecclesie procedere et ibi eum relinquere, quia equus non est creatus ad superbiam hominum sed ad vite utilitatem et ad defensionem et inimicorum Dei expugnacionem. Deinde assumat mantellum, cuius ligatura ponenda est super frontem, ut, sicut diaconus assumit stolam in signum obediencie et paciencie diuine, sic ipse miles assumit mantellum et ligaturam ponit super frontem in signum professe milicie et obediencie pro crucis mee defensione assumenda. Quem eciam precedat vexillum potestatis secularis, ut sciat se potestati mundane in omnibus, que non sunt contra Deum, debere obedire. Ingresso autem eo cimiterium clerici occurrant ei cum vexillo ecclesie, in quo depicta sit passio mea et vulnera mea in signum, quod Ecclesiam Dei et fidem defendere deberet et prelatis eius eciam obtemperare. Cum autem ingreditur ecclesiam, vexillum temporalis potestatis foras ecclesiam remaneat et vexillum meum precedat eum in ecclesiam in signum, quod diuina potestas precedit secularem et quod de spiritualibus plus est curandum quam de temporalibus. Dicta vero missa usque ad "Agnus Dei" prelatus, scilicet rex vel alius, procedat ad militem circa altare et dicat: "Vis tu fieri miles?" Quo respondente "Volo", subiungat: "Promitte", inquit, "Deo et michi te fidem sancte Ecclesie defendere et prelatis eius in omnibus, que ad Deum sunt, obedire!" Quo respondente "Volo", tradat gladium in manus eius et dicat: "Ecce trado tibi gladium in manus tuas, ut non parcas vite tue pro fide et Ecclesia Dei, ut inimicos Dei deprimas et ut amicos Dei defendas." Postea committat ei clipeum et dicat: "Ecce do tibi clipeum, ut defendas te contra inimicos Dei, ut viduis et orphanis tribuas auxilium et ut honorem Dei in omnibus augmentes." Postea manum imponit collo eius dicens: "Ecce obediencie subiectus es/t/ et potestati. Vide ergo, ut, sicut ligasti te professione, sic impleas et opere!" Post hoc autem mantellum adaptet sibi et ligaturam, ut cotidie habeat in memoria, quid Deo vouit et quod ad Ecclesie Dei defensionem plus quam alii se professione in facie ecclesie obligauit.' (Quoted from Bergh's concordance.)

50 See Löfqvist 1935, pp. 107–9. It is worth noting that a similar ritual is used for the initiation of nuns at Vadstena. See Härdelin 1993, p. 207.

France and England at war

As the number of revelations increased it became necessary to have them examined and publicly endorsed, and to this end a commission was set up and held, probably in Uppsala in 1346, by the archbishop, Hemming Nilsson. It consisted of three bishops: Peter Tyrgilsson of Linköping, Thomas of Växjö, and Hemming of Turku (Åbo), as well as a magister (no doubt Mathias of Linköping) and an abbot (normally assumed to be Peter of Alvastra).[51] These men were among the highest-placed churchmen in the country, and some of them were well-known to Birgitta.[52] It is unclear exactly which revelations were the subject of this examination, but they may have included the majority of the revelations that Birgitta had received by the time the commission was convened. The commission gave its full recognition to Birgitta's visionary messages, and soon afterwards, probably somewhere between Easter and September 1347, a number of revelations directed at foreign magnates was sent with a delegation to the pope in Avignon.[53] The enterprise was sanctioned and possibly paid for by the Swedish king, and led by Bishop Hemming, who was accompanied by Prior Peter of Alvastra.[54]

The purpose of this ambitious mission was twofold: Hemming was charged with delivering a message to the pope instructing him to go to Italy for the Holy Year of Jubilee in 1350, and also with taking a sequence of revelations which included a proposed solution to the hostilities between England and France in the opening stages of the Hundred Years War.[55] The long and

51 See Book I 52, in which the Virgin prays that the revelations will take root in people's hearts and extend their branches through the world and bear good fruits. She commands Birgitta to tell her friend (presumably Mathias) 'that he should meticulously lay forth in writing these words before his spiritual father . . . and he will convey them to the archbishop and thereafter to another bishop. When these persons have been thoroughly acquainted with them he will send them to a third bishop.' See further on the commission Undhagen 1978, pp. 47–50.

52 Hemming, for example, was a close friend of Birgitta's and respected by her for his courage and piety. With the small numbers of clerics in Sweden, it was probably difficult to find completely independent investigators who had no prior knowledge of Birgitta, and thus the commission cannot have been totally impartial.

53 A manuscript in Avignon from Gregory XI's library in 1375 notes a volume which fits the description of the texts presented to Clement: 'Item in volumine signato cclxxxiii quidam liber, in quo continentur invocaciones ad deum et ad beatam Mariam virginem et ad dominum Clementem papam sextam et ad reges'. Quoted from Klockars 1960, p. 175. The mention of a 'volume' suggests that a larger, rather than a smaller number of revelations was presented to the pope.

54 See Book I 52, the last part of which is addressed to Hemming. Ex. 85 tells how he is taking a message not to heathens, but to bad Christians, which is a harder task to accomplish. Ex. 104 states that he will carry the message, and in Ex. 51 he is told not to curtail the message but he may add to it if it is necessary for the desired objectives.

55 It is sometimes suggested that Hemming may also have laid before the pope plans for the foundation of the new Birgittine monastery, and also that he sought a bull, on

bitter dispute about territorial possessions in France and the succession to the French throne had reached a head in May 1337 when the French king, Philippe VI, declared Edward III of England's continental possessions confiscate. Edward sailed to the continent in July 1338, with a small English army, and after having negotiated a series of military alliances with the Low Countries and German princes, which were to prove expensive and unreliable for him. In the early 1340s he won the support of Flemish leaders who were anxious to maintain their supply of English wool for their textile industries. After the battle of Sluys he embarked on a lengthy and unsuccessful siege of Tournai, which collapsed due to his severe financial problems, and the failing support of his continental allies. Several lesser campaigns continued to take place throughout France, from Aquitaine to Brittany, and in the summer of 1346, Edward landed at La Hougue in the Cotentin and marched through Normandy, past Paris and towards his fief of Ponthieu, where at Crécy in 1346 he defeated the French army in a crushing battle in which many of the nobility were slain; and he then proceeded to besiege Calais. It was probably in the wake of the battle of Crécy that Birgitta made her abortive attempt to offer a solution for peace.

The message addressed to Clement VI, in Book VI 63, instructs him to arrange peace between the warring parties, and accuses him of partisanship, faintheartedness and lack of resolve in his policy towards the war.[56] Birgitta's judgement of him is severe, since from his election in 1342, he had worked continually on attempts to bring about truces and accords between the two sides. In 1343 he had successfully negotiated a truce and arranged for a peace conference to be held in Avignon in October 1344, which was eventually broken by the battle of Crécy. After the fall of Calais in 1347, another truce was negotiated through his cardinals, which lasted until 1354, two years after his death. However, whether Clement showed the necessary neutrality in his mediation efforts is indeed doubtful and he appears to have sided with the French, as the English repeatedly claimed. He had formerly been a papal legate to Philippe in 1338, and there is evidence that he sent copies of his correspondence with Edward to Philippe, and that he wrote in a letter in 1345 saying that the negotiations were going badly and that Philippe should prepare again for war.[57]

Birgitta is in no doubt about the pope's pro-French position. She herself takes the opposite side, and it is therefore scarcely surprising that her

behalf of the king, to undertake a crusade to Russia, but there is no concrete evidence for these proposals, plausible though they may be. An account of the mission is given by Klockars 1960, pp. 151–78. On the war in general see Allmand 1988 and Curry 1993.

56 One manuscript, MS Falkenberg, says the message was given to the pope two years before the Jubilee, i.e. in 1348.

57 See further Stolpe 1972.

revelations went unheeded. A sequence of revelations describes the warring parties. Book IV 103 tells how St Denis, the patron saint of France, spoke to the Virgin imploring her for mercy for his country where bodies are thrown to the ground like quarry, and souls flutter down to hell like snowflakes. In Book IV 104 St Denis is brought before Christ by the Virgin with his petition, and she uses a likeness 'for the benefit of the woman who is present in spirit', saying she sees two wild animals, one wishing to consume all it can without its hunger ever being satisfied, and the other trying to rise up above all others. They have a terrifying voice, are full of fire and each wants to consume the other's heart, one by biting the other's back and the other by attacking the breast. The voices of the beasts are heard everywhere, and all animals who approach with an open mouth are overwhelmed by the fire, and those whose mouths are closed have all their fur singed off. These two beasts, the vision continues, are the kings of France and England. Both are full of greed and anger; and the one who tries to tear into the other's breast has a greater right to the kingdom than the other which is motivated by greed; the animals with open mouths are the princes who betray them by throwing money into their mouths so they are prepared for war. Both kings deprive Christ of souls, but those who lose their fur are simple people who have their goods left, and who believe the cause is just but they lose their fur in battle, that is, their bodies in death. Then the Virgin hears three voices, one saying he would be content with what he had, but is frightened of losing everything, the second, saying he wishes he had his original position, for he is tired, and the third is the voice of the people who pray daily for peace. Christ ends by reminding the Virgin that the prayers of those who ask will be answered. The following vision, Book IV 105, contains Christ's solution to the war, which is to suggest a marriage match whereby the kingdom can fall to the rightful heir: 'since one of the kings has justice, peace should come about by marriage; in this way the kingdom will fall to the rightful heir'.

The two kings must be at one in heart and soul and they must cease the intolerable taxes and schemes which they impose on their subjects. If the king who has the kingdom does not obey, he will not be successful, and will leave his kingdom in exile and pain; but if the king who has the greater right to the kingdom is obedient, Christ will fight for him. 'But if he does not obey he will not achieve the goal of his desire, but instead lose what he has gained, and a painful conclusion will darken the propitious beginning.'

Birgitta refers to one king (Edward) as having the *maiorem iusticiam*. Legally, she is on his side, but morally, she does not take either side and depicts both men as voracious beasts. The king who has the most just cause attacks the 'heart' or 'breast' of his enemy, implying that he wages open warfare in the midst of the enemy; this attack, and the 'propitious beginning' which ensued, may refer to the English success after Crécy.

Birgitta's reference to a marriage to resolve the hostilities was probably to an alliance between Edward's and Philippe's families, although she gives no further details.[58] Her proposal is an example of her close interest in dynastic power politics. Birgitta's, and the Swedish monarchy's, qualified support for the English may have been promoted by Queen Blanche's family associations with England: in the previous decade the French king's brother-in-law Robert of Artois, having fallen out with the king, had sought refuge with Blanche's brother Jean II of Namur, and then gone to England and fought on England's side against the Scots, before being imprisoned in 1333. The marriage proposal may suggest that Sweden was courting political alliances with England in the mid-fourteenth century, even if economic links were few at this time, and dominated largely by Hanseatic trade.[59]

Whether or not Hemming actually met the warring kings in their respective countries, or simply passed on the revelations through intermediaries, is unknown.[60] What is certain is that Birgitta's messages fell on deaf ears: Prior Peter says that the recipients of the revelations at Avignon showed little interest in the word of God as sent to them by Birgitta, and Hemming is reported as becoming depressed after his unrewarding journey.[61] Although the Avignon mission was ultimately unsuccessful, nevertheless it shows Birgitta's purposefulness and her attempts at active involvement in Swedish foreign diplomacy at the highest level – in this case, with a pope and two foreign kings. The ripples from this enterprise may not have been strong, but they are a sign of her future resolve, shrewdness and moral indignation at the highest political level. Her ambition is to stamp out the moral turpitude and lax standards she sees around her, both in Sweden and abroad; and indeed, this is plainly stated in her revelations addressed to Philippe VI and Edward III: if they are deficient morally, Christ will help neither king. Birgitta's political revelations demonstrate her strong moralistic voice and her belief that politics are about moral issues. This fact is even more strongly borne out in her involvement in the major foreign enterprise undertaken by the Swedish king in the 1340s, the crusades to the east.

58 Another marriage proposal, almost certainly unrelated to the one proposed in Birgitta's vision, but also involving Edward III, is made in a letter preserved in MS 404, Corpus Christi College, Cambridge, from Magnus Eriksson to Edward, in which the copyist writes: 'In the year 1348 in October, the king of Sweden sent a letter to the king of England asking for one of his daughters in marriage.' Magnus can scarcely be asking for marriage for himself, as his wife was still alive, but he may have been making an enquiry on behalf of one of his sons, Håkon or Erik. The letter is supported by a reference to Birgitta's divine calling, and mentions a revelation about the English king's legal right to the French kingdom. See Stolpe 1972, on which the present paragraph is based. See too Colledge 1956, p. 32.

59 Authén Blom 1992, p. 825. The discussion on the marriage proposal re-emerges in fifteenth-century England; see Abergale 1991.

60 As Klockars points out, if Hemming did go to England it must have been after October 1347, when Edward returned there. He was probably back in Sweden–Finland by this date.

61 AP p. 512.

The Russian crusades

Towards the end of the 1340s Magnus Eriksson embarked on a crusade to eastern Finland, ostensibly to convert the heathens there. Swedish foreign policy in the fourteenth century looked eastward, and Magnus inherited a clearly aggressive policy towards the eastern Baltic states at the beginning of his reign. In 1323, the treaty of Orekhov (Swedish Nöteborg) divided the Karelian provinces between Sweden and Novgorod, but border clashes continued to flare up during the next few decades. Finland was still an undefined area, sparsely populated with peoples of different ethnic origins – the Suomi in the western corner, Tavastians in the central lakeland area, and Karelians in the east. The country was visited in friendship and hostility by all of its Baltic neighbours, but was separated from most of them by its language; and the Finnish peoples were caught between the commercial and territorial interests of their neighbours, particularly the Russians, Swedes and Norwegians. Thus when Magnus planned his enterprise to the eastern Baltic in the 1340s he was pursuing an aspect of long-standing national foreign policy, and was not undertaking an impulsive campaign of his own devising, aimed for his own self-aggrandisement.

The events of the crusades can be summarised briefly.[62] Magnus sailed from Sweden in mid-June 1348, and from the island of Björkö, at the north-east end of the Baltic, he sent envoys to Novgorod, to discuss the relative virtues of Roman Catholicism and Greek Orthodoxy. The Novgorodians refused to enter into doctrinal arguments, referring him to the Patriarch of Constantinople, and said they would only discuss Magnus's grievances regarding border territories. He then invaded the areas north of the city of Novgorod where he carried out mass conversions, and he continued along the river Neva and took the town of Orekhov on 6 August 1348. Strategically, the capture of Orekhov was vital. Magnus now effectively held the whole Neva basin; and thus had control over the strip of land between Lake Ladoga and the Swedish frontier in the west. He left Orekhov in the hands of a four hundred strong garrison, and returned to Sweden, but within six months the Novgorodians had recaptured it, in February 1349.

On Magnus's second expedition, in 1350 – in which Birgitta's brother, Israel Birgersson, took part – the Novgorodians were well defended and they surrounded him on all sides, so that he was compelled to make an escape by sea.[63] Most of his fleet was lost at the mouth of the river Narva in a heavy storm; he himself had meanwhile fled to Estonia and Livonia, where he spent the winter of 1350–51, apparently engaged in commercial ventures there. A

62 On the events of the crusades see Fennell 1968; Christiansen 1980, pp. 182–91; Lind 1988.

63 On Israel Birgersson's death in Riga, see Book VI 95.

cease-fire was agreed and a treaty signed at Tartu in 1351, and Magnus returned to Sweden in April or possibly June of the same year.

There are about twenty visions on the justification for the crusades. In Book I 57 Christ laments how contemporary Christians shun God and fill their mouths with stinking and rotten meat; God will go instead to the heathen and fill their mouths with the taste of honey. A debate on the expediency of the crusades is graphically presented by two fierce beasts in a pair of scales in Book IV 2, which is interpreted in Book IV 129.[64] In Book VIII 39, Magnus has asked God for advice on how he should embark on his crusades, and in reply is told that he must go with a good heart and a healthy body; second, that he must take with him morally upright and willing servants. In Book VIII 40 and 43, he is given instructions to carry with him two banners, one of peace and the other of justice; and he must offer the heathens peace before he raises his zealous hand of justice against them. Further, if he has any fears whatsoever, he should not undertake the mission at all. He must take only a specific number of carefully chosen crusading knights with him, and priests and monks of all orders, who will instruct the heathen in the new faith and provide comfort for the faithful, and a bishop whose task will be to build a cathedral and establish a diocese.[65]

Birgitta's attitude towards the crusades is not wholly apparent from such revelations and the question is further clouded by the fact that the revelations cannot be dated accurately; indeed some may even have been revised after the events with the benefit of hindsight. It appears that she is not wholly convinced by the need for the crusades, but she accepts that it would be a tolerable policy if properly carried out. Yet in spite of the failure of the campaign Magnus appears at least to have made the attempt to be a Birgittine king – for instance in his apparent willingness to enter into doctrinal arguments with the Novgorodians – although he becomes a scapegoat in later interpretations of the crusades, not only in the Birgittine tradition in Sweden, but also in Russian sources.[66] For example, in Book VIII 47, which presumably dates from the 1350s, Birgitta expresses her anger at his disobedience on the crusades. She explains how he has contravened all of the Virgin's advice to him, and has become an instrument of the devil for three reasons: first, he withdrew from the crusade on account of poverty and hunger; second, he took with him more men than were necessary and the kind who were professional soldiers who lacked a moral purpose (this is probably a reference to the Danish and German mercenaries he is alleged to have recruited for the second crusade); third, he

64 See further Morris 1993, 'Swedish Foreign Policy . . .'. Images are also used of a child choosing between two apples in Book VI 41, bee-keeping in Book II 19, and a bee seeking a fragrant herb in Book VI 44; and in Book II 3–6 Old Testament parallels are drawn to describe the heathen peoples.

65 Book VIII 45–6.

66 See Lind 1991.

took with him weak-willed clergy and monks who did not know where to preach the Christian faith, or to whom, and therefore they abandoned their mission. Birgitta goes on in this vision to say that the king, who once was appointed by the Virgin as her new son, has now become a son of disobedience. He has sinned in three respects: first, he came to the throne of two kingdoms, but ruled unwisely and unreasonably; second, he was given special grace from the Virgin, who showed him how to govern his kingdom, but he abused that grace; and third, he was commissioned to convert the heathen peoples, but failed in this task. With her deeply traditional view of the crusades, advocating personal honour but spurning worldly ambition, she disapproves of the political motivation for the crusades, as well as Magnus's lack of moral purpose. This revelation is only one of a number dating, presumably, from the 1350s and 1360s, where Birgitta turns against Magnus Eriksson. Her demagogic expressions of reproof and contempt are agitatory, and they frequently amount to incitements to the conspirators among the Swedish magnates to commit acts of treason against him. Even from a safe distance in Rome in the 1350s and 1360s, she demonstrates a continued involvement in Swedish politics, and is a skilled tactician in manipulating political change.[67]

Birgitta seems to have derived her outlook from a different attitude towards kingship and the common good from that which Magnus was pursuing in his reign. Her own scheme is traditionalist, opposed to constitutional monarchy, and she supports group government by the aristocracy as the ideal. Her scheme of politics is controlled by custom which she calls law; and for her custom means the preservation of the rights and privileges of the aristocracy. She sees the king as the chosen servant of his people by whom he can legitimately be deposed if he fails to bring them prosperity and show generosity; and she sees it as part of a king's duty to demonstrate his justice, which for her is best shown by him maintaining the customs of the people, and especially the rights and privileges of the magnates and great families. Many such pieces of advice are outlined in her own 'mirror of kings' in Book VIII.[68] But after the abortive crusades to the east, how could the king be generous if he had nothing to give, especially since he had imposed heavy taxes to fund them in the first place? Or where could he acquire the wherewithal to give except by further taxes or by conquest? For Birgitta, then, the failure of the crusade was a moral condemnation of the king, and a key to the breakdown of their relationship after the crusades.

After the Russian crusades, many of Magnus's supporters rose up against him, disgruntled with the financial burdens he had imposed on them in the wake of the expeditions. Birgitta, now in Rome, supported them in their opposition to the king, and her main arguments against him are summarised in her

67 See further Andersson 1928.
68 See further Gilkær 1993.

so-called 'insurrection' revelation (which text is one of the two autographs in her own hand).[69] There are several areas of discontent: he is accused of sodomy 'for you love men more than your own wife', he has violated his Christian faith by attending mass when he had been excommunicated, he has robbed lands and property from the crown, betrayed his subjects, and abandoned Skåne by mortgaging it to his enemy Valdemar Atterdag. He must repent or hand over his kingdom to his son; if he refuses to mend his ways, the four noblemen to whom the vision is addressed must gather support and elect another king. The revolt was joined by Church leaders whose lands Magnus had confiscated; and eventually he was deposed in 1364, and the throne was offered to his German nephew, Albrekt of Mecklenburg. Albrekt turned out to be an incompetent ruler and abdicated, after which the country was ruled by a council of magnates. When they proved unsuccessful, Magnus's son's widow, Margarethe, daughter of the Danish king Valdemar Atterdag, was called upon to restore power and authority, and her reign marks the beginning of the so-called Kalmar Union of 1397.

Magnus's bequest to Birgitta

Before he embarked on his crusades, Magnus had enjoyed good relations with Birgitta, to the extent indeed, that in May 1346 he bequeathed his palace of Vadstena to her, for conversion to a monastery.[70] In the bequest the king expressed his desire to be buried, with his wife, at the monastery amid rich material tokens in their memory. However, when Birgitta devised her plans for the design of the church, there was little provision for exuberance and adornment; and indeed, many years were to pass before building work started, in 1369.[71]

The fact that Magnus made his bequest in 1346 suggests that already by this date Birgitta had her own plans for founding a monastery, and may even have received the revelation of the new Rule, which is one of her major revelations. It is unknown when or where Birgitta received this vision which was said to have been experienced in a very short time and written down a few days afterwards by her confessor.[72] She must have been ruminating on the idea of establishing a monastery of some kind, possibly even while Ulf was alive, and many revelations in the *Extravagantes* are like early drafts of the Rule, giving advice and guidance on the minutiae of everyday life there; and they express some of her apprehensions about her planned order as well as her dissatisfaction with existing monasticism.

A number of revelations address the indifference of men in holy orders,

69 Högman 1951. For an interpretative discussion see Ferm 1993.
70 DS no. 4069.
71 See further Fritz 1992.
72 Ex. 45.

and their failure to maintain the monastic ideals laid down by their founding fathers. Although it is usually impossible to date such revelations or to establish to which monastic order they refer, it is clear that many of them are an expression of her rejection of existing monasticism. In Book I 13, for instance, she condemns a Cistercian prior who had buried an excommunicate, and in Book VI 92 she attacks a monk, possibly a Dominican, for flaunting his bookish knowledge in reading the *Vitae patrum,* and not showing the appropriate good conscience and humility.[73]

The Liber Questionum

Birgitta's most sustained expression of anti-intellectualism unquestionably dates from the 1340s, and it is the longest of all her revelations. According to the Prologue, she experienced it while on a journey on horseback from Alvastra to Vadstena, a distance of some forty kilometres. It lasted one hour and was so sweet an experience that she was sorry to be disturbed by her servants when she arrived at Vadstena. The vision, contained in Book V, the so-called *Liber Questionum,* is another that may relate, tangentially at least, to the desire to found a new monastic order, for it contains a bitter and hostile attack on a man in holy orders known to Birgitta. The vision makes a sustained denunciation of contemporary clerics and their ideas, and Birgitta is likely to be recording a summary of conversations between clerics she herself had been involved in or had heard. A monk stands on a ladder situated between heaven and earth and engages in dialogue with Christ. There are sixteen *interrogaciones,* each divided into *questiones* and *responsiones,* making eighty-six questions and answers altogether. Occasionally, Christ intervenes with a personal comment, and sometimes God and the Virgin make contributions. In its present form the book has the appearance of a scholastic tract and bears similarities with the scholastic method of disputation, making use of syllogisms and dialectic terms, but also using more discursive forms of exposition which by the fourteenth century had become established among schoolmen.[74]

The themes and topics raised by the querulent monk range over a number of important philosophical and theological issues, but they are not ordered in such a way that they move in a logical progression from one theme to the next. Four major areas can nevertheless be traced. The first *interrogaciones* in the Book are concerned primarily with the nature of free will and the difficulty man has in subordinating his will to God's commands. Why may the monk not use his mouth, ears, hands and feet freely, in a way that delights him;

73 On her attitudes towards monastic orders see further Klockars 1966, pp. 180–208.

74 Especially noticeable in the Book is the use made of *exempla* and metaphors (e.g. gold purified by fire in int. 5, the sun's dazzling brightness as it shines into a house in int. 6, the speed with which the sun's rays pass through glass in int. 12, a bee collecting honey in int. 15, and images of maternal care and devotion in ints. 6, 13, 15).

Plate 3. On a journey between Alvastra and Vadstena, Birgitta receives the revelation known as the *Liber Questionum*. Frontispiece to the Book from the first printed edition of the *Revelaciones*, by Bartholomaeus Ghotan, Lübeck, 1492.
Source: Kungliga Biblioteket, Stockholm.

display his magnificence in the world; indulge his senses; obey people other than God; seek God's wisdom when he has earthly wisdom, and when he has been given free will? In his responses, Christ exhorts the monk to beware of excesses and to curb his will. The second issue taken up concerns natural theology: the monk is baffled by the measure of vicissitude and change in God's creation, and inquires what the purpose of certain gifts of creation is, when apparently they have no function for man? Why are creatures created which are harmful to man; why does Christ send sickness and pain and tolerate iniquitous judges; why is the body afflicted at the point of death; why is one child born alive, capable of receiving baptism while another is stillborn; why do hunger, plague and death come so unexpectedly; why does God permit angry men to enter into conflict; why are some things ugly and others beautiful; why are beasts not endowed with reason or inanimate objects with life; why is there night and day? The general tenet of the responses is that everything in God's creation is created with a purpose, which is to the greater edification of man, and that all troubles and vicissitudes that beset man are a cause for virtue. Nothing in creation acts of its own accord, but by the will of God.

Much of the middle section of the Book is taken up with a range of questions relating to the Incarnation. Some questions ask why God was made incarnate in man, who is so ignoble and imperfect, and why God did not reveal his godhead on earth. Others concern the Virgin Mary, and ask why she specifically was chosen and exalted above all angels and why God did not show her purity with a visible sign. Others indicate the monk's bafflement over the concept of time in the Incarnation: why did Christ not emerge from the womb as soon as he was begotten, or appear at once at the age of thirty; why were his teachings not all heard in one instant; why were his deeds not all performed at once? Christ's responses are that Christ Incarnate was obliged to live according to the decree of nature; that the words of the prophets had to be fulfilled; and that man had to revere God out of love and not fear, and receive his teachings in small portions gradually.

The remaining questions in Book V deal with the nature of and apparent discrepancies in the dispensation of divine justice. Why did Christ give law and justice if not for revenge; why do favourable things happen to the unjust and unfavourable things to the just; why does God tolerate false idols; why does man live in a frail body; why do some have grace in youth and others in old age; why are some clever and others stupid; why are some hard-hearted and others soft-hearted; why are all born in pain; why does a child bear its father's sins when it cannot sin; why does the unexpected often happen; why do the wicked die without affliction and the good not? Why are the prayers of the pious not always heard; why do bad things befall man unexpectedly and why is the devil near some and not others; why do those who have God's spirit sin? Christ answers that he metes out justice to men according to their deserts, that punishments are for man's edification and that hardship and pain are sometimes to be borne for the sake of righteousness.

Certain dominant sentiments seem to underlie the questions. The monk is unwilling to accept the world as it is with all its blemishes and imperfections, and implicit in his questions is the criticism that a perfect God ought not to have created a world so manifestly imperfect. Second, he is frustrated by the limitations which God has imposed on human knowledge. He wants to know why knowledge is not made plainer by God to man, what purpose ignorance serves and why all human knowledge is clouded by uncertainty. Third, the monk is a sceptic, who feels he must question every aspect of his physical and spiritual existence in order to reach a greater certainty about the nature of mankind and the world. He is puzzled by the ordained order of the world and by the fact that God is inaccessibly remote to man. He asks why God has cast a veil over human knowledge, why man's mind is not capable of perfect knowledge, what purpose ignorance serves and why the world is full of evil and imperfection. Christ, for his part, is displeased with the monk for his malice, arrogance and excessive intellectualism.

With its quodlibetal character and allegorising theological schemes, Book V is useful in providing some of the most basic characterising positions Birgitta adopted and her level and range of philosophical and theological knowledge, as well as reflecting the general nature of Swedish debate in the mid-fourteenth century. One of the distinguishing features of the Book is its insistence on justice and legalism, which is uncommon in devotional writings of the period, but which came to dominate her visionary writings. The book may also echo some of the ideas of the Ockhamist school which dominated Europe in the mid-fourteenth century, in which there was a denial of omniscience and an interest in defining the limitations of human knowledge, and in the distinction between divine and human knowledge.[75]

Some scholars have argued that there is an autobiographical element in the *Liber Questionum* and the Book has been seen as a manifestation of her own ideas and a reflection of an inner crisis of faith, by which she moves into a state of spiritual independence.[76] With its attention to reasoned knowledge it focuses on one of the major problems for both Birgitta and her followers during these years: she had a special calling and role as a chosen vessel, filled with divine grace, and had been given the privilege of revealed knowledge, whereas for her followers, knowledge could only be gained through reason. However, the debate in the Book may equally be a reflection of her dismissal of an intellectually arrogant cleric known to her – and by extension, of existing monastic orders – and to whom she objects so strongly that at the end he is 'cast away like a menstrual cloth'.[77]

75 These links are worth further study. See Strömberg 1943.

76 The main studies are Sundén 1973, Koch 1987, and analysis by T. Nyberg in Tjader Harris 1990, pp. 21–30.

77 Interrogacio 16; cf. Isaiah 64.6. The cleric has sometimes been associated with

Departure from Sweden

Within a period of not more than five years (possibly three, if the date of her calling vision is taken as 1346), Birgitta had received as many as half her total number of visions, among them some of her most important ones. She had obtained divine spiritual guidance in the first years of her widowhood; and she had issued comminatory revelations to political leaders in her own country and abroad. In the revelation of the rule she had shown her dissatisfaction with existing monastic orders and expressed her intention to make a new start in Sweden.

Yet these first years of her 'calling' were not an unqualified period of achievement; and indeed, most of the ambitious enterprises she engaged in were unfruitful. The Swedish Church and monastic orders did not heed her reformist warnings to them; the mission to Avignon was a failure; and there were continual murmurings of criticism against her among the nobility. There appears to have been a gradual rift between her and the king in the wake of his failed crusades, and the financial turmoil into which he plunged the country was sharply felt by members of her class. She may also have felt let down by her friends and supporters, like Magister Mathias, with whom she appears to have parted ways at about this time.[78] At the end of the decade, further difficulties were brought to the country with the Black Death, and although very little is known of the extent of mortality or the effects on the economy, they were probably as catastrophic as elsewhere in Europe, and changed the whole face of Swedish society.[79]

Magister Mathias, but there is no unequivocal evidence to link him with the vision (cf. note 27 above).

78 He may have accompanied the king on his crusades, and shortly afterwards he died in 1350, possibly of the Black Death. A late source states that he died in Stockholm in 1350, and that the king laid him in his grave at an altar in the Dominican church. He came to be revered as a saint in Dominican and Birgittine tradition (but not in Franciscan tradition, following a dispute over the worship of Brynolf of Sweden); see Strömberg 1944, p. 28. Birgitta, who was in Rome when Mathias died, received a revelation of him, in which he is blessed for the crown which had been prepared for him (AP p. 83).

79 The *Diarium Vadstenense* states that in 1350 'there was great mortality' that had been foreseen by St Birgitta; Gejrot 1988, p. 116; and see Ex. 27, 74, 77, Book VIII 57. A diploma from Östergötland records that land prices were halved 'because the great mortality which had occurred had left many holdings desolate and tenants could hardly be found', and a later chronicle states that five-sixths of the population was wiped out. There are no other accounts except what can be inferred from the payment of the Peter's pence after 1350 which was reduced by some 40 per cent, and on the basis of the existing figures, it has been estimated that some 30–35 per cent of the population died. Authén Blom 1992 discusses in detail the effects of the plague on the political horizons of Sweden and Norway in the period.

Birgitta's opportunities for reform in Sweden were compromised by the political and economic setbacks of the 1340s, but her compulsion to speak out on public matters had not waned. Her horizons were now extended beyond Sweden to the whole of an integrated Christendom, and in 1349 she set out for Rome, never to return to her native country.

IV

The Rome Years

> Vade Romam, vbi platee strate sunt auro et sanguine sanctorum rubricate, vbi compendium, id est brevior via, est ad celum propter indulgencias, quas promeruerunt sancti pontifices oracionibus suis. Stabis autem ibi in Roma, donec summum pontificem et imperatorem videbis ibidem insimul in Roma et eis verba mea nunciabis.
>
> Go to Rome, where the streets are paved with gold and reddened with the blood of saints and where there is a short cut, that is, a shorter way, to heaven because of the indulgences that the holy pontiffs have merited because of their prayers. Moreover, you are to stay there in Rome until you see the supreme pontiff and the emperor there at the same time in Rome, and you shall announce my words to them.
>
> (AP p. 94)

THE VISION in which Birgitta received the call to go to Rome in 1349 encapsulates the dominating features of the next decades of her life.[1] Rome for her was the place where the saints and martyrs had lived, and which she now wished to see in person. Her immediate motive for going was to join the celebrations of the Holy Year of Jubilee in 1350; and the reference in her vision to the 'shorter way to heaven' alludes to this year of remission for those that made the pilgrimage to Rome. The command to wait in the Holy City until the emperor and pope were there at the same time meant that her stay was to be a long one, but it gave her the opportunity of reflecting on the political crises in her native country and of considering the expediency of returning there. Many of her visions of the next two decades were directed towards members of the Church hierarchy in Rome and contain outspoken calls for the reform of the Church. But throughout the following years she also witnessed a deepening of her spirituality. She followed a life that was a mixture of contemplation and social involvement, living under a quasi-monastic regime within her household, but nurturing friends and supporters among the Roman hierarchy. She also worked relentlessly towards bringing to fruition her hopes

1 See too Ex. 8, which was reworked by the Vadstena monk, Ulf Birgersson; Hollman 1956, p. 90.

for her monastic order, and much of her time was spent in seeking official approval for the Rule, for which she enlisted support from both the pope and emperor.

Milan

Nothing is known of her journey until she came south of the Alps to Milan, where she stopped for some time, perhaps because a friend in her entourage, Ingeborg Laurensdotter, fell ill and died there. Ingeborg, who was married to the Swedish nobleman Nikolaus Dannäs Bielke, had been worried during the journey that her husband was being unfaithful to her, but was told by Christ in a vision to Birgitta that she should continue on her pilgrimage. He also prophesied her death – saying he would fill the 'sack' of her body with sweetness; and it seems likely that she died in Milan.[2]

The powerful Milanese ruler at the time was Giovanni Visconti, whose family had long favoured the imperial cause against the papacy. Having built up a strong power base across all of northern Italy, Visconti had ceased to be dependent on the emperor and governed a powerful territory in his own right; and in January 1349, he became both political and religious leader, after the death of his brother, Luccino. It appears that he offered Birgitta hospitality – although it is unclear how she had made his acquaintance – and the fact that she accepted his generosity makes her strictures against him in a sequence of revelations in Book III 5–9 all the more acerbic.[3] Some of these revelations are put into the mouth of the former incumbent of the archbishopric of Milan, St Ambrose, who by means of images, examples and biblical quotations, makes the thinly veiled allegation that the life of the present archbishop does not live up to the ideals of his predecessor, and he issues a general condemnation of all secular and religious leaders who abuse their power. He compares Visconti to a man who takes his servant as mistress, and spends ten hours with her for every hour he spends with his wife; the mistress represents worldly pleasure, and the wife the Church, and Visconti is urged to spend more time in the service of God and less in pursuing worldly concerns. Further, he is disdainfully compared to a bellows in a smithy, and a snail lying in the slime in which it is born; and one of his confessors is reprimanded for not upbraiding him as he ought. How Visconti himself responded to Birgitta's comminatory revelations can only be guessed at; although in terms of the Church beyond northern Italy, Birgitta probably did herself no harm politically by speaking out so vehemently against the bitter enemy of the papacy, and her reputation may have preceded her as she continued on her pilgrimage towards Rome.[4]

2 AP p. 514, Ex. 101.
3 On the Milan revelations see Lokrantz 1984.
4 This point is made by Stolpe 1973, vol. II pp. 27–8.

The state of Rome

Rome for Birgitta was the very heart of Christendom; and her ideal of it is expressed with illustrations of the saints and martyrs who lived and died there, many of whom she mentions in her revelations, such as St Peter, St Lawrence, St Agnes and St Sebastian. (On the other hand, she never expressed an interest in the secular history of ancient Rome, and always lowered her eyes when she walked in the city.[5]) However, the reality of what the city was like in the mid-fourteenth century was very different. With its drastically reduced population it was little more than a large village, ruled by petty local tyrants, organised by a corrupt city administration, and affected by dissent, neglect and turmoil. In 1346 and 1349 it was afflicted by earthquake and plague. There were power struggles between the leading Roman noble families, the Orsini and the Colonna, and tensions between the populace, the burghers and the nobility. Shortly before Birgitta's arrival, the people of Rome, under the charismatic lawyer Cola di Rienzo, had taken control of the city. Rienzo had antiquarian interests and was encouraged by Petrarch to develop the idea of a Renaissance by making the people of Rome reassert their authority over the city, Italy and the empire. He also wished to introduce a reinvigorated Christian rule in Rome, a city, he declared on the coins he struck, which was mistress of the world.[6]

The Church of Rome was also at a low ebb.[7] For centuries it had held the peoples of Europe together by the tie of a common faith and it was presided over by the divinely instituted office of the pope, who in 'plenitude of power', had supreme and unlimited authority above the law and was not circumscribed by constitutional controls. It had become an increasingly powerful institution, which sought to extend and consolidate its authority throughout the entire Christian world. But by the thirteenth century papal power had started to erode and some of the central tenets of the faith and the very framework of the Church were being brought into question. Individually, these challenges were insufficient to make much impact, but collectively they contributed to a severe undermining of the temporal authority of the papacy and thereby the Church itself. The idea of the crusade led to conflicts of interest with secular rulers. The papacy acted as a counterbalance to the nationalistic tendencies that were emerging throughout Europe at this time, and it strove after a united Christendom with an international outlook by playing down the demands of individual nations. The popes were increasingly involved in secular politics, which led to accusations of national partisanship. A number of sects sprang up which were deemed heretical and became the subject of

5 AP p. 64.
6 Renouard 1970, p. 45. See too Damsholt 1991.
7 The complex causes behind the difficulties within the papacy during the later middle ages have been well documented. See for example Ullmann 1972.

papal inquisitions. The question of Christian poverty provoked a fierce debate which struck at the foundations of faith. Towns and universities were founded which became alternative centres of intellectual activity. An unpredictable, impassioned piety emerged from among the ranks of society and was often at odds with the systems of belief and doctrine officially sanctioned by the Church. There was dissatisfaction with the frequent changes of pope, and vacancies between papacies; and there were voices in favour of oligarchic rule within the institution. The increase in the centralisation of papal power and an efficient bureaucratic machinery to support it also met with criticism. Increased revenues had to be raised to fund the papal enterprises and the Church became increasingly wealthy, which in turn gave rise to allegations of corruption, greed, simony and rapacity. Political writers and theologians were also making their mark. With Thomas Aquinas (c.1225–74) the idea emerged of the individual as a citizen, which was different from the idea of him as a subject of a higher authority. There were also political and theological tracts written criticising the papacy: William of Ockham (c.1300–49) attacked it from a theological angle and criticised the personalities of individual popes; and Marsilius of Padua (c.1275–1342) argued that the papacy disturbed political peace in the world and should be reorganised to reduce its governing authority.

Although it was the historic seat of the papacy, Rome had been without a pope since 1309 when the Curia went into exile at Avignon, under intense pressure from many quarters. During the 'Babylonian captivity' of the papacy, which lasted until 1376, seven popes, of French nationality and largely dominated by French kings, presided over the Church. The Avignonese popes lived in great splendour, and their luxurious lifestyle, supported by an efficient but costly bureaucracy, scandalised their critics – among them Petrarch and Boccaccio. In particular, the lavish-living Clement VI (1342–52) did much to affirm the French character of the papacy and its presence on French soil, which made it deeply unpopular throughout Europe, especially among France's enemies.[8] But it was not always the personal as much as the political failings of the individual popes that were to blame for all the difficulties of the period; the papacy was already in disarray at the beginning of the 'Babylonian captivity', and the pious and devout lives of the popes were no longer a sufficient criterion for exemplary papal rule. Clement VI was succeeded by other popes – Innocent VI (1352–62), Urban V (1362–70) and Gregory XI (1371–78) – who kept the insitution in order and without abuse, held expenditure in check, and dealt with clerical greed; but they had not the political means to remove the Avignon seat until Gregory XI brought about its resettlement in Rome. This event, however, was followed soon afterwards by the Great Schism in 1378, and a full split in the papacy, with competing popes in both Avignon and

8 See further Wood 1989.

Rome. Thus, beset by the papal exile and bitter factional differences within the Church, as well as civil unrest, Rome in the fourteenth century had lost much of its sacred character.

The papacy itself may not have been induced to return to Rome, but for many ordinary Christians Rome had far from lost its attraction. Despite the absence of a pope, vast crowds thronged to the city in the Year of Holy Jubilee. This celebration was instituted by Boniface VIII (1234–1303) in 1300; he had meant it to be a centennial event, but Clement VI changed the period to fifty years, and proclaimed it on 27 January 1343 in a bull that was not published until 18 August 1349. The celebration of 1350 was used by Rome to rebuild the powerful image of the Church, as a means of gaining revenues, and of instilling a sense of peace in the popular imagination. The reformers urging a return of the popes were intending to use it as an opportunity for reconciliation and a resolution of the intractable political differences within the Church. Cola de Rienzo conceived of a universal peace and the dawning of a new, spiritual age, beginning in Rome at the time of the Jubilee when he wrote from Avignon to the Senate and People of Rome in 1343: 'Rise again, O Roman city, for so long fallen prostrate; put off your sad vesture of widowhood; clothe yourself in bridal purple; adorn your head with the diadem of freedom . . .'[9] Birgitta's own call for Clement VI to return is in similar vein: 'Come to Italy, and preach the Word and the year of salvation and divine love, and see the streets, which are spattered with the blood of the saints, and I will give you an unending reward.'[10] As she indicates in her vision, Christ is becoming even more impatient with Clement and has tolerated his excesses for long enough: 'It will not be forgotten how much greed and pride in your time have increased in the Church, and how you could have reformed and improved many things, which you, lover of the flesh, did not wish to.'

The popes could not afford to ignore all the voices of the visionaries and prophets who, like Birgitta, called on them to return to Rome.[11] As Petrarch's phrase, the 'Babylonian captivity', implies, the reformers saw the split in the papacy in terms of a juxtaposition of Babylon (that is, Avignon, which was synonymous with confusion) and Jerusalem (that is, Rome, which gave the promise of peace), and they called for a New Jerusalem to be established in Rome. But as Marjorie Reeves has pointed out, this 'vision is a revolutionary

9 Quoted from Reeves 1992, p. 4.

10 Book VI 63.

11 The Joachimite, John of Roquetaillade, for instance, was listened to by the curia at Avignon, although he was imprisoned for his prophecies; the Infante Pedro of Aragon urged Urban V to return to reform the Church in Rome in 1365; and there is a large collection of prophetic writings at Avignon and in the papal library of Benedict XIII which include the strictures of other prophets on this issue. See further Reeves 1992.

one, threatening the "establishment" rather than enhancing its glory'.[12] For although Rome was historically the cradle of the Church it was at the same time associated with the Antichrist, and perceived as a den of wickedness and corruption by the Avignonese adherents. The waves of pilgrims who entered the city in 1350 brought with them a potential explosion of emotion which helped confirm the ideal of the establishment of a New Jerusalem but at the same time it underlined the threat to the pope and curia in exile. Yet despite the pressures from pilgrims and reformers, the chances of the return of Clement VI in time for the Jubilee celebration looked slim indeed. Rome itself was too full of violence and unrest for him to risk returning there; he was in ill health; and he was closely involved in French political affairs, which were at crisis point following the English successes in the Hundred Years War.

When Birgitta arrived in Rome, then, the papal city was a place of material and moral corruption, and her descriptions of its decay are probably not exaggerated. She attacks the physical state of the city, comparing it to a meadow overgrown with thistles, which needs to be weeded first with a sharp iron, then cleansed with fire and ploughed by a pair of oxen.[13] She attacks its inhabitants for their indifference and slackness in their observance of a Christian way of life.[14] She alludes to its history when St Peter appears to her and comments in apocalyptic terms that Rome had once been the city of champions, where the streets were paved with gold and silver, but that the sapphires had been dulled, its inhabitants had lost their right eyes and right hands, toads and worms dwelt in them, and upright creatures and Peter's fish did not dare lift their heads. For that reason fish would gather there, even if they were not as numerous as before, and when they jumped, the toads and frogs would recede, and the snakes turn to lambs and the lions become as doves at their window. Echoing the vision in which she was 'called' to Rome, St Peter also promises Birgitta that she will hear the cry 'Long live the successor of Peter' and see him in person; 'for I will bury the mountain of desire and those who sit on it shall descend and those who will not descend voluntarily shall be compelled against the expectation of all, for God wants to be raised up with mercy and truth'.[15] In other revelations she uses the idea of God replanting the faithful in the city. In the church of Santa Maria Maggiore the Virgin tells her to tell the papal legate in Rome (Cardinal Annibaldo Ceccano) of the dismal state of the Roman Church in decline.[16] Elsewhere, she prays to the Virgin for Rome, where many of the churches in which the martyrs are buried are in

12 Reeves 1992, p. 4. See also on Birgitta's reformist apocalypticism, Kerby-Fulton 1990, pp. 102–11.
13 Book IV 57.
14 Book IV 10.
15 Book IV 5.
16 Book III 10; and IV 78, which contains the same content in letter form.

ruins.[17] She sees gardens of roses and lilies, signifying martyrs and confessors, and Rome as a field of a hundred feet wide and long, sown with fruitful bundles of wheat, signifying the faithful; and she hears a voice crying for Rome's salvation.[18] Christ explains the vision, drawing a comparison with the words of the prophets about Jerusalem. From Peter's time until that of Boniface VIII (i.e. until 1303) Rome had produced many faithful souls, but now they had abandoned it and its princes were murderers, its gates were unguarded, its altars were laid waste, oblations were spent in the inns, and the sacraments abused. Yet there is a message of hope at the end, and Christ says that Rome is not without friends, and God would indeed show mercy.

Early years

As a woman, and as someone who had turned her back on her worldly life in Sweden, her new life in Rome brought with it demanding challenges. She was without special means, in a foreign country, and with a new language to learn and new people to befriend. Although she had renounced her Swedish inheritance, she clearly continued to make use of her noble origins to establish contacts of similar standing in Italy. The first place where she lived was a house adjoining the church of San Lorenzo in Damaso (where today the Palazzo della Cancellaria is situated), which was owned by the Cardinal of San Damaso, brother of Clement VI (and if the cardinal knew the identity of his tenant, he must have viewed her criticisms of his brother with a considerable degree of tolerance). After she had lived in this house for about four years she was given sudden notice to leave, and with her companions she spent a month seeking a new place to live, in a state of great uncertainty. At the last moment, as they were about to install themselves in pilgrims' lodgings, the notice was withdrawn.[19] Some time after this another house was made available to her by a Roman noblewoman, Francisca Papazzura, whom she had befriended in the year she came to Rome. Francisca was the widow of the Roman noble, Petrus Jacobi Papazzuri. She testified in the canonisation process and later donated the house, situated on Campo di Fiore, to Vadstena monastery on 1 January 1383, and it subsequently became the home of the Birgittine order in Rome.[20] Another influential friend was Niccolò Orsini, count of Nola and Spoleto and a member of one of the leading noble families of Rome.[21] She met him shortly after she came to Rome, through one of his

17 Book III 27.

18 Apart from its Old Testament echoes the image is reminiscent of the apocalyptic Eddic poem, the *Völuspá*, which describes a field a hundred leagues wide in each direction, on which the mighty battle of the twilight of the gods was to be fought.

19 AP p. 528.

20 AP pp. 436–47. See further Collijn 1929, pp. 13–17.

21 On his testimony see AP pp. 225–36.

female relatives, a widow named Selena Orsini. Such highly-connected acquaintances demonstrate that she succeeded in establishing a network of important contacts among the Roman nobility in her early years in the city.

In the 1350s, as she acquired a reputation in Rome, she was no doubt a familiar face as she visited Rome's holy shrines daily and in all weathers.[22] In one of the Roman churches dedicated to the Virgin, she gave advice to a priest, and she must have entered into a close relationship with many clerics in the churches visited.[23] In Santa Maria Rotunda, for instance, she received a response to a question by a Franciscan cleric from Trastevere about whether Christ had owned any personal possessions.[24] Many of the great basilicas and pilgrim churches in Rome are mentioned in the revelations, often in connection with the appearance to her of the saint to which they were dedicated. One church where she developed a close bond was San Lorenzo in Panisperna, which housed a community of Franciscan Clarissan sisters, from whom she sometimes received alms in a gesture of voluntary poverty. Her close contacts with the Clarissan sisters — in whose church, indeed, she expressed her wish to be buried — can be explained by the fact that they were closely supported by the two great noble Roman families, the Orsini and Colonna, many of whose members were sisters, and many family members had their graves in the church.[25]

During her years in Rome, Birgitta also visited holy shrines in Italy, although most of the visits cannot be dated. She probably visited Pavia, the burial place of St Augustine, Bologna, where St Dominic was buried, and Assisi, where she received visions concerning St Francis.[26]

The fact that Birgitta's reputation established itself rapidly is shown by that fact that in 1355, the pope granted her some money for her son Birger to travel back to Sweden after a visit to Rome. Writing to the governor of Perugia, Gerardus, abbot of the Benedictine monastery of Marmoutier at Tours, in France, Innocent sends instructions, saying: 'It has come to our knowledge that our beloved son, Birger from Sweden, and his sister, our beloved Katarina, who are both living in Rome, are in difficulties; we command you

22 AP pp. 15, 367, 579.

23 Book IV 79–80.

24 Book VII 8, AP p. 382. She visited this church before she travelled to the Holy Land, AP p. 382. According to Klockars 1971, p. 154, the church of San Paulo fuori le Mura (which had contained frescoes by Cavallini, but been damaged during an earthquake of 1348) contains a statue of Birgitta; tradition has it that she frequently prayed there in front of a crucifix.

25 See further Collijn 1929, pp. 65–92. He writes (p. 89) that Birgitta may have drawn inspiration from this community for her own order.

26 The visions on St Francis are in Book VII 3 and Ex. 90. See further on her pilgrimages to the kingdom of Naples (probably in the late 1360s) and elsewhere, Klockars 1971, pp. 147–59.

this day to see that they are paid without delay, through a bank in Rome or another town, as a gift from us, four hundred gold florins.'[27]

As the pope's intervention suggests, not the least of her hardships in the early years were financial uncertainties. She worried about mounting debts and the daily demands from her creditors; for a period of three years no money was sent from Sweden, but she was reassured that money would be sent on the octave of Epiphany 'when the head cloth is shown' – a reference to the relic of St Veronica.[28] Other accounts of financial worries during the years in Rome include her taking a loan from a German, and her receipt of the bridal crown of her Norwegian daughter-in-law, Karl's wife Gyda, upon the latter's death, the proceeds of which granted Birgitta's household the means to live for a whole year afterwards.

Birgitta may have had her friends in Rome but she also was viewed with deep suspicion by many. Her attacks on Rome and the Romans were so severe that they provoked an angry reaction among the citizens, such that 'they were filled with a deep hatred of St Birgitta, for which some of them threatened to burn her alive, others defamed her as a heretic and witch'.[29] She was not unnaturally intimidated by these threats, but mostly on account of her servants and kinsmen, whom she feared might take fright and leave her; and afterwards she vowed not to visit any place, town or pilgrim site without God's command.

Among clerics there was also hostility to her. In the summer of 1350 she visited the Benedictine monastery of Farfa in the Sabine hills, where she was told that a room was ready for her in the new wing at the monastery.[30] However, when she arrived there she was given wretched accommodation by the brethren on the grounds that they were unaccustomed to living with women. The episode is reminiscent of the initial misogyny of the brethren at Alvastra. Christ told her she should humbly accept the accommodation and experience what it was like for the early Christian saints who had lived in the desert. She took her disdainful treatment badly, however; and spoke disparagingly about the worldly abbot as 'a fallen angel'.[31] As elsewhere in her attacks on clerical excess, she is critical of the falling away of the standards set by the founding fathers, and elsewhere she attacks several Benedictines individually, such as the abbess of a nunnery, a monk at the monastery of San Lorenzo fuori le Mura, and the Benedictines of San Paolo fuori le Mura, Rome.[32]

27 Quoted from Jørgensen 1954, vol. II p. 115.
28 AP p. 516, Ex. 103. The cloth, allegedly containing the imprint of Christ's face, had been in Rome since the eighth century and was much revered in the fourteenth century. Financial hardship during a pilgrimage is also described in AP p. 636.
29 Ex. 8.
30 AP p. 491, Ex. 97.
31 See Book VI 45, Ex. 105 and Book III 22.
32 Book VI 98, 19, 45, 18. Note that Book VI 19 is almost identical to Book V revelacio 8, which is supposed to date from the Sweden years.

During her early years in Rome, Birgitta was also engaged in studying Latin grammar, with her instructor, Magister Peter. Peter Olofsson had been the head of the Swedish Dominican house at Skänninge, not far from Alvastra, but when Birgitta left Sweden in 1349 he travelled with her, and remained with her in Rome, along with his namesake, Prior Peter, for the rest of her life.[33] In her Latin lessons there are insights into the struggles she had with learning the positive, comparative and superlative grammatical terms; and she hears the Virgin tell St Agnes (her spiritual mentor) that an adjective needs to be added to a noun; on another occasion the Virgin asks why she is downcast and she replies that it is because she is not visiting the holy shrines in Rome; the Virgin gives her leave to visit them but not to use this permission as an excuse not to study her grammar or not to obey her confessor.[34]

Birgitta came to Rome with at least a rudimentary knowledge of Latin, as is suggested by Book I 58, which describes some Latin comparative adjectives.[35] Those who knew her at the time of her arrival in Rome say she was ignorant in the grammar but that she learned quickly. Prior Peter corroborates this, saying that after she left Sweden she was instructed by God to cease some of her prayers and instead learn Latin grammar; and he says that she made good progress.[36] Lorenzo, one of the canons at the Lateran church, says he had conversations with her in around 1350 and had to use an interpreter, as she only spoke her native tongue.[37] Of her knowledge of Italian little is known, but she must have learnt to use it fluently as an everyday means of communication, as is suggested by her instinctive outburst about the spiritual state of her son Karl, who had recently arrived from Sweden: 'Questo core!'[38]

The household established by the small Swedish party in Rome bears the stamp of a pious religious community and can be seen in many ways as a continuation of the daily routines they had adopted at Alvastra, and a prototype of the monastery she later founded. Ex. 65, which is given here in full, describes the daily routine:

33 See further Aili 1995. His life was edited by Schück 1895.

34 Books III 27, VI 105.

35 This text is also one of the 'Birgittiner-norske' texts and dates from the Sweden years. See Wessén 1968, p. 82.

36 AP p. 545. Article 38 in the canonisation process deals with her knowledge of Latin, but the answers given do not give a completely consistent picture. Niccolò Orsini, for instance, when questioned on the article, avoids a direct answer, saying she spoke to him 'litteraliter' but that he did not know whether or not it was correct. It was Niccolò who acted as interpreter when she met Urban V in Montefiascone because she did not know sufficient grammar and did not easily understand the pope's language (perhaps his French Latin accent). This suggests she must have spoken Italian to Niccolò.

37 AP p. 420.

38 AP p. 436.

Christ speaks: 'I advise you to sleep four hours before midnight and four after midnight. If this is impossible and there is a good intention, that will be acceptable. For anyone who somehow can reasonably reduce eight hours' sleep without weakening the body, senses or power, shall be granted a greater reward. Then you may have four hours for reading your prayers and fulfilling other devout and useful works so that no hour is wasted. Then you may sit for two hours at table, but if you can use a shorter time, God will reward you. However, this time may in no way be lengthened without reasonable cause. Then you may have six hours to attend to the necessary deeds which are allowed and commanded of you. You should spend two hours at vespers and compline and in pious prayers, and afterwards two hours in eating and drinking at evening meal in honourable refreshment for the body's comfort. When you have left your bed you should observe silence for four hours so that you do not speak without permission and only say the necessary and that with as few words as possible, in case anyone demands a response from you. You are allowed to have moderate and honourable refreshment for corporeal comfort and relaxation. After table prayers you should keep silence until you read the prescribed and ordained prayers. Six hours in accordance with the prescription of your Magister Peter you should use to learn or achieve something useful and then you may speak with whomever you wish, and speak honourably and never against God. At vespers and compline you should observe silence and in the short time which afterwards remains until evening meal, you may speak honest words with each other and have recreation until you go to bed.

I have said in the gospel that anyone who gives a vessel of cold water in my name shall not go unrewarded. Likewise every privation, however small, which is taken for the sake of my honour and piously carried out, shall deserve a worthy reward from me. Keep account of the fasting you observe while you are out on journeys. If you were in a monastery you might perhaps have more freedom and superfluity. Take therefore what is necessary for the body with reasonable moderation. Use a sort of soup – be it of cabbage or any other broth – but leave other kinds alone, to honour God. You may eat meat or fish of two kinds at the table. You should refrain from anything more, to honour me. Eat the bread which is placed before you and if you need more than what you have been given, ask for it in my name from your magister. And the same rule, which has been given concerning bread, also concerns drink. Know also that the sick cannot observe the rule to the same extent as the healthy and strong; therefore they may ask for what they need and it should not be refused them.

Since you have decided to own nothing, you should not give away anything without permission or receive anything offered you without permission. I warn you also that the devil sets snares and ambushes for you all the time. I advise you therefore to pay attention to the words you speak during times when silence is prescribed, and make true confession, arranging a suitable penalty for speaking. And if in your words there is a bad or unwisely deliberated speech or answer, then the penance and penalty should be all the greater. If anyone in a quick temper or anger abuses another, you should seek a suitable place as quickly as possible and there read an 'Ave Maria' and humbly pray to God for forgiveness. Every Friday you should come to confession in church with the purpose of not hiding or repeating your weaknesses but humbly improve all that is given to you to do.[39]

The mixture of private prayer and devotion from four o'clock in the morning until breakfast at eight o'clock, with active work and learning during

[39] 'Christus loquitur: "Consulo vobis habere quatuor horas pro dormicione ante mediam noctem et quatuor post. Sed qui hoc non potest, habeat voluntatem, et proderit ei. Qui vero potest minuere aliquid de sompno racionabiliter in hiis octo horis, ita quod non deficiat in corporalibus sensibus vel viribus, proficiat ei in maius premium. Deinde habeatis quatuor horas pro oracionibus legendis vel pro aliis deuotis et vtilibus operibus perficiendis, vt nulla hora pretereat sine fructu. Deinde per duas horas sedeatis ad mensam, quod si breuius feceritis, premium a Deo ide recipietis. Et illud tempus nullatenus sine causa racionabili prolongetis. Deinde habeatis sex horas ad operandum opera necessaria, quo vobis permittuntur et iniunguntur. Deinde habeatis duas horas ad vesperas et completorium et deuotas oraciones. Postea duas horas ad comedendum et bibendum in cenis cum honesta consolacione ad alleuiacionem corporis. Surgentes autem a lecto teneatis silencium per quatuor horas, ita quod nichil loquamini sine licencia et nec nisi vere necessaria sum paucioribus verbis, si quid a vobis queritur, respondendo. Postea permittitur vobis habere moderatam et honestam consolacionem ad solacium et recreacionem corporalem. Post gracias teneantis silencium, donec legeratis oraciones vobis iniunctas et ordinatas. Sex autem horas ordinetis secundum preceptum magistri vestri vel ad discendum vel ad operandum aliud aliquid vtile, et tunc loqui potestis, cum quibus volueritis, que sunt honesta et non contra Deum. In vesperis et completorio teneatis silencium. Et in illa modica hora, que deinde protenditur ad cenam, potestis loqui adinuicem, qua finita potestis verbis honestis, vsque dum lectos intraueritis, consolari. Ego dixi in euangelio, quod qui dederit calicem aque frigide in nomine meo, non perdet mercedem suam. Ita omnis abstinencia, quamuis minima, pro honore meo assumpta et deuote completa, meretur a me condigna premia. Vos scitis ieiunia vestra in itinere tendenda. Si essetis in monasterio, esset forsitan vobis maius ocium aut superfluitas. Sumatis igitur corporis necessaria cum parcitate discreta. Vtamini brodio vnius generis, siue sit olus siue aliud quodcumque sorbile, plura autem relinquite ob honorem Dei. Carnes vero vel pisces de duplici genere liceat vobis in mensa habere, et id, quod maius est, ob honorem meum dimittite. Panes, qui vobis apponuntur, comedatis, et si pluris, quam apponitur, egueritis, petatis in nomine meo a magistro vestro. Eadem lex sit de potu, que de pane data est. Sciatis eciam, quod infirmus non eque potest tenere regulam vt sanus et fortis viribus, et ideo potest sua necessaria petere et sibi, que habentur pre manibus, exhiberi. Et cum nichil decreueritis possidere, nichil debetis sine licencia dare vel data vobis sine licencia acceptare. Vos eciam precauto, quod dyabolus omni hora ponit vobis laqueos et insidias. Ideo consulo vobis, vt notetis verba, que tempore silencii protulistis incaute, et faciatis de hiis veram confessionem, assumentes satisfaccionem, debitam pro eisdem. Et si in verbis inuenitur inutilis et non discrete premeditata locucio vel responsio, tunc oportet, quod penitencia et satisfaccio sit maior. Si vero aliquis subito motu vel ira obloquitur alteri, statim, cum fieri potest, queratis locum aptum legendo vnum 'Aue Maria' et a Deo indulgenciam humiliter postulando. Qualibet sexta feria veniatis in capitulum ea voluntate, quod nichil velitis de delictis vestris abscondere vel iterare sed omnia, secundum quod vobis iniungitur, humiliter emendare." ' (Hollman 1956, pp. 187–9)

the day, followed by worship and an evening meal, gave Birgitta time for both contemplation as well as an active life in the community.[40] The revelation states explicitly that the regime is stricter than that of a monastic life, and recommends extreme asceticism, based on a monastic model, for the 'lay' community. As in the Birgittine rule, however, allowances are made for those with greater or lesser needs than are prescribed, and personal privation is commended.

Birgitta's role of subordination and obedience is marked by her handing everything she owned to Magister Peter, who was in charge of the practical affairs of the household. Now she was no longer mistress of her own affairs, and learnt obedience and submission to her confessor's advice, to the extent that whenever they walked out on the streets of Rome together she asked his permission even to look up from the ground.[41]

The Sermo Angelicus

About four years after her arrival in Rome, in 1354, while she still lived next to the church of San Lorenzo in Damaso, Birgitta received the lengthy revelation known as the *Sermo Angelicus*, which contained the daily readings for matins intended to be used at the new monastery.[42] According to the Prologue, she could see the altar of the church from her house and would sit daily 'with pen, paper and tablet' ready to receive the text dictated in sections to her by an angel. Her Swedish version was then translated into Latin by Magister Peter. This 'revelation' marks another important stage in the preparations for the new order and forms a distinctive part of the Birgittine nuns' liturgy. It is devoted to the Virgin Mary and is probably the most eloquent expression of Birgitta's Mariology throughout her work.[43]

The *Sermo Angelicus* is a well crafted, polished and lyrical piece of writing. For each weekday there are three readings. For Sunday the Angel tells how God has loved Mary in her perfection from eternity; Mary is compared to

40 Note that the day's routine is listed twice in the first paragraph, with the second time embellishing the first; perhaps this is an example of textual reworking.

41 Later, when visiting Naples, without asking his guidance, she wanted to help a merchant called Antonius, whose good character she had misjudged, and she smelt a foul smell in her nose. AP p. 391.

42 See Eklund 1972. On the date see pp. 18–20; and see also Collins 1969. The *Sermo Angelicus* survives in three forms today: first, as part of the main Revelation corpus; second, as part of the Breviary composed for the nuns at Vadstena, known as the *Cantus sororum*, to which liturgical sections were added by Magister Peter (see Lundén 1976); and third, as part of Alfonso's compilation of Revelations dating from c.1380, known as the *Celeste Viridarium*.

43 Birgitta's Mariology was first discussed by Vernet 1937 and Roschini 1973, but has only recently begun to be examined in more depth. The collection of essays edited by Brodd and Härdelin 1996 contains a number of articles on Marian attitudes in various Birgittine contexts.

Noah's ark and God's love for Mary is compared to Abraham's love for Isaac. The Monday readings tell how the angels knew after the fall of Lucifer that the Virgin would be created; how much they rejoiced in her creation, and how, still increate, she stood before God and the angels after the creation of the world. The angels, knowing great things would be achieved through Mary, did not grieve about the fall of man, having seen the divine vision of Mary standing before God. In the Tuesday readings the angel tells of Adam's penance after the fall, and of how Adam in his fallen state found consolation in the knowledge of the future creation of Mary and her great humility and dignity; and likewise Abraham, Isaac, Jacob and all the prophets found comfort in her future birth. For Wednesday, the readings concern Mary's conception and birth, and tell how God, who loved Mary before he created her, also loved her when she was in her mother's womb. The Thursday readings describe Mary when she had received wisdom from God and how she was beautiful in soul and body in the eyes of all who saw her, and not disposed to any sin. She conceived the Son of God in her womb, and gave birth with her virginity intact. The Friday readings deal with Mary's sorrow and anguish at the death of Christ and her spiritual constancy and patience during her suffering. The angel explains to Birgitta that Mary knew, in fulfilment of Scripture, that Christ must suffer for the salvation of mankind; nonetheless her grief was overwhelming at the Passion of Christ. But as soon as Christ was laid in the tomb, she took heart in the knowledge that he would rise from death to eternal glory. The Saturday readings depict the steadfastness of Mary's faith in the resurrection, even when others voiced doubts. Her life and doctrine were an example for the others around her; and because of her great merits she was assumed into heaven in body and soul after her death.

The *Sermo Angelicus* places the Virgin firmly in the plan of God. Birgitta reflects aspects of the rise in Marian devotion in the later middle ages, and exemplifies the shift that had taken place from the presentation of the Virgin as a distant, liturgical figure who was depicted mainly in terms of her relationship to Christ, into a personalised image of an individual who experienced human joys and sufferings and who was depicted in terms of her saving work for man.[44] She is the *mater dulcissima* and *regina misericordiae*, who is presented as the object of pious praise and as an instrument of intercession between God and man.

The *Sermo Angelicus* reflects a blend of Marian popular devotion and learned argument on doctrinal issues, and contains innovative elements, such as its interpretation of the Assumption, the traditional belief that the Virgin was assumed into heavenly glory in body and soul three days after her death. This doctrine was debated from the sixth century onwards although it was not generally accepted until the second half of the thirteenth century. The *Sermo*

44 See further Johnson 1987.

Angelicus teaches that Mary was assumed into heaven a 'a few days' after her burial, in body as well as soul:

> ... so the body of his most gracious mother, because it never committed any sin, by God's power and might was assumed into heaven, together with her most holy soul, a few days after her burial, and was venerated in all honour.[45]

Birgitta expounds further on the doctrine in Book VII 26, where she states that the number of days spent in the grave before the assumption was fifteen (a point that was taken up and criticised in debates following the canonisation):

> Hear carefully, daughter! After my son ascended into heaven I lived for fifteen years in the world and in addition the time as passes between the ascension day of my son and the day of my death. Then I lay dead in the grave for fifteen days. Thereupon I was assumed into heaven with unending honour and joy. The clothes in which I was buried remained in the grave and I was instead clothed in such clothes as my son and Lord Jesus Christ is clothed in. You shall know also that in heaven there is no human body except my son's noble body and my body.[46]

Another doctrine affirmed in the *Sermo Angelicus* is the perpetual virginity of the Virgin. 'By this wonderful union neither the divinity of the Son was reduced nor the virgin integrity of the mother.' Birgitta defies anyone to doubt that it was in God's power to execute a state of affairs by which Mary's virginity remained eternally intact. (SA 15)[47]

A further teaching that was associated with the Virgin was the doctrine of the Immaculate Conception. The doctrine, which argued that Mary was free from the stain of original sin from the first moment of her conception, had been keenly debated since the seventh century. St Anselm of Canterbury in the

45 '... ita et corpus sue dignissime matris, quod numquam aliquod peccatum commisit, aliquantis diebus post eius tumulacionem Dei virtute et potencia fuit cum eiusdem sacratissima virginis anima assumptum in celum omnique honore simul cum eadem extitit glorificatum.' (Eklund 1972, p. 134)

46 'Attende, filia! Ego, postquam filius meus ascendit ad celos, vixi in mundo per XV annos et tanto tempore plus, quantum est de festo Ascensionis eiusdem filii mei vsque ad mortem meam. Et tunc mortua iacui in isto sepulchro per XV dies. Deinde fui assumpta in celum cum infinito honore et gaudio. Vestes autem mee, cum quibus fui sepulta, tunc remanserunt in sepulchro isto et ego fui tunc induta talibus vestibus, qualibus indutus est filius meus et Dominus meus Ihesus Christus. Item scias, quod nullum corpus humanum in celo est nisi corpus gloriosum filii mei et corpus meum.' (Bergh 1967, p. 195.) See further on the doctrine Schmid 1933, p. 112 note 2.

47 Cf. also Book VII 25, where it is said that her virginity would remain intact in eternity and Christ was born of her 'in all purity'. Books I 10 and VI 57 reiterate the same argument.

eleventh century provided the intellectual argument in favour of the Immaculate Conception, whereas St Bernard denied it. The great scholastic tradition of the Dominicans, like St Albert and St Thomas Aquinas, also denied the doctrine on the grounds that in every natural conception the stain of original sin is transmitted, and Mary was not exempt from this. Thirteenth-century Franciscan writers, like Duns Scotus, however, took the view that Mary was sanctified and set free from original sin in her mother's womb, and thus she was always free from original sin.

In the *Sermo Angelicus* Birgitta does not touch directly on the doctrine but speaks of Mary's parents' exemplary marriage in general terms: 'The will of such couples may be compared to fruit-bearing branches, since they fear God in all their deeds, and according to God's will, they love each other only in order to produce children for God's praise.' (SA 10) Elsewhere in the Revelations, however, there are direct references to the Virgin's immunity from sin. In Book VI 49 Mary tells Birgitta how she was conceived 'without original sin and not in sin' because her parents had the most perfect marriage and their sexual union was against their own will and by God's will. In Book VI 55, it is said that she was conceived without any concupiscence of her parents and there is a reference to the doubt some feel about this doctrine. Birgitta appears to reflect the argument of Mary's sanctification in the womb of her mother in Book I 9. Although Mary's parents did not sin when they conceived Mary, they were born in original sin themselves and therefore there was an 'infectio carnis' in her being. This argument is reiterated in Book V revelacio 13 : 'Mary was a vessel pure and impure, pure because she was all beautiful and because there was not found in her even enough impurity in which to fix the point of a needle; not pure because she was descended from the kin of Adam and born of sinners although conceived without sin in order that, of her, my Son might be born without sin.'

Mary is also depicted as an integral part and instrument of God's saving presence on earth. She is the intermediary in salvation history, the mother of mercy who intercedes on men's behalf in their petitions to God. Her reference to the Virgin as *salvatrix* (Ex. 56: the vision in which see sees her husband in purgatory) and to the Virgin and Son together as *redemptrix* (Book I 35) may illustrate further the active part the Virgin plays in the work of redemption and suggests that divine grace comes through Mary as well as Christ; in the latter vision, indeed, the Virgin declares that just as Adam and Eve sold the world for an apple, she and her son redeemed the world 'as it were with one heart'.[48]

Chapter 19 of the *Sermo Angelicus* outlines a view of Mary as the mother of wisdom and draws attention to her active and intellectual qualities. In being the instrument of the incarnation, the Virgin possesses a special

48 See Graef 1963, vol. 1 p. 309, and Børresen 1991.

wisdom superior to that of learned men. She rejoiced in the resurrection, which she witnessed – contrary to scripture – before Mary Magdalene and the apostles. Her name, *magistra apostolarum*, suggests that after the ascension she instructed the apostles in those things they did not know about Christ.[49] She is also presented as one who comforts martyrs, teaches believers, gives an example to virgins, consolation to widows, counsel to the married, and support for all who embrace the faith.

Without doubt Mary dominates Birgitta's spirituality, as is seen across the entire corpus of texts (in approximately one third of them she is addressed by the Virgin) and in the monastic order, which is dedicated to the Virgin and in which the office of the abbess is moulded on emulation of the Virgin. It is seen too in the Birgittine liturgy which repeatedly resonates with praise of the Virgin, as well as in Birgitta's life, where Mary has a palpable role to play, which is perhaps best symbolised when she assures Birgitta of the authenticity of two Marian relics, a drop of her milk and a hair from her head.[50]

The Virgin appears to Birgitta as her comforter, friend and mentor who explains the contents of her visions and reassures her in her prophetic calling. More significantly and uniquely, as Claire Sahlin has argued, is the way in which Birgitta sees her role as the channel of God's works as analogous to the Virgin's role in incarnating Christ: just as Mary is a vessel and channel, the instrument of God's grace, so Birgitta places herself in a similar role as mediator of God's reforming message to mankind.[51]

Katarina Ulfsdotter

As we have seen, the Virgin provides comfort to Birgitta in her struggle to place her special calling above her family. The daughter–mother relationship which she clearly felt in her intense feelings towards the Virgin may be more fully explored in an examination of her own attitude towards her daughter Katarina, who for most of her years in Rome was her mother's companion. Direct information about their daily life can be obtained from Katarina's testimony in the canonisation process, which she gave in August 1379, as well as the *Vita sancte Katerine*, written by Ulf Birgersson, who entered Vadstena as a brother in 1407 and became general confessor there until his death in 1433.[52] It is the type of saint's life in which there is a transformation from a young, beautiful, worldly girl to a humble, patient and obedient woman.[53] It contains

49 See further Nyberg 1993 and Nyberg 1996.
50 AP pp. 628, 527–8, 634–5.
51 See further Sahlin 1996, 'The Virgin Mary . . .'.
52 AP pp. 303–51. His *vita* was included in the application for Katarina's canonisation in 1415 (see Collijn 1942–46) which resulted in her beatification on 14 June 1488, and meant that she could be revered in certain dioceses in Sweden as well as within the Birgittine order.
53 On the typology see Weinstein and Bell 1982, pp. 19–99.

popular, everyday and even gossipy details, giving a colourful picture of a young aristocratic woman who underwent an enormous emotional upheaval and inner conflict before her complete dedication to a life of monastic service. It concentrates largely on her difficult life in Rome when she was beset by all kinds of hardships, not least by the amorous advances of admiring noblemen.

Her *vita* states that from an early age she showed signs of piety, refusing to take the breast of a wet nurse who did not lead a chaste life. She was placed in the Cistercian nunnery of Riseberga, where the devil appeared to her in the guise of an ox when she was in bed one day, and with its horns threw her lifeless on the floor. At the age of seven, having been persuaded by playmates to play with some dolls, she dreamt of devils in the shape of dolls entering her bedroom and beating her so much that the following day she was covered in bruises.[54] She married a nobleman, Eggard Lydersson van Kyren (whose family originally came from Holstein); and asked him on their wedding night to agree not to consummate the marriage.[55] A public affirmation of her virginity was given one day when Eggard was out hunting; a hind – an animal which symbolised chastity, and later became Katarina's saintly emblem – sought refuge with her and buried its face in her lap as she sat in the carriage accompanying the hunt – for she 'had suppressed all animal desires'. In private their chastity was protected by prayer and genuflections, and by sleeping on the floor with little bedding, even in winter; and in public their life consisted of self-denial and exemplary deeds. Having heard of their exceptional domestic arrangements, her brother, Karl Ulfsson, crept into their bedroom one night to find them sleeping separately and uncomfortably on the floor; for which he remonstrated with them for being naïve and highly strung. Their ascetic lifestyle, however, soon caught on: when Katarina abandoned the fashionable dress of noble ladies she was followed by other women in her circle, including Karl's wife, which incurred further his wrath against his sister. He accused her of dressing like a beguine and of encouraging other women to follow her example.[56]

A few months after Birgitta had departed for Rome, Katarina, then aged about nineteen, set out to visit her. Eggard consented to let her go although he was concerned for her safety on such a hazardous journey. Karl Ulfsson, however, wrote to Eggard threatening to kill him if he allowed Katarina to leave Sweden, but she intercepted the letter and sought support from her uncle Israel, who encouraged her to go. She arrived in Rome in August 1350, while her mother, accompanied by Magister Peter, was away in Farfa monastery. Peter felt a sudden urge to go back to Rome, and they returned to find Katarina who had been searching for her mother for eight days. A few weeks later, as Katarina was preparing to return to Sweden, she was asked by her

54 On children's play see Krötzl 1989.

55 On Eggard see further Klockars 1976, pp. 96–8.

56 See above p. 50. On the beguines in Sweden see Morris 1999.

mother to stay on. She humbly agreed to give up everything, including her husband, and her mother received a revelation stating that she would be more useful in Rome than in Sweden, and that she should stay there as her mother's companion.

Katarina's new life in Rome was not without great trauma and after a while, so the *vita* continues, she started to suffer from homesickness and a yearning for her old freedom. Yet as she still longed for Sweden, even after she was widowed, she asked her mother for a remedy. Birgitta had her confessor whip her daughter severely until all her worldly inclinations were removed. Her life continued to be lonely and miserable and, moreover, her mother forbade her from undertaking pilgrim walks in the city because of the dangers of robbers and attackers; and she was forced to stay at home with the servants while her mother and her confessor visited the holy shrines in Rome. With resentment and bitterness, and envy at the freedom of her brothers and sisters back in Sweden, she refused to tell her mother why she was so depressed at being incarcerated in the house in a strange country, but the following night she was comforted by the Virgin who instructed her to be obedient to her mother and confessor. Nevertheless, it was not easy for her to submit in humility and obedience, and her mother's demands were rigorous, for Birgitta feared that Katarina would fall into worldly sin and temptation.

Much of Ulf's biography of Katarina deals with accounts of her flight from the attentions of admirers; Katarina was still only about twenty and allegedly extremely beautiful, and she had vowed to preserve her chastity and never remarry. Attempts were made by suitors to ambush her: a Roman count lay in wait for her as she walked on her way to the church of San Sebastiano with her companions and servants; but the abduction attempt was foiled. Afterwards she would only worship in the church nearest her house, unless her mother's visions could confirm that she would be able to travel safely. On another pilgrimage to the church of San Lorenzo, in the company of her mother, the same count again lay in waiting in a vineyard but he fell asleep and was blinded by the daylight when he awoke. Recognising his wrong he at once sought Birgitta and Katarina at the church and asked for their forgiveness, offering his services as their protector, at which point his sight was restored; this count later testified to Urban V and the cardinals about these miracles. Another time, on a pilgrimage to Assisi they stayed overnight at a poor inn and as they huddled in a corner, a band of robbers entered, who, seeing Katarina's beautiful face in the firelight, began to make advances to her, and were about to attack her when a sudden commotion outside made them flee. The next day the same robbers lay in wait at the roadside for Birgitta's party to pass by, but this time the women were protected by a cloud of darkness over the road while the surrounding countryside was bathed in light, and so they continued safely on their journey.

In the sources, Katarina's sanctity is suggested through her gift of prescience. One day, she met a pilgrim nun who told her to pray for a Norwegian woman's soul and then disappeared. Her servants said that although they heard her talking to someone they had seen no one; and Birgitta then received a vision informing her that her son Karl's Norwegian wife, Gyda, was dead. Katarina's behaviour in her renunciation of worldly pleasure, her generosity, charity to the poor and voluntary poverty are also exemplary, according to the *vita*. Some Roman noblewomen invited her to go out with them one day, and having obtained permission from Birgitta, they walked outside the city and came to some vineyards where the grapes were hanging down over the walls. Because she was tall her companions asked her to pick the grapes. She stretched up, not the least embarrassed by her ragged and patched dress. What the noblewomen saw, however, was that she was wearing a magnificent garment bedecked with jewels. In the same way, when she lay ill in bed one day, a Roman nobleman called on her, and her humble bed of straw was suddenly transformed into splendid bedclothes with scarlet and golden covers.

Ulf's biography is a colourful account, rich in detail, drawing on monastic tradition and using the stereotypes of the later medieval saint's life. At a time when the cult of the Virgin's mother, St Anne, was strong, Katarina is part of a pattern in which saintly families, consisting of more than one generation of saint, are created.[57] Once she overcomes the emotional and physical struggles of her early widowhood, the impression is given of a complete conversion to a saintly life, and the picture that emerges in the sources is of a tireless and selfless piety, and a gentle and passive personality who worked with dedication towards the foundation of the order and her mother's canonisation. The virtues of obedience to her confessor (which probably also implies obedience to her mother's wishes) and confession are emphasised, and she is portrayed as having deep spiritual integrity which is underpinned and moulded by the patterns of a monastic existence, but which contrasts with the politically astute and outspoken actions of her mother.[58] She came to be a great and respected woman in her own right; and according to her *vita*, she was called upon in times of difficulty in Rome, as when the banks of the Tiber overflowed and she was invited to pray for a retreat of the waters. Her gifts of rhetoric and persuasion were also renowned, and she was able to speak among princes and scholars, as (according to her *vita*) Urban VI (1378–89) commented after she had addressed him and the cardinals: 'Daughter, you have truly drunk your mother's milk.'

In spite of the apparent physical proximity in which the two women lived, however, it seems that they were not very close emotionally; nor did Birgitta confide in her daughter or reveal her divine experiences to her; many of Katarina's testimonies, indeed, are derived from what she had heard from the

57 See Vauchez 1988, p. 211.
58 See further Nyberg 1991, 'Birgitta som mor . . .', on the monastic character of her sainthood.

confessors rather than what her mother had told her in person.[59] *Extravagantes* 69 contains probably the best insight into the relations between the two women. Birgitta is given a salutary chastisement for over-indulging her contemplative states at the expense of her worldly needs, and she is reminded of the great sacrifices her daughter has made by renouncing everything – husband, family and friends. In a pointed reminder of the tension between the active and contemplative life, Birgitta is instructed to interrupt her continual prayerful state and instead humbly to mend Katarina's ragged clothes.[60]

Part of Birgitta's and Katarina's life in Rome involved the pastoral care of the poor of the city, a subject which is addressed in article 20 of the canonisation process. They provided hospitality to foreigners visiting Rome and always had their doors open for Scandinavian pilgrims. Book IV 16 recounts how a Swedish bailiff from Östergötland received hospitality from Birgitta during his pilgrimage to Rome but that Christ chastised her, saying that the man was not pious. In Book VI 102, she comforts a Swedish woman who is ill in Rome; and in Book VI 115 she tells a Finn from Turku diocese, who could not find a confessor in Rome who could speak Finnish, that the will to confess is sufficient.[61] *Extravagantes* 100 tells of a Swedish woman who visited Santiago de Compostela where she heard a voice speaking from a crucifix on a church fresco; she returned to Sweden and then embarked on a pilgrimage to Rome. At Montefiascone she saw a similar image in a house and heard a voice telling her to stay there: she took up a pious life, 'with tears, fasting and prayers'. One day she had a vision of a woman with dew and fragrant white and red roses pouring out of her mouth: this was Birgitta 'who is in Rome and will bring there wine from foreign parts, mixed with roses and give it to thirsting pilgrims'.[62] The woman may have been an early Birgittine pilgrim following in the footsteps of Birgitta and visiting the religious shrines in Europe.

Restoration of the papacy

Birgitta's own programme, even before she left Sweden, was for the restoration of the papacy to Rome, which had been absent since the pontificate of Pope Boniface VIII at the very beginning of the century, and at whose door she placed much of the blame for Rome's present problems in Book III 27. Several revelations concerning the popes occur at the end of Book IV, but they are also gathered, in chronological order and with further circumstantial detail, in Alphonso of Jaén's *Tractatus de summis pontificibus*.[63] Her strictures against

59 This point is made by Nyberg 1991, 'Birgitta som mor . . .'.
60 There is also advice to Katarina in Book VI 120.
61 What language she communicated with him in is unclear, as it is extremely unlikely that she could understand Finnish.
62 Ex. 101. See too AP p. 503.
63 The collection was made sometime before 1380, which is the date when they are mentioned by Prior Peter in his testimony. The exact number of revelations included

individual popes are fierce, but her criticisms are always carefully directed at the incumbent of the papal office, and not at the institution itself.

In the 1340s she had issued comminatory messages to Clement VI, including the message taken in person to him by Prior Peter and Bishop Hemming of Turku.[64] She also criticised his legate in Rome, Pocius de Péret (bishop of Orvieto 1348–61), prophesying his death away from his native land, in Avignon: 'He will be like a dog which is captured by smearing a knife with meat so that when it tries to taste the meat it is slit by the knife.'[65]

Her shock at the state of the city when she arrived there led her to continue her calls on the pope to return to the city. In Book IV 33 she addresses one of the Avignon popes, whose identity cannot be determined, about the wretched state of the papal city, saying its princes are like wild robbers, its buildings are dilapidated, its churches abandoned, and its canons, priests and deacons, 'the devil's whoremongers', openly keeping mistresses in their own homes. Monks are accused of not following their original rule, nunneries are likened to brothels, and usury and simony are rife. The laity are also immoral, failing to attend confession and Mass, and many practise polygamy and take pleasure in hearing the cries of their wife and mistress giving birth at the same time in the same house. Thus Birgitta warns the pope that the Catholic faith is in danger of ruin unless someone appears who will work to abolish all evil in Rome.

During the time she spent in Rome Birgitta endeavoured to bring about the return of the papacy there. As well as having a general purpose in hoping to rescue Christendom from its imminent decline, as she saw it, she also had a personal reason for wishing to see the papacy restored to the Holy City: she needed to obtain papal authorisation for her new order, and therefore made several appeals for the popes to listen to her. She was indifferent to their high station and ignored any need to pay court to them. Of Innocent VI, for instance, she comments that he is made 'of better metal' than his predecessor, Clement VI, but would do well to heed Christ's messages to her.[66] His successor, Urban V, is likened to excellent quality gold within a ball of thread symbolising worldly concerns. He is told that the monastic rule which has been sent to him should be ratified, for Christ has equipped the monastery 'in the place Vadstena in Sweden' with spiritual gifts, and granted indulgences which can be gained in the church of San Pietro in Vincoli in Rome.[67]

The plan to restore the papacy was opposed by the emperor Charles IV, the French king, the Visconti family in northern Italy, and the Guelph towns of

in this tract is unclear, but there is a core of nine, viz. Book IV 136–44, with several others which are included as part of the tract in certain manuscripts. The tract is discussed and edited by Jönsson 1997.

64 Book VI 63.

65 Ex. 102.

66 Book IV 136.

67 Book IV 137.

Plate 4. Frontispiece of Book VIII, in a Neapolitan manuscript dating from the late fourteenth century. Birgitta receives her Revelations from Christ and the Virgin, and hands them to Alphonso of Jaén and Prior Peter of Alvastra. In the bottom part of the picture, flanked by a group of laymen and clerics, and possibly also Katarina in the foreground, they hand the Revelations to a number of kings and queens. (See interpretation by J. Svanberg in Aili, Ferm and Gustavsson 1990, p. 124.)
Source: Pierpont Morgan Library, New York, MS M. 498 fol. 343v.

Italy. However, it was welcomed by the supporters of the Florentines, whose ambassador wrote to Urban: 'Rome calls to her spouse, who will also be her saviour'; as well as Italian poets like Petrarch who wrote 'Holy Father, Israel has left Egypt at last. The House of Jacob is no longer in the midst of a strange people.'[68] Presumably, however, Charles IV overcame his objections.[69] The emperor in the fourteenth century had a symbolic role as the highest secular authority, as is suggested by Birgitta who speaks of a division between canon law, Roman law and Swedish common law: 'there are three laws, one the Church's, the second the Emperor's, and the third that of the commoners'.[70] She used every means to influence Charles to ensure the return of the papacy, as well as to help in obtaining recognition for her order, and she writes instructing him (through the mouth of Christ) to work with the pope to obtain authorisation for her order.[71] However, she appears not to have had any direct contact with the emperor, and most of her messages to him are of a general nature only.[72]

Birgitta's wishes were fulfilled – albeit only temporarily – in October 1367, when Urban returned to Rome. He spent the summer months of 1368 at Montefiascone, and on 21 October 1368, led by the emperor, whose wife a few days afterwards was crowned empress in San Pietro church, the pope made his ceremonial entry into the Holy City. Magnus Petri testified that he himself was present and saw how the pope and emperor entered the city together, in fulfilment of Birgitta's early prophetic vision.[73] Urban's first year in Rome was full of promise, but his continued preference for French appointments led to resentment and unrest in neighbouring states with which the Romans sided; thus amid political and social unrest, on 12 April 1370, he removed first to Viterbo, and then to Montefiascone, with the probable intention of returning to Avignon. It was here, in the summer of 1370, that Birgitta met him in person and made further appeals to him to stay in Rome. Her message was delivered first to Cardinal Beaufort (later Pope Gregory XI), who was reluctant to let her see the pope, but she was nevertheless granted an audience, possibly on even more than one occasion.[74] Her friend Niccolò Orsini acted as mediator and interpreter at one of her meetings with the pope; and it appears that Alphonso

68 Quoted from Holland Smith, 1970, p. 115.

69 Charles IV was regent in Bohemia during the 1330s, and became king of Bohemia in 1346. He had sided with the French in their hostilities against the English, and his father fell in the battle of Crécy. He came to Rome in 1355 where he was crowned by a cardinal on behalf of the pope in exile as 'emperor of the Romans', illustrating, as Ullmann 1972, p. 290, has written, the 'shadowy character of Roman emperorship'.

70 Book IV 111.

71 Book VIII 51. Book IV 45 also concerns the emperor.

72 Birgitta's revelations concerning the emperor are discussed by Klockars 1971, pp. 88–96.

73 AP p. 267.

74 On this point, see the summary of discussions by Jönsson 1989, pp. 44–7.

and Magnus Petri were also present at one meeting. In Book IV 138, the Virgin urges Urban 'to strengthen the Catholic faith, establish peace and thus renew the holy Church'. She accuses him of having been weakened by his spiritual work and tempted into material enjoyment; and she notes that he longs to go back to France, 'for his homeland is to him excessively attractive, by worldly people's standards'. If he does return to Avignon she prophesies that 'he will receive a blow or a puff of wind so that his teeth will gnash or be knocked out, his sight will become dim and dark and his limbs tremble'. When he died in Avignon a few weeks later, her prophecies were seen as having been fulfilled.

V

The Last Pilgrimage

> Mary said: 'I am the queen of heaven, and mother of the suffering. I wish to show you how my son lived in his humanity, and how he suffered on the cross. And this is a sign to you, that you will come to the places where I dwelt on earth, and where you will see my son with your spiritual eyes.'
>
> Maria loquitur: 'Ego sum regina celi et mater miserorum, ego tibi ostendere volo, qualis filius meus erat in humanitate sua et qualis, quando paciebatur in cruce, et hoc erit tibi signum, quia venies ad loca, in quibus ego corporaliter conuersabar, et ibi videbis spiritualibus oculis tuis filium meum.'
>
> (Ex. 66)

NOW NEARING THE END of her life and in failing health, Birgitta had one last pilgrimage to make, a journey to the Holy Land. This pilgrimage would be a realisation of the prophecies she had received, dating back to the 1340s, concerning the earthly life of Christ, and it would allow her to see in person the places connected with the Incarnation. It was to be a journey of emotional prayer and meditation, which brought her closer to the human Christ, and which also increased her identification with the Virgin. Yet at the same time, her emotional responses to the holy shrines she visited during her pilgrimage sharply contrasted with her continued outspoken involvement in secular matters.

Alphonso of Jaén

At Montefiascone the Virgin appeared to Birgitta 'and instructed her to tell her friend Alphonso, the priest and hermit' to write and copy the books of revelations which were divinely given to her and which until then had been kept secret.[1] Alphonso Pecha was the former bishop of Andalusian Jaén, and was Birgitta's last, and in some ways most influential confessor. He was born at Segovia sometime between 1327 and 1330, and his parents were Fernán Rodriguez Pecha, who was chamberlain to King Alphonso XI of Castile, and

1 AP p. 98.

Elvira Martinez, grand mistress of the queen's household.[2] He studied canon law and became archdeacon of Saldaña in the diocese of León; and at the early age of about thirty, on account of his exceptional learning and aided no doubt by the petitions of his elder brother, who was the royal chamberlain, he was made bishop of Jaén by Pope Innocent VI in 1359. He resigned his bishopric in 1368 for reasons which are disputed.[3] He may have preferred a contemplative life, and wished to follow the example of his brother who had joined a community of hermits in the desert; he may have disliked the political situation during King Pedro I of Spain's despotic rule; or he may have been outmanoeuvred when a rival bishop, named Andres, was elected to his see. Having tendered his resignation to Pope Urban V at Montefiascone, he settled in Italy and undertook a religious profession, perhaps in an eremetical order, since he is said later to have come to Rome 'de heremo'.[4]

Alphonso first learned about Birgitta from a Spanish hermit named Laurencius who belonged to a community at Monteluco near Spoleto.[5] Probably he met her for the first time around 1368 and the two must have become well acquainted during the three months they spent together at Montefiascone in the summer of 1370; Birgitta's being without her two Swedish confessors, who were both ill in Rome, meant that Alphonso became her confessor as well as her spiritual director, and he may even have been involved in writing down some of her revelations during this period. Both Birgitta and Alphonso had much in common in terms of their noble background, knowledge of secular and political affairs, and a disenchantment with contemporary secular and religious life. Both too had an interest in new models of monastic life that would represent a break with existing monasticism and a fresh beginning for its members: Alphonso had espoused a spiritually pure and élite form of life in choosing to follow the eremitical life, and for Birgitta, contemplation was a central part of her monastic ideal. Furthermore, Alphonso was well-connected and had an excellent knowledge of canon law, which would prove vital for Birgitta to obtain papal authorisation for her order, and later for him as a petitioner for her canonisation.

Alphonso's duties towards Birgitta are described in an *additio* to Book VII 16, in which the Virgin uses female likenesses to describe their relationship, which is one of mutual spiritual dependence: 'My friend [i.e. Alphonso] ought to love you as a mother, as a lady, as a daughter and as a sister': a mother, because of Birgitta's age, a lady, because of the grace given to her by God, a daughter, by teaching and consoling her, and as a sister, by reproving her

2 On Alphonso's life, which is clouded by uncertainties, see Seidlmayer 1930, Colledge 1956, Jönsson 1989 and Gilkær 1993.

3 On this debate see Colledge 1956, p. 27, Jönsson 1989, pp. 40–7, and Gilkær 1993, pp. 48–52.

4 AP p. 327.

5 AP p. 364.

when necessary, and by showing her more perfect things through words and examples:

> Also, tell him that he ought to be like one who carries the best of flowers. These flowers are my words, which are sweeter than honey to those who savour them, sharper and more penetrating than arrows, and more effective in their reward. It is therefore the duty of the bearer to protect the flowers from the wind, the rain, and the heat: namely, from the wind of wordly talk, from the rain of carnal delights, and from the heat of worldly favour.[6]

Predictions of the pilgrimage

Pilgrimage to the Holy Land was an established tradition within Birgitta's family, as it was among other members of the nobility in the later middle ages.[7] Several times during her life Birgitta had been told she would travel to Jerusalem. The *vita* tells how in Arras, on her return from her pilgrimage to Santiago with her husband Ulf, she was informed that she would go to Jerusalem and that she would receive a vision of the nativity of Christ.[8] The same message is also conveyed in the last vision in the *Liber Questionum*, a striking symbolic vision in which she is addressed directly by God. He relates a parable in which a servant tells his master that his field is ready for cultivation, but the master replies that he must wait patiently for the time of sowing until the stubble has been loosened by rain and wind.[9] In the meantime, the master tells him to seek five places in which five objects are found:

> In the first place there was a vessel, closed and not closed; a vessel, small and not small, luminous and not luminous, empty and not empty, clean and not clean. In the second place a lion was born, which was seen and not seen, heard and not heard, touched and not touched, known and not known, held and not held. In the third place there was a lamb, shorn and not shorn, wounded and not wounded, calling and not calling, suffering and not suffering, dying and not dying. In the fourth place there was a serpent that lay

6 'Item dic ei, quod ipse debet essse sicut ille, qui portat flores optimos. Hii sunt verba mea, que dulciora sunt melle sapientibus ea, acuciora et penetrabiliora sagittis, efficaciora remuneracione. Oportet ergo portantem cauere floribus a vento, pluuia et estu: a ventu scilicet mundane locucionis, a pluuia carnalium delectacionum, ab estu mundani fauoris.' (Bergh 1967, pp. 170–1) See also Sahlin 1997, pp. 37–8, who refers to this revelation in a study of the relationship of Birgitta to her confessors.

7 In Scandinavia the tradition goes at least back to the eleventh century, and includes reference to viking kings who travelled to Jerusalem, and a runic inscription which names a woman, Inigunn, who went to Jerusalem (see Gräslund 1988–89); and it continues with the pilgrimage of Erik of Pomerania in 1423. See further KLNM s.v. 'pilegrim'.

8 AP pp. 80, 96.

9 The wait for the sowing time is echoed in the opening chapters of the Rule, where there is reference to the planting of a new vineyard. See further Chapter VIII.

> and did not lie, moved and did not move, heard and did not hear, saw and did not see, felt and did not feel. In the fifth place there was an eagle that flew and did not fly, that came to a place and never left it, that rested and did not rest, that was renewed and not renewed, rejoiced and did not rejoice, that was honoured and not honoured.[10]

In the exposition, the significance of the five places is explained, and each is associated with aspects of the humanity of Christ: the vessel with the Virgin, the lion with Bethlehem, the lamb with Calvary, the serpent with the garden of Gethsemane, the eagle with the Mount of Olives. The common image of the Virgin as vessel is used elsewhere in the revelations, and the animals here are Messianic titles, each associated with places and points in Christ's life on earth: the lion, which is traditionally associated with the Resurrection (for example Book VI 94), is used here for the birth; and its opposite, the lamb, is the type of the crucified Christ. The serpent occurs in the New Testament (John 3.14) as a figure of the risen Christ, although Birgitta uses it less as a symbol of the triumph over injury and death than as a symbol of the ignominy of death before resurrection, thus connecting the serpent with suffering before the salvation of mankind, and emphasising her characteristically incarnational theology. The eagle plays the role of heavenly messenger in Christian typology and in patristic tradition it is a symbol of ascension and prayer; here, however, Birgitta appears to use it to denote the risen Christ. At the end of the vision, the promise of more revelations is made to her:

> Therefore, he who comes to these places pure and with a good and perfect will, shall see and taste how sweet and pleasant I, God, am. And when you come to these places, I will show you more.[11]

10 'In primo loci fuit vas clausum et non clausum, vas paruum et non paruum, vas luminosum et non luminosum, vas vacuum et non vacuum, vas mundum et non mundum. In secundo loco nascebatur leo, qui videbatur et non videbatur, qui audiebatur et non audiebatur, qui tangebatur et non tangebatur, qui agnoscebatur et incognitus fuit, qui tenebatur et non tenebatur. In terco loco fuit agnus tonsus et non tonsus, agnus vulneratus et non vulneratus, agnus clamans et non clamans, agnus paciens et non paciens, agnus moriens et non moriens. In quarto loco ponebatur serpens, qui iacuit et non iacuit, mouebatur et non mouebatur, audiuit et non audiuit, vidit et non vidit, senciebat et non senciebat. In quinto loco fuit aquila, que volauit et non volauit, que et venit in locum, vnde numquam recessit, que requieuit et non requieuit, que innouabatur et non innouabatur, que gaudabat et non gaudebat, que honorabatur et non honorabatur.' (Bergh 1971, p. 173)

11 'Ergo, qui ad ista loca venerit mundus cum bona et perfecta voluntate, habebit videre et gustare, quam dulcis et suauis sum ego Deus. Itaque, cum veneris ad ista loca, ostendam tibi plura.' (Bergh 1971, p. 175) This vision has been the subject of a variety of interpretations; see for example Sundén 1973, pp. 85–9, who adopts a Jungian interpretation, and Nyberg 1990, p. 26, who gives a theological interpretation.

Her preoccupation with a pilgrimage to the Holy Land in the 1340s, however, was not to be realised until the end of her life. In May 1371 she was instructed to prepare to travel to Jerusalem to visit Christ's grave and other places there; and at the end of the year she was told to depart, and not be anxious about her weak physical condition but to place her trust in God's protection and strength. Although she was now nearly seventy years old and years of self discipline and rigorous fasting must have had their effect on her, she apparently accepted the prospect of pilgrimage cheerfully. The author of the papal bull issued at her canonisation, indeed, in true hagiographic style, makes the comment that neither the summer heat nor the winter chill could put her off her pilgrimages, and that she did not travel by horse but by foot, and made so many genuflections that her knees were as hard as camels' knees![12]

Giovanna I of Naples

The source materials are detailed on the itinerary and chronology of the pilgrimage.[13] Birgitta's party left Rome on 25 November 1371 and included three of her children – Katarina, Birger and Karl – as well as Alphonso, Prior Peter, Magister Peter, two Spanish anchoresses named Elvira and Praxedis, who were probably Birgitta's handmaids, and two Swedish chaplains, Gudmarus Frederici and Magnus Petri.[14] The journey took them first to Naples, which Birgitta had visited earlier for two years in 1365–67, and where she made the acquaintance of the Neapolitan archbishop Bernard, and the queen, Giovanna I (1326–82), daughter of Robert of Anjou. Naples was a prosperous commercial centre and its court had been a focus of culture and learning under Giovanna's uncle, Charles of Anjou, in the early fourteenth century. Boccaccio had been a member of Robert of Anjou's court, and was invited there by Giovanna's chief adviser, the banker and statesman, Niccolò Acciaiuoli, in 1363 and again in 1365, although his stays at the court were short. Niccolò (d.1365) was also a patron of Birgitta's during her stay in Naples, where she

12 See further Ellis 1991, p. 94. The detail of the camels' knees is probably not unique, and occurs in other saints' lives; see for instance the description of St James the Less in the homilies of John Mirk, which describes his knees as having such hard skin that they were as lumpy as camels': 'he vset forto knell soo moche yn hys prayers, þat hys kneus wern soo þekke of ylle, þat þay weren boched lyke a camele' (Erbe 1905, p. 140). I am grateful to Dr Veronica O'Mara for drawing my attention to this parallel.

13 On the pilgrimage see Andersson 1973.

14 Birger was made a knight of the Holy Sepulchre in the Holy Land. See further on this practice Keen 1984, pp. 48–9. Magnus Petri was a close friend of Birgitta's and later became confessor general at Vadstena. The main biographical detail on him is contained in the *Diarium Vadstenense*; see Gejrot 1988.

also befriended his sister, Lapa, after curing her son of a severe illness.[15] Under Giovanna's rule, however, Neapolitan prosperity and culture started to disintegrate, and her court was notoriously full of corruption.[16] Birgitta gives her view of conditions there in Book VII 28:

> . . . in this said city many buy pagans and infidels to be their slaves and some masters of these slaves do not bother to baptise them and do not want to convert them to the Christian faith . . . Moreover, some keep their female servants and slaves in such abjection and ignominy, as if they were dogs – selling them, and, what is worse, frequently exposing them in a brothel to earn money that is a disgrace and an abomination. Others, in fact, keep them in their own houses as mistresses both for themselves and for others . . . many men and women, with various inordinate marks of respect, keep about them and consult wicked fortune-tellers and diviners and the most evil enchantresses. Indeed, sometimes they ask them to perform witchcraft and incantations in order that they may be able to conceive and beget children.[17]

Even without Birgitta's strictures, Giovanna had the reputation of being a pleasure-loving and worldly woman whose name was involved in endless scandals, including her involvement in the death of her first husband. When Birgitta came to Naples in 1371, she was in her third marriage, to a Spanish prince, Jacobus III, king of Mallorca. Birgitta makes the most bitter attack on her wantonness in Book VII 11, although the full force of her criticism is hidden in the official version of the vision and included only in the *additio*.[18]

15 AP p. 331.

16 Barraclough 1968, p. 162, sums her up as 'infamous, dissolute and incompetent'.

17 'in dicta ciuitate multi emunt paganos et infideles ad seruitutem suam, et aliqui eorum domini non curant eos baptizare neque volunt ad fidem christianam eos conuertere . . . Item aliqui tenent suas seruas vel sclauas in tanta abieccione seu ignominia, ac si essent canes, vendentes eas et, quod deterius est, exponentes ipsas frequenter in lupanari ad lucrandum pecuniam turpitudinis et abhominacionis. Alii vero tenent eas in suis domibus vt meretrices, et pro se et pro aliis, et hoc valde abhominabile et odiosum est Deo et michi ac eciam toti celesti curie. . . . multi homines et femine habent secum et consulunt aliquos malignos sortilegos et diuinatores et aliquas pessimas incantatrices diuersis respectibus inordinatis. Nam aliquando petunt ab eis, quod ipsi faciant aliqua maleficia et incantaciones ad finem, vt possint concipere et generare prolem.' (Bergh 1967, pp. 204–6)

18 The title states: 'This is the beginning of a revelation that Birgitta had in Naples for the queen of the same city. But other things contained in it are not set down here because they are secrets that pertain to the status and person of the said queen.' 'Hic est principium cuiusdam reuelacionis, quam domina Birgitta habuit pro domina regina Neapolitana in eadem ciuitate, sed alia, que ibi continentur, non ponuntur hic, quia secreta sunt, que pertinent ad statum et personam dicte domine regine.' (Bergh 1967, p. 140) The main revelation is short: after an introduction (in which God declares he has given free will to all, but it is the devil who impedes the will), the text is stopped abruptly with the word 'etc'. This is an example of a vision

The *additio* lists fourteen pieces of advice as to how Giovanna should mend her ways: observe confession, reflect on her marriage, repay her debts, not burden her people with new changes, have trusty counsellors, contemplate the Passion, sustain the poor, give gifts wisely, show compassion to the unjust, ensure peace in her kingdom, not paint her face, show humility and contrition, and set aside worldly customs and female flatterers. Then follows a grotesque description of a woman who is presumably the queen. She is dressed in a shift covered in semen and mud. 'This woman is a monkey that sniffs at its own stinking posterior.' Again she appears wearing a crown of twigs, covered in excrement and mud, and sitting naked on a trembling beam. The next time she is seen the woman is seated on a golden throne, with two devils before her, one offering her blood and the other fire. The Virgin says that the woman is in need of tribulation as penance. Christ then intercedes on the woman's behalf, stating that she had done some things to please him.[19]

Birgitta could not approve of Giovanna's personal conduct; nor did she agree with her on political matters, especially with regard to the papacy. Giovanna saw the pope's presence in Rome as a threat to her own territories and she had sold part of her inheritance at Avignon to Pope Clement VI, for which she had received the highest form of papal recognition from Urban V, the golden rose. She was later drawn into internal strife in Italy and joined the factions of the Avignon papacy, but eventually she was accused of being a schismatic and excommunicated by Pope Urban VI. She was driven into exile and imprisoned, and the new king of Naples, Charles of Durazzo, had her smothered in her bed in 1382.

It is of interest, therefore, why Birgitta should apparently have become such good friends with the queen, and why the queen should have taken her part in the canonisation process. In spite of Birgitta's harsh words about the queen and their differences on papal politics, Giovanna appears to have paid heed to Birgitta, and there seems to have been a strong bond of respect and friendship between the two women, as is confirmed by *Margareta Clausdotters krönika*, which recounts that Giovanna 'was a particularly good friend of Birgitta's and loved her greatly'.[20] However, according to the same source, their relationship was complicated by the philanderings of Birgitta's son Karl.

The meeting between Karl and Giovanna, if it is to be believed, is colourfully recounted in the same chronicle. As well as greeting the queen in the

addressed to a famous person which is sensitively censored in the official record of it.

19 The *additio* ends with statements concerning Gomez Garcias of Albornoz (nephew of Ægidius of Albornoz who held posts in the administration of the papal states and whom Birgitta called her 'spiritual son'), and Antonius of Carleto (a merchant of Naples, who entered the service of Giovanna and was another good friend of Birgitta's).

20 Annerstedt 1876.

customary way of kneeling down and kissing her feet, Karl also kissed her squarely on the lips, thus winning her affection, so much so indeed that the queen then declared she would like to keep him in Naples as her husband, to Birgitta's horror, especially since Karl's wife was still living in Sweden. Much concerned, Birgitta turned to God for help, and fifteen days afterwards, on 12 March 1372, Karl was taken ill and died, and was given a royal burial by Giovanna. Birgitta's stern judgement in preferring the death of her favourite son to the ignominy of his adulterous relationship with the queen of Naples is well illustrated in this account. But her personal grief for his death continues for long afterwards despite her lack of display of any public emotion as she sat with him when he was dying. Alphonso, who was also present, says she remained without tears 'immobile as a pillar'.[21] In Book VII 13, the Virgin tells Birgitta she had been present at the parting of the soul from Karl's body, using a metaphor of a woman giving birth:

> I acted like a woman standing by another woman who is giving birth, so that she might help the infant, lest it die in the flow of blood or suffocate in that narrow place through which an infant exits and so that, by her watchful care, the infant's enemies, who are in the same house, might not be able to kill it. I acted in the same way. Indeed I stood near your son Karl, shortly before he died, in order that he might not have such thoughts of carnal love in his memory.[22]

A few days later she saw a soul in judgement which was as vulnerable as a new-born infant and she heard an angel and a devil argue over his many sins.[23] The angel insists that his sins are atoned for by the continual prayers, thoughts and tears of his mother, but this incurs the devil's wrath:

> When the devil heard this, he cried out impatiently roaring, and said: 'Woe is me. For all my memory has been taken from me! I do not now recall in what respect that knight followed my will; and – what is more amazing – I have forgotten what name he was called by while he lived.'
>
> The angel answered: 'You know that now, in heaven, he is called "Son of Tears" '. The devil cried out loudly and answered: 'What a cursed sow his mother, that she-pig is, who has a belly so expansive that so much water was poured into her with the result that her belly's every space was filled with liquid for tears! She is cursed by me and all my company!'

21 AP p. 370.

22 'Feci quidem sicut mulier alteri mulieri parienti astans, vt iuuaret infantem, ne ex fluxu sanguinis moreretur et ne in illo arto spacio, per quod exiret infans, suffocaretur, cauens eciam, ne infantis hostes, qui in eadem domo essent, ipsum interficere possent. Simili modo ego feci. Ego quippe steti prope eundem filium tuum Karolum, paulo antequam emitteret spiritum, vt carnalem amorem non sic in memoria haberet . . .' (Bergh 1967, p. 152)

23 The motif of the struggle between an angel and a devil is common in the revelations; see further Bergh 1973.

Then the angel answered: 'Your curse is God's honour and the blessing of all his friends.' Then Christ the Judge spoke saying this: 'Depart, devil, my enemy!' And he said to the knight, 'Come, my chosen one!' And at once the devil fled.[24]

The reference to Karl as the 'son of tears' echoes the anxieties of St Augustine's mother before her son's conversion to a spiritual life, and illustrates Birgitta's concern for the salvation of her most worldly child.[25] Karl's soul was caught in a bitter struggle with the devil and he needed the intercessions of two 'mothers', his earthly mother as well as the Virgin, to keep him from eternal punishment. The revelation lasted intermittently for many days and it continued as she boarded a ship bound for Palestine. Her next stop was Famagusta.

Cyprus

Cyprus at this time was in a state of turmoil.[26] The island had been under Western rule since King Richard I of England had conquered it during the Third Crusade in 1191, and it was a kingdom ruled by a French dynasty, the Lusignans, who came from Poitou in western France. They imposed a Western system of government and land ownership on the indigenous Greek population, and until the end of the fourteenth century it was a stable, prosperous island, with a sound administration; it was also one of the easternmost outposts of the Catholic Church. King Peter I was murdered in 1369, shortly after he was engaged in a crusade against the Muslims on behalf of the pope. His young son Peter II was proclaimed king, but the boy's mother, Eleanor of Aragon, was passed over as regent in favour of Peter I's brother, Prince John of Antioch, whom Eleanor suspected of her husband's murder. She became the focus of opposition to the new regime and wrote to the pope and other Western rulers calling on them to allow her to make her case for justice before them, and she received letters from Pope Gregory XI in 1371 admonishing the young prince to rule well and telling her to look after him. But the pope also

24 'Tunc dyabolus hec audiens clamauit impacienter rugiens et dixit: "Ve michi, qui tota memoria mea michi ablata est! Iam enim non recolo, in quibus iste miles meam secutus est voluntatem, et quod est mirabilius, eciam oblitus sum, quo nomine, dum vixit, vocabatur." Respondit angelus: "Scito, quod modo in celo vocatur 'filius lacrimarum'." Dyabolus vero clamans alte respondit: "O quam maledicta est illa scrofa seu porca mater eius, que tam prolixum habuit ventrem, quod tanta aqua in ipsam infusa fuit, quod omnia ventris eius spacia impleta fuerunt humoribus lacrimarum! Sit ipsa maledicta a me et a tota mea societate!" Respondit angelus: "Tua malediccio est honor Dei et omnium amicorum suorum benediccio." Tunc autem loquebatur iudex Christus sic dicens: "Recede tu, inimice dyabole!" Deinde dixit illi militi: "Veni tu, o mi electe!" Et sic statim fugit dyabolus.' (Bergh 1967, p. 161)

25 See Atkinson 1991, pp. 178–9, on this vision.

26 See further Hill 1948, pp. 364–70, Edbury 1991, pp. 197–211.

sent envoys in person to intervene in what looked like a deteriorating situation, and he ordered Peter II's coronation to take place immediately. In December 1371 he was duly crowned king of Cyprus, and in October 1372 he was crowned titular king of Jerusalem. However, the coronation was followed by a riot involving Genoese and Venetian merchants in Cyprus and led to the Genoese demanding compensation for death and heavy losses. Because of the weak internal position, with Eleanor and John both contending for power, the Genoese saw the opportunity of launching an invasion fleet against Cyprus. In October 1372 Eleanor was accused of appealing to the Genoese for help against John; and she again sought support from the pope, the king of Aragon and Giovanna of Naples. The pope attempted to intervene to head off the confrontation in October 1372 and in May 1373 he told Giovanna and others not to help the Genoese expedition by donating provisions. The pope's efforts at intervention throughout 1373 failed and the invasion began. Famagusta and the capital, Nicosia, were taken, and the king, his mother and John were all imprisoned. The Genoese success was shortlived, however, and a peace treaty was signed on 21 October 1374. In the long term, although the treaty imposed severe financial restraints on the Cypriots, the foundations of the kingdom and its dynasty were not permanently damaged.[27]

Thus when Birgitta came to Cyprus in mid April 1372, the island was on the brink of war.[28] She had with her a letter of recommendation from the queen of Sicily and empress of Constantinople, who was probably Mary of Bourbon, a former sister-in-law of Peter I.[29] Eleanor welcomed Birgitta to her palace and took advice from her, asking when she should have her son crowned king, whether she should avenge her husband's murder, and whether she should enter into a new marriage or return to her native country. In Book VII 16, which is a compilation of comments and *additiones* dealing with Cyprus, Christ describes the island in apocalyptic prophetic terms:

> This town is like Gomorrah, burning with the fire of sloth, excess and pride. Therefore its structures shall fall, and it shall be desolated and diminished, and its inhabitants shall depart, and they shall groan in sorrow and tribulation, and they shall die out, and their shame shall be mentioned in many lands because I am angered at them.[30]

27 These events are described by a witness in the canonisation proceedings by the Genoese knight, Carolus of Malocello (AP pp. 429–31). Birgitta's pronouncements on Cyprus were also later used to explain the capture of Cyprus in 1376 by the Genoese.

28 The chronology here follows Andersson 1973, although he does not substantiate his dates. Some dates are given in the chapter titles in Book VII, and others are given in the canonisation proceedings.

29 See further Jönsson 1989, p. 100.

30 'Hec ciuitas est Gomorra, ardens igne luxurie et superfluitatis et ambicionis. Ideo ruent structure eius et desolabitur et imminuetur, et habitatores eius migrabunt et pre dolore et tribulacione ingemiscent et deficient, et nominabitur confusio eius in

There follow other pieces of advice to the court entourage which contain some harsh political realism. The duke (John of Antioch) who knew of his brother's death should do penance or he would experience a harsher death; God would avenge Peter's murderers. The court is corrupt and confessors appear to be like simple sheep but really are foxes and flatterers. Eleanor should not return to Aragon, or think of remarriage, but she should stay and nurture her son and appoint good counsellors for him. On the subject of the crowning of a new king, she speaks of the burdens and dangers of a rule by so young an heir. There is also personal advice for the queen; she is to cease wearing tight dresses and clothes which reveal her breasts, nor must she use perfumes, but she should follow instead the example of holy queens and saints.

While she was in Cyprus Birgitta was asked by Eleanor to pray for the new young king. Some time later, now in Jerusalem, she received advice for Peter II and John of Antioch, on how they should rule the kingdom, that urged them to work together and always observe the love of God in their political dealings. She sent this guidance back to Cyprus, although according to Alphonso's editorial title of Book VII 18, Christ 'instructed her to write those things to them as if from herself and not from the part of Christ', in other words, in letter form, rather than as a revelation.

The following revelation, Book VII 19, was also received in Jerusalem but sent back to Cyprus in letter form. Its strictures are directed in crusading terms at those who espouse Greek Orthodoxy and are not followers of the pope in Rome:

> Let the Greeks also know that their empires and kingdoms or domains will never stand secure and tranquil in peace, but that they themselves will always be subject to their enemies from whom they will always sustain the gravest of losses and daily miseries until, with true humility and charity, they devoutly subject themselves to the Church and faith of Rome, totally conforming to the sacred constitutions and rites of that same Church.[31]

According to the title, the revelation was sent back to Cyprus to be published in the kingdom but John ignored it and thus on her return from Jerusalem,

multis terris, quia iratus sum eis.' (Bergh 1967, p. 169) There are several *additiones* in Book VII 16; see Bergh 1967, p. 79. The sequence is positioned between two Holy Land visions, and some of its contents may therefore date from the Jerusalem period.

31 'Sciant eciam Greci, quod eorum imperium et regna siue dominia numquam stabunt secura neque in pace tranquilla, sed inimicis suis semper subiecti erunt, a quibus semper sustinebunt grauissima dampna et miserias diuturnas, donec ipsi cum vera humilitate et caritate ecclesie et fidei Romane se deuote subiecerint, eiusdem ecclesie sacris constitucionibus et ritibus se totaliter conformando.' (Bergh 1967, p. 182) See on this revelation in terms of her prophetic self-awareness and the use of Old Testament prophetic models Costello 1989, pp. 116–19.

Birgitta herself let it be made public ('publicauit') in the presence of Eleanor, Peter II, John of Antioch and the royal council. There is no evidence, as some have suggested, that she took to the streets and preached in public in Cyprus; although it might be argued that in this vision she comes very close to adopting a role of public preacher.[32] Alphonso's words 'narrauit' and 'publicauit' suggest that she delivered her own message (presumably in Latin, but of course Alphonso or another male companion may have spoken or interpreted on her behalf). Preaching was a role that for women was regarded as dangerous and could have led to accusations of heresy against her. The incident aptly illustrates the growing confidence with which she spoke out publicly in her moral crusade, especially in secular political affairs, towards the end of her life. She was now elderly and unwell, and a complete stranger in Cyprus, and yet she was more determined in her strictures, and even less compromising, than she had ever been in previous secular matters.

It is clear that the king and John of Antioch paid Birgitta scant regard in Cyprus; and there were other voices of derision and incomprehension. A Dominican named Simon, who was confessor to John of Antioch, said she was demented, with 'una mente capta', and another dismissively called her an ignorant little woman 'ignara muliercula'.[33] Among those who did not ridicule her, however, was the English knight and courtier, William Williamson, who followed her to Jerusalem; as did the queen's confessor, the Franciscan, Martin of Aragon, who was the bearer of the message in Book VII 19. He had sought advice on the poverty ideal preached by his order, which he confessed to having difficulty in pursuing, and after his stay in Jerusalem with Birgitta he returned to Famagusta where he sold all his possessions.[34]

The vision of the Passion

On the next stage of the journey the party experienced bad storms. Alphonso relates in the canonisation proceedings that Birgitta remained quite calm through these adversities amid the general panic around her, showing no sign of fear, but sitting quietly in the boat without any anxiety for the loss of her property which had been thrown overboard.[35] Having arrived at the port of Jaffa, they made their way to Jerusalem, apparently shunning the advice given to them in Cyprus to blacken their faces to adopt an Arab disguise.[36]

The ordering of Book VII in its present form probably reflects the order of the pilgrimages she undertook in the Holy Land. She appears to have made

32 E.g. Jørgensen 1954, p. 280, Costello 1989, p. 114. For discussion of the role of women as public preachers see Sahlin 1997, 'The Prophetess . . .'.
33 AP pp. 430, 390.
34 Book VII 20.
35 AP p. 314.
36 Book VII 16.

the standard tour of the stations of the cross, starting with the church of the Holy Sepulchre, which comprises several shrines and includes the chapel over the site of the crucifixion. In this church she was told that those with devout hearts will receive God's grace, and she appears to gain absolution for the deceased members of her family: 'some souls of your relatives that were in purgatory have today been freed and have entered into heaven in my glory'; presumably her son Karl was uppermost in her mind at the time.[37] In the church, too, her important vision of the Crucifixion was experienced, which is quoted here in full.

> While I was at Mount Calvary, most mournfully weeping, I saw that my lord, who was naked and scourged, had been led by the Jews to his crucifixion. He was being guarded by them diligently. I then saw too that a certain hole had been cut into the mount and that the crucifiers were round about and ready to work their cruelty. The lord, however, turned towards me and said to me: 'Be attentive; for in this hole in the rock the foot of the cross was fixed at the time of my passion.'
>
> And at once I saw how the Jews were there fixing and fastening his cross firmly in the hole in the rock of the mount with bits of wood strongly hammered in on every side in order that the cross might stand more solidly and not fall. Then, when the cross had been so solidly fastened there, at once wooden planks were fitted around the trunk of the cross to form steps up to the place where his feet were to be crucified, in order that both he and his crucifiers might be able to ascend by those plank steps and stand on top of the planks in a way more convenient for crucifying him. After this, they then ascended by those steps, leading him with the greatest of mockery and scolding. He ascended gladly, like a lamb led to the slaughter. When he was finally on top of those planks, he at once, willingly and without coercion, extended his arm and opened his right hand and placed it on the cross. Those savage torturers monstrously crucified it, piercing it with a nail through that part where the bone was more solid. And then, with a rope, they pulled violently on his left hand and fastened it to the cross in the same manner. Finally, they extended his body on the cross beyond all measure; and placing one of his shins on top of the other, they fastened to the cross his feet, thus joined, with two nails. And they violently extended those glorious limbs so far on the cross that nearly all of his veins and sinews were bursting. Then the crown of thorns, which they had removed from his head when he was being crucified, they now put back, fitting it onto his most holy head. It pricked his awesome head with such force that then and there his eyes were filled with flowing blood and his ears were obstructed. And his face and beard were covered as if they had been dipped in that rose-red blood. And at once those crucifiers and soldiers quickly removed all the planks

[37] 'alique anime consanguineorum vestorum, que erant in purgatorio, hodie liberate sunt et intrauerunt in celum in gloria mea.' (Bergh 1967, p. 163)

fastened to the cross, and then the cross remained alone and lovely, and my lord was crucified upon it.

And as I, filled with sorrow, gazed at their cruelty, I then saw his most mournful mother lying on the earth, as if trembling and half-dead. She was being consoled by John and by those others, her sisters, who were then standing not far from the cross on its right side. Then the new sorrow of the compassion of that most holy mother so transfixed me that I felt, as it were, that a sharp sword of unbearable bitterness was piercing my heart. Then at last his sorrowful mother arose; and as it were, in a state of physical exhaustion, she looked at her son. Thus, supported by her sisters, she stood there all dazed and in suspense, as though dead yet living, transfixed by the sword of sorrow. When her son saw her and his other friends weeping, with a tearful voice he commended her to John. It was quite discernible in his bearing and voice that out of compassion for his mother, his own heart was being penetrated by a most sharp arrow of sorrow beyond all measure.

Then too his fine and lovely eyes appeared half dead; his mouth was open and bloody; his face was pale and sunken, all livid and stained with blood; and his whole body was as if black and blue and pale and very weak from the constant downward flow of blood. Indeed, his skin and the virginal flesh of his most holy body were so delicate and tender that, after the infliction of a slight blow, a black and blue mark appeared on the surface. At times, however, he tried to make stretching motions on the cross because of the exceeding bitterness of the intense and most acute pain that he felt. For at times the pain from his pierced limbs and veins ascended to his heart and battered him cruelly with an intense martyrdom; and thus his death was prolonged and delayed amidst grave torment and great bitterness.

Then, therefore, in distress from the exceeding anguish of his pain and already near to death, he cried to the Father in a loud and tearful voice, saying: 'Father, why have you forsaken me?' He then had pale lips, a bloody tongue, and a sunken abdomen that adhered to his back as if he had no viscera within. A second time also, he cried out again in the greatest of pain and anxiety: 'Father, into your hands I commend my spirit.' Then his head, raising itself a little, immediately bowed; and thus he sent forth his spirit. When his mother then saw these things, she trembled at that immense bitterness and would have fallen onto the earth if she had not been supported by the other women. Then in that hour his hands slipped slightly from the place of the nail holes because of the exceeding weight of his body; and thus his body was as if supported by the nails with which his feet had been crucified. Moreover, his fingers and hands and arms were now more extended than before; his shoulder blades, in fact, and his back were as if pressed tightly to the cross.

Then at last the Jews standing around cried out in mockery against his mother, saying many things. For some said: 'Mary, now your son is dead'; but others said other mocking words. And while the crowds were thus standing about, one man came running with the greatest of fury and fixed a lance in his right side with such violence and force that the lance would have passed almost through the other side of the body. Thus when the lance was extracted from the body, at once a stream, as it were, of blood spurted out of that wound in abundance; in fact the iron blade of the lance and a part of the shaft came out of the body red and stained with the blood. Seeing these things, his mother so violently trembled with bitter sighing that it was quite discernible in her face and bearing that her soul was then being penetrated by the sharp sword of sorrow.

When all these things had been accomplished and when the large crowds were receding, certain of the lord's friends took him down. Then with pity, his mother received him into her most holy arms; and sitting, she laid him on her knee, all torn as he was and wounded and black and blue. With tears, she and John and those others, the weeping women, washed him. And then, with her linen cloth, his most mournful mother wiped his whole body and its wounds. And she closed his eyes and kissed them; and she wrapped him in a clean cloth of fine linen. And thus they escorted him with lamentation and very great sorrow and placed him in the sepulchre.[38]

38 'Ad montem Caluarie dum essem mestissima plorans, vidi Dominium meum nudum et flagellatum ductum per Iudeos ad crucifigendum. Qui diligenter ab eis custodiebatur. Vidi quoque tunc foramen quoddam excisum in monte et crucifixores in circuitu paratos ad operandum crudelitatem. Dominus autem conuersus ad me dixit michi: "Attende tu, quia in isto foramine petre infixus fuit pes crucis mee tempore passionis."

Et statim vidi, qualiter ibi crux eius a Iudeis figebatur et firmabatur fortiter in foramine petre montis cum lignis confixis cum malleo valentissime circumquaque, vt crux solidius staret, ne caderet. Cum igitur crux ita solide firmata esset ibidem, statim adaptabantur tabule lignee in circuitu stipitis crucis per modum graduum vsque ad locum, vbi pedes eius crucifigi debebant, vt possent per illos gradus tabularum tam ipse quam crucifixores ascendere et super tabulas illas apciori modo stare ad crucifigendum eum. Post hec autem ascenderunt ipsi per illos gradus, ducentes eum cum irrisione et vituperio maximo. Qui gratanter ascendens velut agnus mansuetus ductus ad immolandum, cum esset iam super tabulas illas, non coactus sed statim voluntarie extendit brachium suum et aperta sua dextera manu posuit eam in cruce, quam illi seui tortores immaniter crucifixerunt, et perforabant eam clauo per illam partem, qua os solidius erat. Tunc eciam trahentes cum fune vehementer manum eius sinistram cruci affixerunt eam simili modo. Deinde extento corpore vltra modum in cruce posita fuit vna tibia eius super aliam et sic iunctos pedes affixerunt in cruce duobus clauis, et in tantum extenderunt illa gloriosa membra in cruce vehementur, quod quasi omnes vene et nerui eius rumpebantur. Quo facto coronam de spinis, quam deposuerunt de capite eius, cum crucifigeretur, iterum imposuerunt et aptauerunt capiti suo sanctissimo. Que tam fortiter pupugit reuerendum caput eius, quod oculi sui repleti fuerunt illico fluente sanguine, aures quoque obstruebantur et facies et barba quasi tegebantur et intincta erant illo roseo sanguine. Et statim illi crucifixores et milites amouerunt velociter omnes tabulas illas, que adherebant cruci, et tunc remansit crux sola et alta et Dominus meus crucifixus in illa.

Cumque ego repleta dolore respicerem crudelitatem illorum, vidi tunc matrem eius mestissimam in terra iacentem et quasi trementem et semimortuam. Quam consolabantur Iohannes et alie sorores eius, que tunc stabant non longe a cruce ad eius partem dexteram. Dolor igitur nouus compassionis illius sanctissime matris in tantum transfixit me, quod quasi senciebam, quod cor meum pertransibat quidam gladius acutus importabilis amaritudinis. Surgens tandem tunc illa eius mater dolo-

This is one of four major visions on the crucifixion scene, received at different stages in her life.[39] It is representative of the intensity of the new devotionalism and affective piety of the fourteenth century, which appealed directly to

rosa, quasi exinanita corpore, respexit ad filium suum, et sic sustentata stabat a sororibus, tota stupore suspensa et velut mortua viuens, gladio doloris transfixa. Quam cum Filius respexisset et alios amicos plorantes, voce flebili commendabat eam Iohanni, et bene cernebatur in gestu eius et voce, quod cor ipsius ex compassione matris penetrabatur acutissima sagitta doloris immensi.

Tunc autem oculi eius amabiles et decori apparebant semimortui, m os eius erat apertum et sanguinolentum, vultus pallidus et submersus totusque liuidus et intinctus sanguine, corpus quoque totum erat quasi liuidum et pallidum et languidum valde ex continuo fluxu decurrentis sanguinis. Cutis eciam et caro illa virginea sanctissimi corporis eius ita delicata et tenera erat, quod ex modica percussione illata signum liuidum exterius apparebat. Aliquando vero conabatur ipse extensiones facere in cruce pre amaritudine nimia, quam senciebat, intensi doloris acutissimi. Nam quandoque dolor de membris eius et venis perforatis ascendebat ad cor et vexebat eum crudeliter intenso martirio, et sic mors eius prologabatur et dilatabatur cum tormento graui et ingenti amaritudine.

Tunc igitur ille anxius pre nimia doloris angustia et vicinus iam morti ad Patrem clamauit alta voce et flebil dicens: "O Pater, quare dereliquisti me?" Habebatque tunc labia pallida et linguam sanguinolentam, ventrem submissum coherentem dorso, ac si nulla intus habuisset viscera. Secundo quoque clamauit iterum cum anxio dolore maximo: "O Pater, in manus tuas commendo spiritum meum." Et tunc caput eius erigens se aliquantulum statim incluinauit se et sic emisit spiritum. Que tunc mater eius videns contremuit pre immensa amaritudine, volens cadere in terram, nisi quod sustinebatur ab aliis mulieribus. In illa igitur hora manus illius aliquantulum se retraxerunt a loco perforacionis clauorum pre nimio pondere corporis, et sic corpus eius quasi sustentabatur a clauis, quibus pedes crucifixi erant. Digiti autem et manus et brachia magis iam extenta erant quam ante, spatule vero et dorsum eius quasi strinebantur ad crucem.

Tunc denique circumstantes Iudei irridentes clamabant contra matrem eius multa dicentes. Alii namque dicebant: "Maria, iam mortuus est filius tuus", alii vero dicebant alia verba irrisoria. Et sic stantibus turbis in circuitu venit vnus accurrens cum furia maima et infixit lanceam in eius latere dextro tam vehementer et valide, quod quasi per aliam partem corporis lancea voluit pertransire. Quod cum extraheretur lancea de corpore, statim habundanter exibat de vulnere illo cum impetu quasi quidam fluuius sanguinis, ferrum vero lancee et aliqua pars haste rubicanda exibat de corpore et intincta sanguine. Que videns mater ita vehementer contremuit cum amaro gemitu, quod bene cernebatur in eius facie et gestu, quod anima eius tunc penetrabatur acuto doloris gladio.

Hiis autem expletis cum turbe multe recederent, deposuerunt Dominum quidam amici eius. Quem tunc pie mater recepit inter sua brachia sanctissima et reclinauit eum sedens in genu totum dilaceratum, vulneratum et liuidum. Quem lauabant cum lacrimis ipsa et Iohannes et alie mulieres plorantes. Et tunc tersit eius mater mestissima cum lintheo suo totum corpus eius et vulnera clausitque eius oculos deosculando eos et inuoluit eum in sindone munda. Et sic duxerunt eum cum planctu et dolore maximo et posuerunt eum in sepulchro.' (Bergh 1967, pp. 164–8) Translation (with some modifications) by A.R. Kezel in Tjader Harris 1990, pp. 188–90.

39 The other major accounts of the Passion are: Books I 10, I 27 and IV 70. They are com-

the emotion rather than the reason, and emphasised the pain and humiliation of the crucified Christ.[40] The motif of Christ Triumphant of older medieval tradition was now transformed into that of Christ Suffering, and the devout Christian was invited to become an active participant in the event itself, and to feel its bitter reality at first hand by entering into the scene and empathising with the physical pain. From a doctrinal point of view, the increased insistence on the physical features of the Passion compromised the significance of its place in the redemption of mankind, for the emphasis on corporeality all too easily overlooked the part played by the Trinity and the Resurrection in salvation history.[41]

Fourteenth-century mystics demonstrated a range of responses in their Passion visions. They felt a gratitude for Christ's sacrifice, and penitence for human sin; they felt the inner response of compassion which entailed (as the word itself suggests) a sharing in the Passion; and they were compelled to outward imitation in following the example of Christ. For Birgitta, gratitude for what Christ had suffered was seen in her constant reminders of the event in what Richard Kieckhefer calls 'the ongoing passion of Christ'.[42] It pervaded her whole life and became firmly engrained in her consciousness, going right back to her childhood vision of the crucified Christ and the meditations and prayers of her marriage years. In her daily life, her compassion is suggested by her pouring boiling wax on her body every Friday, and always shedding tears when she contemplated the Passion.[43] She also possessed a relic of the true cross which had been given to her while she was in Sweden.[44] Further, she used the crown of thorns as the model for the distinctive head-dress of her order.

In her Holy Land vision of the Passion, unlike her other Passion visions, the narrative perspective is Birgitta's: she gives an eye-witness account of the events as experienced through her own ears and eyes. Not only does she enter completely into compassion with Christ, but she also identifies wholly with the suffering of his mother. She reproduces in the vision the common idea of the Virgin swooning at the foot of the cross 'trembling and half-dead', at the

pared by Ellis 1993, who shows how overlapping motifs are borrowed from one vision to another, and notes some distinctive features which are not reflected in other descriptions of the Passion at the time: for instance, the four nails which had long since been replaced by three in the iconography of the scene; the tau-shaped cross which is suggested in Book IV 70; and the flagellation in Books I 10 and IV 70, which is brought to an end by a man who frees Christ from his bonds.

40 See further Kieckhefer 1984, pp. 88–121, Cousins 1987, Beckwith 1993.

41 The themes of the Trinity and the Resurrection are of course dominant elsewhere in her visions, although they have no role in this one. See Koch 1991.

42 Kieckhefer 1984, p. 97.

43 AP p. 99. On her tears, see Bergh 1993, p. 295.

44 Ex. 106.

sight of her son's pain.[45] Furthermore, Birgitta's compassion for Mary's suffering extends into imitation: Mary's pain becomes her pain, as is suggested when Birgitta herself feels that 'a sharp sword of unbearable bitterness was piercing my heart'.[46]

The vision of the Nativity

Birgitta's vision of the Passion of Christ is centrally placed in Book VII (chapter 16) shortly before the other most famous vision: that of the Nativity (chapter 21). The visions are separated only by the Cyprus revelations which, as we have seen, refer back to earlier events. The Nativity was the other great meditative event for the later medieval mystics, although it was generally overshadowed by the Passion.[47] The positioning of the Nativity after the Passion in the ordering of Birgitta's visions is also a poignant reminder of the reduced pleasure of the Virgin at the foreknowledge of the Passion. In the church in Bethlehem Birgitta sees the Virgin, dressed in a white mantle and finely-woven tunic through which her swollen womb can be seen. Joseph prepares the cave and goes outside; Mary removes her mantle and veil, and makes ready the garments for the baby:

> . . . And when all these things had been prepared, the Virgin knelt with great reverence, she began to pray; and she kept her back toward the manger and her face lifted to heaven towards the east. And so with raised hands and with her eyes intent on heaven she appeared to be suspended in an ecstasy of contemplation, inebriated with divine sweetness. And while she was thus in prayer, I saw something lying in her womb move; and then, in a moment and the twinkling of an eye she gave birth to a son, from whom there went out such great and ineffable light and splendour that the sun could not be compared to it. Nor did the candle that the old man had put in place give light at all because that divine splendour totally annihilated the material splendour of the candle. And so sudden and momentary was that manner of giving birth that I was unable to notice or discern how or in what part of her body she was giving birth. But yet, at once, I saw that glorious infant lying on the earth, naked and glowing in the greatest gracefulness. His flesh was most clean of all dirt and uncleanness. I saw also the afterbirth, lying wrapped very neatly beside him. And then I heard the wonderfully sweet and most gentle songs of the angels. And the Virgin's womb, which before the birth had been very swollen, at once retracted; and her body then looked wonderfully beautiful and delicate.
>
> When therefore the Virgin felt that she had now given birth, at once,

45 See Graef 1963, p. 309.

46 See Sahlin 1993, p. 220. The pierced heart, whether Birgitta's, Christ's or Mary's, is another common theme in the Revelations.

47 Cousins 1987, p. 384, notes that the birth and crucifixion meditations are central to Franciscan observance in particular.

having bowed her head and joined her hands, with great dignity and reverence she adored the boy and said to him: 'Welcome my God, my lord, my son!' And then the boy, crying and slightly trembling from the cold and the hardness of the floor, where he lay, rolled a little and extended his limbs, seeking to find refreshment and his mother's comfort. Then his mother took him in her hands and pressed him to her breast, and with cheek and breast she warmed him with great joy and tender maternal compassion. Then, sitting on the ground, she put her son in her lap and deftly caught his umbilical cord with her fingers. At once it was cut off without any flow of liquid or blood. And at once she began to wrap him carefully, first in the linen cloths and then in the woollen ones, binding his little body, legs and arms with a ribbon that had been sewn into four parts of the outer woollen cloth. And afterwards she wrapped and tied on the boy's head those two small linen cloths that she had prepared for this purpose. When these things therefore were accomplished, the old man entered; and prostrating himself on the ground, he adored him on his knees and wept for joy. Not even at the birth was that Virgin changed in colour or by infirmity; nor was there in her any such failure of bodily strength as usually happens in other women giving birth, except that her swollen womb retracted to the prior state in which it had been before she conceived the boy. Then she arose, holding the boy in her arms; and together both of them, namely, she and Joseph, put him in the manger, and on their knees they continued to adore him with gladness and immense joy.[48]

48 'Cumque hec omnia sic parata essent, tunc virgo genuflexa est cum magna reuerencia, ponens se ad oracionem, et dorsum versus presepe tenebat, faciem vero ad celum leuatam versus orientem. Erectis igitur manibus et oculis in celum intentis stabat quasi in extasi contemplacionis suspensa, inebriata diuina dulcedine. Et sic ea in oracione stante vidi tunc ego mouere iacentem in vtero eius, et illico in momento et ictu oculi peperit filium, a quo tanta lux ineffabilis et splendor exibat, quod sol non esset ei comparabilis. Neque candela illa, quam posuerat senex, quoquomodo lumen reddebat, quia splendor ille diuinus splendorem materialem candele totaliter annichilauerat. Et tam subitus et momentaneus erat ille modus pariendi, quod ego non poteram aduertere nec discernere, quomodo vel in quo membro pariebat. Verumptamen statim vidi illum gloriosum infantem iacentem in terra nudum nitidissimum. Cuius carnes mundissime erant ab omni sorde et immundicia. Vidi eciam pellem secundinam iacentem prope eum, inuolutam et valde nitidam. Audiui eciam tunc cantus angelorum mirabilis suauitatis et magne dulcedinis. Et statim venter virginis, qui ante partum tumidissimus erat, retraxit se et videbatur tunc corpus eius mirabilis pulchritudinis et delicatum.

Cum igitur virgo sensit se iam perperisse, statim inclinato capite et iunctis manibus cum magna honestate et reuerencia adorauit puerum et dixit ille: "Bene veneris, Deus meus, Dominus meus et filius meus!" Et tunc puer plorans et quasi tremens pre frigore et duricia pauimenti, vbi iacebat, voluebat se paululum et extendebat membra, querens inuenire refrigerium et matris fauorem. Quem tunc mater suscepit in manibus et strinxit eum ad pectus suum, et cum maxilla et pectore calefaciebat eum cum magna leticia et tenera compassione materna. Que tunc sedens in terra posuit filium in gremio et recepit cum digitis subtiliter vmbilicum eius, qui statim abscisus est, nec inde aliquis liquor aut sanguis exiuit. Et statim cepit eum

Plate 5. Wearing a pilgrim's hat and staff, Birgitta witnesses the birth of Christ. Fresco in Undløse parish, Sjælland, c. 1440.
Source: Danmarks kirker (Nationalmuseet, Copenhagen).

The vision of the Nativity is widely recognised as one of Birgitta's most important revelations in terms of its devotional content and lyricism; and it is followed by three short revelations on the same theme, which may originally have been a continuation of the same vision.[49] The first looks like a commentary on the vision itself, confirming the truth and novelty of the depictions. The second describes the visit of the shepherds, who, having heard that the (male) *salvator* had been born and not a (female) *salvatrix*, were given confirmation of the child's sex. The third revelation in the sequence contains a

inuoluere diligenter, primo in panniculis lineis et postea in laneis et stringens corpusculum, tibias et brachia eius cum fascia, que suta erat in quatuor partes superoris panniculi lanei. Postea vero inuoluit ligando in capite pueri illos duos panniculos lineos, quos ad hoc paratos habebat. Hiis igitur completis intrauit senex, et posternens se ad terram genibus flexis adorando eum plorabat pre gaudio. Nec tunc in partu virgo illa immutabatur colore vel infirmitate, nec in ea deficit fortitudo aliqua corporalis, sicut in aliis mulieribus parientibus fieri solet, nisi quod venter eius tumidus retraxit se ad priorem statum, in quo erat, antequam puerum conciperet. Tunc autem surrexit ipsa, habens puerum in vlnis suis, et simul ambo, scilicet ipsa et Ioseph, posuerunt eum in presepio et flexis genibus adorabant eum cum gaudio et immensa leticia.' (Bergh 1967, pp. 188–190) Translation (with some modifications) by A.R. Kezel in Tjader Harris 1990, pp. 203–4.

49 A detailed commentary of these revelations is provided by A.R. Kezel in Tjader Harris 1990, notes 768–825, pp. 305–9.

comment by the Virgin to Birgitta, on how what had been ordained and foreknown had now happened. The Nativity revelation contains innovative elements that are not found in mainstream representations of the scene; and the fact that the Virgin tells Birgitta in Book VII 22 that her vision of the birth is the true record, indeed, suggests that Birgitta was aware that it deviated from standard depictions of the scene. The Virgin reminds Birgitta of a traditional picture of the birth which she had seen while she was in Naples, and implies that the true record was not exactly as depicted there: 'yet you may know for certain that I was in such a state and gave birth in such a manner as you have now seen: bending on my knees, praying alone in the stable'.[50]

This, then, is the most striking departure from traditional iconography: the Virgin is depicted as kneeling down in an attitude of prayer at the moment of birth, rather than in the traditional posture of lying down. Other details, while not necessarily completely original, echo features within various monastic traditions in the later middle ages, such as Franciscan tradition in which Joseph is given prominence, and in which he takes off his own shirt for the swaddling clothes, and lights a candle before withdrawing from the scene before the birth itself.[51]

Compared to the majority of Birgitta's visions, where the visual element is subordinated to the locution, this vision is essentially visual, and Birgitta is a participant witness who describes the unfolding scene in all its minute material detail. In iconographical representations of the scene in art, indeed, she is sometimes depicted as an onlooker of the scene. Scandinavian art historians have argued that this vision revolutionised depictions of the Nativity in Christian iconography.[52] From now on, it is argued, starting in Italian art, the stable scene with the Virgin lying on her childbed is replaced by the outside stable scene. In c.1380 the new depiction is represented in the church of San Antonio extra Muros in Naples, according to a witness testimony in the canonisation process.[53] At about the same time, a fresco by Ugolino de Prete Ilario in the cathedral at Orvieto depicts the Virgin on her knees in an attitude of prayer. The Tuscan painter, Niccolò di Tommaso, was one of the first to make a direct

50 'Et licet aliquid ostendi tibi in Neapoli super hoc, scilicet qualiter stabam, quando peperi filium meum, tamen scias certissime, quod ego sic steti et tali modo peperi, sicut nunc vidisti flexis genibus orando sola in stabulo.' (Bergh 1967, p. 190)

51 See further Nordenfalk 1961, p. 372. Halborg 1993 suggests that several details may have been stimulated by her veneration of relics connected with the Nativity, which were situated in churches in Rome.

52 See especially Cornell 1924, who first argued this case. Modern art historians have not significantly modified Cornell's argument, e.g. Andersson 1973, pp. 107–13, Lindgren 1991, p. 105, Svanberg 1997. I am grateful to Ulla Sander Olsen for making available material which has helped clarify my interpretation of the iconography.

53 AP p. 233. The witness records that Birgitta saw a depiction of the Nativity in this church – possibly the one referred to in Book VII 22, although the latter vision suggests a conventional iconography. See Klockars 1971, p. 158.

allusion to Birgitta, in a painting dated c.1380–1400 now in the Vatican's Pinoteca: Birgitta is an onlooker in the right-hand foreground, and the words of welcome by the Virgin to the child are quoted from the vision in scrolls.[54] From around the same time, a mural depicts Birgitta as a spectator at the scene in the church of Santa Maria Novella in Florence, as does a painter from the Sienese school, in a painting now in the Museo Civico in Pisa; and there are early depictions of her in four churches in Naples.[55] A few decades later, she is depicted in the foreground of a fresco in Castilione d'Olona, Piedmont, by the Florentine painter, Masolino.[56] By the early fifteenth century, therefore, the new iconography had become established and was beginning to spread northwards, manifesting itself above all in areas of Birgittine influence, as exemplified by Meister Franke's reredos in Hamburg, and the reredos in Lye (Gotland) which was executed in Lübeck at the beginning of the fifteenth century.[57]

Death

In Book VII 26, the Virgin instructs Birgitta to prepare to return to Rome, and the command is repeated during her pilgrimage to the river Jordan, where she is told that 'there were still messages to be sent to the world's princes'.[58] Here there is a sense of impatience to leave the shrines of the Holy Land and return to the secular intrigues in the Mediterranean area in which she had become involved. To the last, she wished to fulfil her role as mediator of divine words to secular potentates, and she worked tirelessly towards achieving her ambitions for the papacy.

On their return to Rome, they stopped again in Naples in January 1373. At Giovanna's court at Aversa, she again issued messages in public 'to Archbishop Bernard, three masters of theology, two doctors of canon and civil law,

54 See Svanberg 1997, who draws attention to two further depictions by the same painter, one now in the Yale University collection and the other in Philadelphia Art Museum.

55 See Klockars 1966 'De tidigaste'. See AP pp. 166–73, where four Neapolitan churches are mentioned: Santa Maria del Carmelo, San Giorgio Maggiore, San Eligio and San Antonio de Vienna extra Muros.

56 In this fresco, she is depicted next to another woman, and together they appear to represent the two midwives who, according to legend, came to Bethlehem to witness the birth. One of them, who did not believe in Mary's post-partum virginity, points with her hand, while the other, who did believe, appears to represent Birgitta. This interpretation has been suggested in a private communication from Professor Jan Svanberg.

57 The question remains of whether the iconographic shift was prompted by Birgitta's vision, or indeed whether the new iconography was already in the process of development in the late fourteenth century, and her vision simply helped to precipitate and disseminate the development.

58 AP p. 96.

and some knights and citizens of the city' on the slackness and superstition of the Neapolitans.[59] The *vita* uses the adverb 'intrepide' to describe her boldness in speaking out thus.[60] By this point in her life, she had gained an authority and could command an audience which enabled her to issue her messages more forcefully than before, having them read from pulpits and in public places, and gathering high-ranking audiences to attend. In Naples, perhaps, she comes closer to public preaching than she had ever done before, although she always trod a fine line between the public proclamation of her comminatory messages, from which women were banned, and the private disclosure to individuals, which was permitted for women with wisdom and knowledge.[61]

One of the last revelations recorded in Book VII reinforces the admonishing tone of her last years, as well as the message for all mankind, beginning with the top of the hierarchy. It depicts Christ in glory, together with the Virgin, reprimanding his people who have ceased listening to him:

> Listen, all my enemies in the world, for I am not addressing my friends who follow my will. Listen, all you clerics, archbishops, and bishops and all of lower rank in the Church! Listen, all you religious, of whatever order! Listen, you kings and princes of the earth and all you who serve! Listen, you women, princesses and all ladies and maidservants! All you inhabitants of the world, of whatever condition or rank you are, whether great or small, listen to these words that I myself, who created you, now speak to you![62]

Her determination to see the papacy restored to Rome likewise had not diminished in the last year of her life, and further messages to Pope Gregory XI were sent from Naples.[63] Only five days before her death, she appealed to him for the last time. In this vision, Christ reveals that in the last few months of her life she had received no revelations:

> I have done to you what a bridegroom does concealing himself from his bride so that he may be more ardently desired by her. Thus I have not visited you during this time; for it was the time of your testing. Therefore, now that

59 'Quam reuelacionem ipsa domina Birgitta publicauit in presencia dicti domini Bernardi archiepiscopi et trium magistrorum in theologia et duorum doctorum in iure canonico et ciuile et aliquorum militum et ciuium dicte ciuitatis.' (Bergh 1967, p. 196)

60 AP p. 100.

61 See Sahlin 1997 'The Prophetess . . .', p. 40 note 25.

62 'Audite omnes inimici mei in mundo viuentes, quia ad amicos meos non loquor, qui sequuntur voluntatem meam. Audite omnes clerici archiepiscopi et episcopi et omnes inferioris gradus Ecclesie! Audite omnes religiosi, cuiuscumque ordinis estis! Audite reges et principes et iudices terre et omnes seruientes! Audite mulieres, principesse ac omnes domine et ancille, et omnes, cuiuscumque condicionis et gradus estis, magni et parui, qui habitatis orbem, verba hec, que ego ipse, qui creaui vos, nunc loquor ad vos.' (Bergh 1967, p. 211)

63 Book IV 141–3.

> you have been tested, go forward and prepare yourself; for now is the time when – as I had promised you – before my altar, you shall be clothed and consecrated as a nun. And henceforth you shall be counted not only as my bride, but also as a nun and a mother in Vadstena.[64]

Birgitta died on 23 July 1373.[65] The words of Christ in the above vision suggest that she was to be buried in nun's clothing, and Katarina confirms in her testimony that her body was taken to the monastery of San Lorenzo in Panisperna, where she had had many friends, among the sisters, from the Roman nobility.[66] In accordance with her wishes she was buried at the monastery on 27 July. Preparations were then begun to have her remains transported back to Sweden; and at the end of that year the arrangements were completed for the translation of her relics back to her native country. A travel permit, dated 13 November 1373, describes the items that accompanied the coffin, and the fact that they included altar vessels, Mass vestments and books suggests that permission had been granted for Masses to be held during the long journey homewards.[67]

According to a letter from Francisca Papazzura, the cortège set out from Rome on 2 December 1373, with Birger and Katarina accompanying their mother's remains back to Vadstena, as well as the two Peters and Magnus Petri, several of Birger's and Katarina's servants, including a squire, Petrus Frijs, and a girl called Maria.[68] Also in the party was presumably the Turkish slave whom Queen Giovanna had given to Birgitta and who became a nun at the monastery with the name Katarina Magnusdotter (taking her adopted name from the two founding figures at the monastery, Katarina Ulfsdotter and Magnus Petri). In addition there were two nobles from Gdańsk, who accompanied the cortège as far as their native city.[69] Many other devoted admirers probably joined the party at the first stage of its journey through Italy. Francisca Papazzura wrote to her friend Lapa Buondelmonte saying that she had never felt such sadness and melancholy as when the Swedish party departed from the city.[70]

64 'Ego faceram tibi, sicut sponsus solet facere, qui abscondit se a sponsa sua, vt ardencius desideretur, sic ego non visitaui te consolacionibus isto tempore, quia tempus probacionis tue erat. Jdeo nunc probate procede et para te, quia iam tempus est, vt, sicut promiseram tibi, ante altare meum in monacham vestieris et consecraberis, et amodo reputaberis non solum sponsa mea, sed eciam monacha et mater in Wastenis.' (AP p. 101)

65 Her death day was not her feast day, which was 7 October; but in 1969 the feast day was changed to 23 July. On the date of the translation of her relics, see Jönsson 1987. Her relics have been investigated by Bygdén 1954.

66 AP p. 343. See further on her relations with this nunnery Collijn 1929, pp. 65–92.

67 See Collijn 1929, p. 80.

68 See Collijn 1929, pp. 14–19.

69 On the journey back to Sweden see Lindblom 1955 and Lindblom 1962.

70 Collijn 1929, pp. 17 and 20.

The exact route taken northwards is unclear but it is known from accounts of miracles that occurred on the way that they passed through Montefalco, and then took an easterly route northwards, stopping in Moravia and Bohemia – where near Brno, they were set upon by bandits – and travelling through Poland – where there is an account of a woman being safely delivered of a child as the party entered her house. They arrived in Gdańsk at the end of March 1374, where, according to Katarina's *vita*, Katarina made allegations against the Teutonic Knights who dominated the city, thus following in the footsteps of her mother in pronouncing judgements on secular potentates, and corroborating the pope's recognition of her gift of rhetoric and persuasion.

From Gdansk they made the journey over to Sweden on 28 May – according to a miracle account, safely led by a star – to the fishing port of Sikavarp on the island of Öland. The miracle stories shed light on political uncertainties in Linköping diocese at the time, especially because the region bordered with disputed Danish territory. A Swedish local magnate, for instance, who had been abducted by German soldiers, was miraculously rescued from a nearby fortress as Birgitta's relics passed nearby.[71] Accompanied by a growing following, the party travelled to the town of Söderköping on 29 June, where other miracles occurred: a small mute boy was cured after he sought shelter under the coffin; and a man who had sneered at local reverence for Birgitta was seized by a fit of madness. The procession passed through Linköping cathedral and on to Vadstena where it arrived amid great ceremony on 4 July 1374.

71 AP pp. 105–110. See further on the miracles Fröjmark 1992, pp. 105–28.

VI

The Making of the Saint

Devotæ autem et convenientes viduæ, et aliæ sexus utriusque personæ, piis sanctisque operibus semper intentæ, se ante Dei tribunal cum plenis manipulis repræsentant . . .

Godfearing, temperate widows and others of both sexes, continually occupied with good and pious works, come before the seat of Judgement with full sheaves. . .

(Canonisation bull 1391, *Acta Sanctorum, Octobris*, vol. 4 p. 469)

WITH THE RETURN of the papacy to Rome apparently secured, Birgitta's supporters, who numbered some of the most loyal supporters of Urban V and had been zealous in their efforts to restore the Roman papacy, seized an opportune moment to submit an application for her canonisation. The Urbanists likewise had an interest in having a saintly candidate of stature who would reaffirm the position of the pope at the heart of the Church.[1] Birgitta had been a passionate advocate of religious reform and closely involved with the Urbanist camp, and there was now widespread recognition of her special gift of prophecy. The complex history of the canonisation, which was the first canonisation in the fourteenth century to have taken place in Rome, was highly charged politically, and achieved only after much hard lobbying, dedicated persistence and skilled manipulation of curial law. With the frequent change of pope, however, and amid the partisan rifts and tensions within the Church hierarchy in the troubled years before and during the Great Schism, it was a far from smooth passage to sainthood.

The entire procedure of canonisation by the later middle ages was characterised by a concentration of power and influence from the pope and his close circle: it was they who imposed their own idea of sanctity on the faithful. In the course of the middle ages, a shift in papal preferences took place, from the canonisation in the early period of 'insiders' – monks, clerics and hermits – towards the selection of laymen and women from the ranks of the ordinary

1 Vauchez 1988, p. 318, comments: 'Mais seules des saintes comme Brigitte de Suède ou Catherine de Sienne, dont la glorification pouvait renforcer la position de l'une des obédiences rivales – en l'occurrence le camp "urbaniste" –, ont réussi, non sans difficultés, une percée qui devait être sans lendemain.'

faithful, even if such saints came mostly from the noble and upper classes of society and the success of their candidature depended crucially on an influential clerical entourage.

The act of canonisation declared in canon law that individuals could be honoured as saints once their faith, life and miracles proved them to be worthy candidates; and also that an office appropriate to the rank of the person should be performed on the anniversary of their death.[2] By the fourteenth century procedures had reached a new level of legal and procedural complexity, due in part to the centralisation of the process a century before, when the principle of the papal prerogative of canonisation was established, which effectively prevented canonisations by bishops at local level and introduced the veneration of all saints by the whole of Christendom. The procedure as it had developed by the later middle ages was briefly the following. An initial request was generally made by the home territory or metropolitan centre from which the candidate came, but there also had to be solid support from within the papal circle as well as from kings and secular rulers. An enquiry, or *processus*, was established, consisting of three commissioners, including at least one bishop, whose task was to examine the life and miracles of the candidate, to give witness statements to the pope and to report on the progress of the investigation. The *processus* was attended by a large following of clerics and friars, including interpreters – for witnesses were not always literate – and canon lawyers, whose work it was to put down the depositions formally and edit copies, which were then authorised by the commissioners' seals. When the commission had gathered its evidence the pope met his cardinals in secret, and a report, or *summarium*, was read by those in charge of the enquiry. At a second consistory the pope consulted with bishops and archbishops at the curia, and at a third, he made public his intention to add the new name to the canon of saints. A liturgical ceremony followed a few days afterwards, and bulls were published outlining the course of the *processus*, listing the saint's special virtues, and reminding the faithful of the papal prerogative of canonisation. The pope also gave the text of the proper prayers to be incorporated into the office, and made announcements on the preservation of the relics and observation of the new saint's feast-day.

Preparations

There is probably no better illustration of the procedure of canonisation in the later middle ages than Birgitta's, for the Birgittine records are copious as well

2 The distinction between beatification and canonisation was not held then, as it is today. See Vauchez 1988, pp. 99–120. See too pp. 47–67 and Kemp 1948, pp. 106–40, on which the following description is based. A discussion of the criteria for consensus on what constitutes sanctity is given in Kleinberg 1989.

as complete.[3] At the end of the year of Birgitta's death the first overture was made when an examination of her miracles was held in Montefalco, in the presence of her son Birger and daughter Katarina, by Bishop Galhardus of Spoleto.[4] The *vita*, written by Prior Peter of Alvastra and Magister Peter of Skänninge, was added to the report of his findings. Events in Italy were then interrupted while Birgitta's remains were translated back to Sweden where the Birgittine supporters actively set about promoting the cause among leading magnates in her homeland. In November 1375 a message was sent from Avignon to the archbishop of Lund, instructing him to set up a commission to examine Birgitta's life and miracles in Sweden; and this task was assigned to Bishop Valdemar of Odense who travelled to Vadstena in March 1377 and began the investigation, with the help of Bishop Nikolaus Hermannson of Linköping. It was perhaps fortunate that King Magnus Eriksson (from whom Birgitta had gradually become estranged) had died in 1374, and that his successor, Albrekt of Mecklenburg, was well-disposed towards the cause; he submitted a supporting petition to the pope in October 1376.[5]

Having set in motion the formal procedures in her native country, Katarina returned to Rome in 1375, bringing with her a collection of miracles that had been reported in Sweden. However, they proved to be inadmissible on the grounds that the records of them had not been presented according to correct protocol: they had not been commissioned by the diocesan bishop, and their supporting testimony was inadequate. In response, Nikolaus Hermansson wrote to Pope Gregory XI in 1377 protesting that the Swedes did not use notarial attestation to prove the authenticity of documents (an essentially Italian practice), but rather they used the seals of religious and secular authorities.[6] Alphonso of Jaén saved the situation by seeking legal advice on the presentation of the documents, and specific instructions were sent to the bishop of Linköping to ensure that the proper procedures were followed. The miracles were then resubmitted successfully.[7] This incident is an excellent reminder of Alphonso's shrewd handling of curial law, and without him Birgitta's case is far less likely on technical and procedural grounds to have succeeded.

When Katarina returned to Rome in 1375, Gregory XI had still not returned to the Holy City. In 1376 she visited Naples, where an investigation had been

3 It should be remembered that the popes were lobbied on two separate, but often overlapping, counts by the Birgittine supporters: for Birgitta's canonisation and for the official recognition of the Birgittine Rule and Order. See further Chapter VII on the order.

4 The account here follows Höjer 1908, pp. 102–10, and Collijn 1924–31, introduction, who modifies Höjer on some points. See too Jönsson 1989 and Nyberg 1991, *Birgittinsk festgåva*, pp. 401–29.

5 AP pp. 48–9.

6 Vauchez 1988, p. 53 note 53.

7 AP pp. 393–4.

set up by Archbishop Bernard, concerning Birgittine miracles alleged to have taken place in the kingdom of Naples. Under increasing pressure to settle the disputes among the warring factions in Rome, the pope eventually made his solemn entry into Rome on 17 January 1377, and Katarina was now able to put her petitions to him in person. With further supporting petitions from Queen Giovanna of Naples and the emperor Charles IV in 1377, Gregory set up a committee of cardinals and learned theologians, including Alphonso, to investigate the Rule and revelations. One of the members, Johannes of Corfu, formally applied for her canonisation on 29 May 1377 at a consistory at the papal palace near the church of Santa Maria Maggiore. A second petition, by Bishop Petrus of Orvieto, followed in the same year, but proceedings were brought to an abrupt halt with the death of Gregory on 27 March 1378.

The new pope, Urban VI, was Bartolomeo Prignano, former archbishop of Bari, who was elected at the famous – farcical – conclave of 7–8 April 1378. This was the first papal election to be held in Rome almost since the beginning of the century, and there was pressure from the Roman crowds to elect a Roman, or at least an Italian, which might prevent the new pope from returning to Avignon. Prignano was a compromise choice, being a Neapolitan; but when he was called to accept the throne, the crowd fell into uproar, and the cardinals instead presented the city with an octogenarian imposter. On the following day Urban's election was properly confirmed. Katarina, who was one of 145 witnesses called by Urban to prove the legitimacy of his election, betrayed no awareness of the open revolt on the streets of Rome at the time but she did acknowledge that the cardinals, for fear that the new pope would be killed because he was not a Roman, went through the pretence of having elected a pro-Roman pope to pacify the crowds.[8] Alphonso wrote a detailed commentary of Urban's election, known as the *Informationes . . . super creacione Vrbani*, in which he outlines Birgitta's relations to the popes and argues that God allowed dissent to arise between the cardinals in order that Rome could retain an Italian pope who would stay in Rome.[9] Urban's attempts at reform, his over-zealousness, and his Italian provenance angered the French-dominated college of cardinals who united in their opposition to him, and on 29 September 1378 they elected instead Cardinal Robert of Geneva as anti-pope, with the name Clement VII, and he promptly moved to Avignon. This split at the very heart of the papacy ushered in the damaging period known as the Great Schism, which lasted from 1378 to 1417. Kings and countries around Europe favoured either the Urbanist or Clementist cause: Sweden and England, for instance, supported the former, while Naples, France and Spain chose the latter.

Under Urban VI two further applications for the canonisation were submit-

8 See further Ullmann 1967, pp. 9–11; and on Katarina's testimony, Höjer 1907, Brilioth 1925, p. 112 note 4, Jönsson 1989, p. 72.

9 See Jönsson 1989.

ted, and on 15 December 1378 the pope authorised a formal examination and received for scrutiny the corpus of Revelations with supporting material. The examining committee consisted of four cardinals (rather than the customary number of three): Thomas of Grado, Agapitus of Colonna, Johannes of Corfu and Gentilis of Sangro (the latter two turned against Urban and were executed in 1386). They each appointed their own examining representatives who shared in the work of interrogating witnesses. In July 1379 the Spaniard Ludovicus Alfonsi of Cabezon (who was Katarina's spokesman during the canonisation proceedings) submitted fifty-one articles concerning Birgitta's life and work and arranged for witness statements to be made.

The fifty-one articles are in two groups: articles 1–39 concern events which took place in Birgitta's life, her family, upbringing, marriage, pilgrimages, virtues and prophetic gifts, her ability to cure the sick, and other supernatural gifts (including her ability to learn Latin quickly!), and articles 40–51 concern the miracles which took place after her death.[10] The interviews of some twenty-six witnesses in Rome began on 18 July 1379 and continued until 29 February 1380. The witnesses were all questioned with regard to their relation to Birgitta and memory of her; and although the most eminent witnesses are questioned on all fifty-one articles, the remainder deal with a smaller number of issues. There were ten main witnesses, of whom four were Swedish: the three who had worked so closely to bring about the canonisation – her daughter Katarina, Magnus Petri (confessor general at Vadstena 1384–94) and Prior Petrus – and Hartlevus, bishop-elect of Västerås. Katarina introduces details which are not encountered elsewhere, telling for instance how she put a pillow under her mother as she slept on the floor to mortify her flesh, and how her mother confessed all her temptations to her confessors and submitted herself completely to their instructions, 'whether or not they were justified' – a suggestion, as Birger Bergh suggests, of her irritation with their exacting expectations.[11] Katarina also tells of Birgitta's constant danger from her enemies, and describes how one of her own messengers one day pretended to hand over a letter to her, but in fact held a knife with which he intended to kill her. The bishop-elect, Hartlevus, was not part of Birgitta's close circle, but had visited her in Rome where he saw her attend pilgrim shrines, 'weep devoutly' in the chapel of the house where she lived, and sing the praise of the Virgin. He also testified about her continued contacts with Sweden, telling of how she reprimanded King Magnus to mend his ways, and of how he had heard his predecessor, Bishop Mathias of Västerås, inform the new king Albrekt of a blind man who had been cured by her prayers.

The other key witnesses included Alphonso of Jaén, who relates that she exhausted herself on her visits around the churches of Rome so that he would

10 They are summarised by Collijn 1924–31, pp. 643–59. See too Bergh 1993.

11 Bergh 1993, p. 295.

give her a lump of sugar to restore her energy, and he relates how after a heated argument with him she fell on her knees beating her breast and asking for his forgiveness. Other key witnesses who testified concerning their acquaintance with her in the latter part of her life were Cardinal Elziarius of Sabrano (who was related to the lay saint Elzear of Sabrano, d.1323), for whom Birgitta had prophesied a religious life in Book VII 5; her noble friend Latino Orsini and his wife Golicia, Laurentius who was prior of San Giovanni in Laterano, and Francisca Papazzura. There were a further sixteen partial witnesses, and other testimonies concerning the miracles which were recorded in other places in Italy and incorporated into the officially ratified reports, together with testimonies already gathered in Vadstena and Naples.

After the completion of the papal examinations and cross-examination of the witnesses there was nothing formally to prevent the canonisation from being ratified. However, because of the political turmoil that had arisen in the papacy, the canonisation process lost momentum, and although Urban VI was well-disposed towards the canonisation he did not bring it to a conclusion. Katarina returned to Sweden in 1380, having obtained a number of important bulls in support of the monastic order, but not her mother's canonisation.[12] Still showing her unfailing support for Urban, however, she wrote to Archbishop Birger Gregersson on 18 July 1380 saying that the pope was hampered by the dissension between himself and the anti-pope, but had nevertheless made her mother 'a saint in his heart'.[13] Urban wrote to Katarina and Nicolaus Hermansson in April 1381 stating that he hoped to conclude the canonisation, and a new embassy prepared to travel to Rome. In 1383, however, the pope went into exile from Rome, and spent five years travelling in Italy before he returned there in September 1388. In April 1389 he sent another letter to Sweden saying he wished to complete the canonisation, but before he could see it through he died, on 15 October 1389. His successor, Boniface IX, was well-inclined to support the cause, and following petitions from royal quarters in Sweden, and agreement from the cardinals, a new commission was set up in October 1391. One of the most influential cardinals of this committee was Adam Easton (c.1330–97), a learned Benedictine from Easton, near Norwich.[14] After his studies at Oxford he went to Rome in 1367, where he was quickly promoted. At the election of Urban VI he gave evidence against the cardinals who had opposed the election, and was raised to the cardinalate as titular priest of the church of Santa Maria in Trastevere. However, he later fell foul of the pope, was stripped of his cardinalate and imprisoned, although not – unlike a number of his fellow cardinals – put to death, perhaps because of the intercessions from England on his behalf. He was not released and

12 Brilioth 1925, p. 114 note 2.
13 '. . . dicens, quod sanctificauerat eam in corde suo'. Quoted from Undhagen 1960, p. 120 note 3.
14 See Schmidtke 1982.

restored to the cardinalate until the election of Boniface IX, after which he began to take an active part in securing Birgitta's canonisation.

The commission of 1391, in which Adam Easton took part, was concluded by the handing over of a handsome book with a gilt binding to the pope, which contained the Revelations, and the *Liber attestacionum*, a summary of all the cross-examinations and supporting documents. Sumptuous copies were also made for the sixteen cardinals, which would no doubt have made any remaining sceptics among them better disposed to accept the canonisation.

The canonisation 1391

The canonisation celebrations are fully described in the *Diarium Vadstenense* in the entry for 1391:

> After a commission had been appointed and three cardinals had conducted a satisfactory examination about her life, miracles and reputation, the lord pope appointed the day for the canonisation, and ordained that at vespers the day before the canonisation bells should be rung in all the churches of Rome. And so it happened also during the night before and the day of the canonisation.
>
> Further, on the day of canonisation all the cardinals met in the early morning with the patriarchs and Church prelates in the papal court. And dressed in white mass clothes they all processed with the lord pope with great solemnity into the pope's palace, into the great chapel which was decorated with lights and torches and completely adorned with tapestries, and the floor was strewn with leaves and sweet-smelling herbs. In the middle before the altar was situated a throne, properly fitting for the pope. The pope sat in it and gave a sermon to all and its subject was: 'Viduam eius benedicens benedicam etc.'. And he read out what was demanded for such a high occasion, that is canonisation, and showed that everything had been lawfully undertaken in the holy affair from beginning to end, and said that it was not possible or fitting to deny justice in a so clear and obvious a case: for St Birgitta's exemplary life and the large number of her miracles which had occurred through her merit and her reputation among people all bore witness to her sanctity.
>
> When the sermon was completed, but before he concluded, he instructed all to call upon the Holy Spirit and the Virgin herself, so that God might not allow the Church to be mistaken in this affair. And the singers began the antiphon 'Veni sancte Spiritus', which finished with the versicle about the Holy Spirit and St Birgitta, 'Ora pro nobis etc.', and the pope said, 'Let us pray to God, qui corda fidelium etc.' and the collect for St Birgitta: 'Domine Iesu Christe, qui beate Birgitte tantam etc.'. And so he declared that her canonisation was a fact, and that a saint was inscribed in the catalogue of saints. Her feast with the proper office should be held in the Church throughout the world, as other saints are venerated. And the cantor began, 'Te Deum laudamus', and the pope and all the others processed through the palace.
>
> Further, to all who were present at the canonisation, and who would have

been involved if they had been able to, and to all those who visited St Peter's church and the monastery of San Lorenzo in Panisperna, where St Birgitta was buried, on the day of canonisation and the following Sunday, he granted a true indulgence as in the year of Jubilee.

Further, to all who truly repented and confessed and who were in a state of grace or would be within eight days, and who in spiritual intent in the month of October visited the said San Lorenzo monastery in Panisperna, he granted the same indulgence as in the year of Jubilee.

Further, on the second day after the canonisation the pope celebrated a mass in honour of St Birgitta in St Peter's church.

Further, in St Peter's church thirty thousand lamps and a very large number of candles and torches burned from midnight until after the papal mass.

Further, during the same papal mass oblations were made by the three cardinals who were representatives in the canonisation process, and by the brethren from Vadstena, Magnus Petri and Andreas Olafsson, who in this affair laboured faithfully and brought it to a successful conclusion.

Further, the foremost cardinal, who was called the bishop of Ostia, held a very stately feast in his house in honour of St Birgitta on the same day as the papal mass.

Further, the three cardinals arranged for Birgitta's relics to be displayed in the church of San Lorenzo in Panisperna.[15]

15 'Post enim factam commissionem in negocio canonizacionis beate Byrgitte et per tres cardinales habita probacione vite eius, miraculorum et fame sufficienti, dominus papa constituit diem canonizacionis precipiens, ut hora vesperorum in die precedente diem canonizacionis pulsarentur omnes campane per totam Romam. Et sic factum est eciam in nocte et die canonizacionis. Item, ipso die canonizacionis, summo mane, convenerunt omnes cardinales cum partiarchis et ecclesiarum prelatis in curia pape. Et omnes induti albis cum domino papa processionaliter cum magna sollempnitate intrant magnam capellam in palacio pape, que fuit ornata cum candelis et faculis ac per totum cum vestibus circumdata, pavimento cum foliis arborum et herbis odoriferis strato; ubi posita in medio ante altare cathedra bene apta pro summo pontifice. In qua papa sedens fecit sermonem coram omnibus, cuius thema erat Viduam eius benedicens benedicam etc., narrans eciam ea, que requiruntur ad tam arduum negocium, scilicet canonizacionis, et probans, quod legittime processum est in hoc sancto negocio a principio usque in finem, dicens non posse nec licitum esse negare iusticiam in tam claro et evidenti facto, quia excellens vita beate Byrgitte et turba miraculoruom, que facta sunt meritis eius, et fama populi testimonium dabant ipsius sanctitati. Sermone tandem completo ante conclusionem tamem ammonebat omnes ad invocandum Spiritum sanctum et ipsam Virginem gloriosam, ne Deus permitteret errare ecclesiam in hoc facto. Et cantores inceperunt antiphonam Veni sancte Spiritus, qua finita cum versiculo de sancto Spiritu et de beata Byrgitta, Ora pro nobis etc, dominus papa dixit: "Oremus. Deus, qui corda fidelium etc." cum collecta de sancta Byrgitta "Domine Iesu Christe, qui beate Byrgitte tantam etc.", pronuncians eam iam de facto canonizatam et sanctam et in sanctorum cathalogo asscriptam; de qua festum cum officio proprio fiat in ecclesia per totum orbem, sicut de aliis sanctis. Et cantor incepit Te Deum laudamus; et papa et omnes in processione ieverunt per palacium. Item, onmibus, qui interfuerunt can-

The formal celebrations took place on 7 October 1391, and were supported by a bull and sermon preached by Boniface IX. Boniface had probably not known Birgitta in person, but although the sermon he delivered was impersonal in tone, it touched on two main characteristics of Birgitta's sanctity, the fact that she was a 'vere vidua', and that she was a 'mulier fortis'. In developing the description of her as a good widow, he cites biblical examples of prophetic widows, praising her piety, her care for her household, the poor and needy, and her voluntary poverty and espousal of a chaste life. He also praises her passionate concern for the salvation of those she met, her humility, and her contemplative life, which example is now followed by the 'spiritual daughters' of her monastic order. In stressing the perception of her as a powerful woman, Boniface quotes the biblical widow Judith and tells how Birgitta revealed 'in the feminine sex a masculine soul in fervour of spirit'.[16] Like Judith, Birgitta has helped free the Church from heresy and schism, and worked relentlessly to condemn unorthodox views and restore unity. The biographical detail contained in the sermon is often at odds with the evidence of witnesses in the canonisation process and with the revelations themselves, and as a biographical source it is thus of little value; Roger Ellis indeed describes it as 'holy whitewash', and a skilful attempt at concealing the ambi-

onizacioni et qui libenter interessent, si comode potuissent, et omnibus visitantibus ecclesiam sancti Petri et monasterium sancti Laurencii in Panisperne, ubi sancta Byrgitta sepulta fuit, ipso die canonizacionis et dominica sequenti, quando papa celebravit, concessit veram indulgenciam anni iubilei. Item, omnibus vere penetentibus et confessos et qui fuerunt in statu gracie, vel feirent infra octo dies, visitantibus causa devocionis per totum mensem Octobris dictum monasterium sancti Laurencii in Panisperna concessit eandem indulgenciam anni iubilea. Item, altero dei post diem canonizacionis celebravit dominis papa missam de beata Byrgitta in ecclesia sancti Petri. Item, in ecclesia sancti Petri ardebant a media nocte usque post missam pape xxx milia lampadarum et candele et facule valde multe. Item, in ipsa missa pape fuit facta oblacio per illos tres cardinales, qui fuerunt commissarii in negocio canonizacionis et per fratres de Vazsteno, dominum Magnum Petri et dominum Andream Olavi. Qui in isto facto fideliter laboraverunt et usque ad consumacionum per Dei auxilium perduxerunt. Item, summus cardinalis, qui intitulatur episcopus Ostiensis, fecit valde sollempne convivium in domo sua in honore beate Byrgitte ipso die, quando papa celebravit. Item, tres cardinales commissarii fecerunt ostensionem reliquiarum beate Byrgitte ad sanctum Laurencium in Panisperna.' (Gejrot 1988, pp. 124–6) The description in the *Diarium Vadstenense*, by Thorius Andreæ and written in 1402 at the latest, is based on the eye witness accounts of Vadstena monks, and it is corroborated by two other accounts: that of Laurencius Romare, a cleric who accompanied the general confessor at the proceedings, and gave a colourful account of the festivities and banquet after the canonisation, with details of the sumptous food and costs incurred (see Karlsson 1901), and the first-hand record of Petrus Amelius, Patriarch of Grado (see Annerstedt 1876, pp. 241–4).

16 '. . . femineo sexui masculinum animum in feruore mentis inuenit.' Quoted from the discussion of the sermon by Ellis 1991, p. 103. See too Hedlund 1993. The sermon has not been edited; a copy exists in Lincoln Cathedral Chapter Library MS 114, fols. 49v–53v.

guities of the newly-elected pope's own position, while at the same time strengthening his standing within the Church. Nevertheless, the sermon does convey the pope's acceptance of inspired prophetic discourse by women such as Birgitta and it expresses his approval for the new mysticism which she embodied.

Apologists and opponents

Birgitta's reputation had spread rapidly in élite circles in the years before the canonisation. According to a letter written by Alphonso in 1378 to the archbishop of Uppsala, Birger Gregersson, the revelations were already known in Spain and being copied in Italy and Sicily; and while the canonisation was under way the bishop of Worms took a copy to the emperor, one was taken to France and others were obtained by ambassadors to the Holy See of Castile, Cyprus and Naples, and by universities, cities and religious orders.[17]

Yet there were those who opposed her elevation to the status of saint. In her lifetime, as we have seen, she had alienated her acquaintances and been the object of criticism by laymen and clerics alike; and after her death and canonisation there were openly critical factions and impassioned arguments conducted between her defenders and detractors. When Pope Boniface IX formally announced his intention to canonise her, for instance, he invited objections to be put formally on an appointed day. Two men came forward. One was a magister who said that the examination ought to have been more thoroughly conducted, whereupon he was expelled from the room by the cardinal of Alençon (who presumably was not expecting objections to be made and had offered dainties and wine to the assembled gathering). The cardinal remarked 'It would have been better and more useful for you . . . to have eaten straw like a cow or an ass than to have discussed and argued about things that are above your intellect and knowledge.'[18] The other dissenter came with a booklet listing his objections which he was forced to relinquish, and it was judged by the cardinal and Magnus Petri to contain nothing but falsehoods.

In answer to, or in anticipation of, the criticism, Birgitta's supporters wrote robust defences of her prophetic gifts. Alphonso, for instance, cites a number of doubters, such as a man from Subiaco whose genitals swelled up after he

17 See Colledge 1956, p. 31 note 70.

18 'melius et utilius sibi fuisse . . . et comedisse stramina instar bouis et asini, quam tractasse et disputasse de rebus super intellectum et scientiam suam constitutis.' (Karlsson 1901, p. 7) The voices of opposition were recently examined in detail by Claire Sahlin, in her Ph.D. thesis, 1996. I am grateful to Dr Sahlin for allowing me to draw on, and quote from, her unpublished material in the following account, especially from ch. 6 ' "*Vera Prophetissa Dei*"? Attacks and Defenses of Birgitta's Prophetic Authority, 1373–1391', pp. 242–304, and ch. 7 'The Cry of Divine Wisdom or the Delusions of a Presumptuous Woman?: Conflicting Fifteenth-Century Perspectives on Birgitta's Prophetic Voice', pp. 305–73.

had questioned her sanctity, and a German squire who was tormented in his body after he mocked her.[19] To counter criticisms, Alphonso wrote a defence of the Revelations, the *Epistola solitarii ad reges*, in c.1375, which was included as the Prologue to Book VIII, and was probably intended to solicit support among influential rulers and princes for the canonisation; indeed this tract may have prompted the petitions in the late 1370s of King Albrekt in Sweden, Queen Giovanna of Naples and Emperor Charles IV.[20] In his *Epistola* Alphonso provides advice on learning to distinguish the true forms of spiritual life and discusses the concept of *discretio spirituum* in classical literature, patristic and biblical writings, and he outlines the criteria which should be used to distinguish genuine from illusory revelation.[21]

Magnus Petri likewise wrote a missive sometime between 1384 and 1391, the *Epistola contra calumpniantes sanctissimas reuelaciones beate Birgitte.* Its purpose, according to Claire Sahlin, was 'to persuade "calumniators" of the truth of the *Revelations* by presenting evidence, which "thus far had been suppressed" (*hactenus suppressa*). This evidence included a series of unequivocal, favorable pronouncements on the orthodoxy and authenticity of the *Revelations* by "the most circumspect and learned men" (*circumpectissimis et peritissimis viris*), many of whom were cardinals and masters of theology.'[22] Magnus quotes some of the prophetic revelations which had been fulfilled and shows that leaders in many countries had received copies of the Revelations.[23] During the later years of Birgitta's life and particularly after her death, great men and women in Europe sought enlightenment on contemporary issues, and read her revelations for practical information about imminent and future events, much in the same way as they had systematically searched the prophecies of Hildegard of Bingen two centuries earlier.[24]

However, the voices of criticism could not be stemmed. The earliest critic known by name was Heinrich of Langenstein (d.1397), a theologian from the University of Paris, who wrote some of the first theoretical works on the conciliar movement. He argued for the end of the Schism and for the reform of the Church which he saw as open to corruption; and he was concerned about the true spirit of grace, and about the burgeoning list of saints as he feared that new saints displaced devotion to older ones. He argued that if Urban V, Birgitta of Sweden and Duke Charles of Blois, duke of Brittany (who was supported by the Avignon papacy), were canonised, this would add only more to the already over-full calendar of saints.[25] As Sahlin argues, 'Although he

19 AP p. 412.
20 Jönsson 1989, pp. 62, 106.
21 As was indicated in Chapter III, Mathias of Linköping also was expert in the discretion of spirits. See also on the *discretio spirituum* Voaden 1996.
22 Sahlin 1996, p. 264.
23 See Undhagen 1960.
24 See further on this point Southern 1970, p. 170.
25 '. . . si conveniat Urbanum V^{um}, Brigidam de Svecia, ducem Britanniae Carolum, non

never made any direct allegations against Birgitta, he may have had her in mind when he also questioned the reasonableness of allowing fools to predominate over wise people and ignorant people to discuss difficult matters. He may also have had the *Revelations* in mind when he indicated that uncanonical scriptures (*Scripturae apocryphae*), hymns, and prayers were brought forward in ignorance to the detriment of the faith.'[26]

Another critic, who is not known by name, was a 'dominus et magister' from Perugia who questioned at length Birgitta's claims to speak and write in God's name. His tract does not survive, but in 1390, Adam Easton wrote a vigorous defence of her Revelations, in response to the Perugian master's attack, whose arguments he paraphrases. Adam's *Defensorium Sancte Birgitte* makes clear that the Perugian had brought into question the orthodoxy of the Rule, the *Sermo Angelicus* and the *Quattuor Oraciones* in particular, but above all, he had questioned the promotion of a woman as a Church teacher and recipient of divinely dictated messages. Concerning the Rule, the adversary argues that God cannot have proclaimed such a monastic rule through a female intermediary, but Adam's rejoinder is to draw attention to the biblical instances in which Christ appears to women, equating their unique and special standing with Birgitta's, and thereby placing her above ordinary women. Another objection to the Rule is that it is written in an unacceptably simplistic style, to which Adam retorts that women, being 'weak in intellect, more unlearned in the capacity for doctrine, and more simple than men' are better served by a Rule that is simply written. A further charge expresses doubt that Christ revealed the Rule because women are forbidden from speaking and teaching publicly in church; and Adam's rebuttal is that the Rule on the contrary was to be delivered to a community of nuns, and not in church. The adversary also argues that Christ might instead have dictated the Rule to one of the established Church fathers, to which Adam responds by arguing that Christ did not favour one gender over the other. Adam's mildly feminist defence shows him to be more liberal-minded than the persistently hostile Perugian whose first objection to Birgitta was her sex.[27] Like Boniface in his sermon and other advocates of the canonisation, Adam makes the case for her being an exceptional and unique woman, who did not share all the characteristics of ordinary members of her sex, and therefore was eligible for elevation to the canon of saints.

Indeed, the question of Birgitta's gender appears to have been a central criticism of many objectors. Sahlin has drawn attention to a little-known treatise in Lincoln Cathedral Chapter Library, written in her defence by a

obstante sanctorum multitudine, canonizari, et si deceat quorumdam novorum sanctorum festa solemnius peragi quam praecipuorum apostolorum.' (von der Hardt (ed.) 1697, col. 56)

26 Sahlin 1996, p. 266.

27 See further Schmidke 1982.

Franciscan cleric between 1391 and 1409.[28] While supporting the traditional prohibitions on women's public teaching, the cleric argues against Birgitta's critics, saying that it was part of God's plan to make a woman the instrument of prophecy. He states that some of her detractors had suggested that it was absurd that a woman from Sweden, on the edge of the Christian world, should be chosen as a vehicle to communicate God's word. He defends her Swedish origins by citing other examples of chosen people from obscure corners of the earth and compares her achievement with Amazon women's triumphs, saying that God endowed women from the North with special gifts, even in pagan times.[29] The main aim of the letter, Sahlin states, is 'to counter detractors who claimed that women were not appropriate conduits of God's revelations. Arguing against those who judge it "not fitting that God revealed such things to the female sex and not to the masculine" ("... *indignum estimantes quod muliebri sexui et non masculino Deus talia revelaverit*") he portrays Birgitta as a "strong woman" ("*feminam fortem*") who serves as a legitimate vehicle of divine revelation.'[30]

While examining Birgitta's life and the manner in which she received her visions against the evidence of other authorities, her supporters were implicitly attacking the detractors of other female mystics. The cause of Caterina of Siena, for example, was also championed by Alphonso and her case for canonisation was taken up in 1411–16. The vehemence of the learned arguments illustrates the growing polarisation within the debate over the sanctity of visionary women. By the early fifteenth century there was a swell of opinion arguing that Birgitta should not have been canonised, and theologians were ranged into two camps, the ancients and moderns, each taking a strong line in defence of, or opposition to the canonisation. At the Council of Constance in 1414–17, Swedish delegates asked for the canonisation to be confirmed, and in so doing, they drew attention to the voices of dissent in some quarters and also the bitter debates arising over the privileges granted to the Order. Perhaps spurred on by a wave of nationalistic religious fervour, the Swedish delegates also applied for proceedings to be opened for Katarina Ulfsdotter, Nikolaus Hermansson and Ingrid of Skänninge. The Council of Constance was a landmark in the history of the medieval papacy, for it spelt the end of the descending principle of papal power, by which the pope as the vicar of Christ, while retaining his power, delegated parts of it to members of the Church. The Council instead spelt the complete victory of the conciliar system; from now on, the pope owed his position to the general Council, and

28 Lincoln Chapter Library MS 114, fols. 18v–24v.

29 As Sahlin 1996, p. 320, points out, the suggestion here is that he believes that these fierce fighting women were married to the Goths, which explains their association with the North.

30 Sahlin 1996, pp. 320–21.

Plate 6. Confirmation of St Birgitta's canonisation at the Council of Constance. Detail from a colour drawing from Ulrich von Richenthal's Chronicle of the Council, written in a south German dialect, c. 1450. To the left, a liturgy is performed; while to the right, archbishop Peder Lykke of Lund, aided by other bishops, holds up a reliquary in the shape of Birgitta's head.
Source: New York Public Library, Astor, Lenox and Tilden Collection, no. 32, pp. 70–71.

became its chief officer.[31] Apart from bringing an end to the Schism through the election of Pope Martin V, the Council of Constance also sought to condemn a number of heretics and heresies (among them Jan Huss, the Bohemian theologian from the University of Prague, and some of the teachings of the Oxford scholar John Wyclif whose body was ordered to be exhumed). Birgitta's works also came under consideration by the Council. Her foremost critic was Jean Gerson, chancellor of the church and University of Paris, and a prominent member of the Council. He was interested in the spiritual and doctrinal discernment of experienced teachers within the Church, and also in the *via mystica*. He supported the rights of the institutional hierarchy in the tasks of discernment, and showed scepticism about claims to mysticism that were not ratified institutionally. His work *De probatione spirituum*, written in August 1415, is in part a commentary on the deliberations of the Council over the canonisation of Birgitta and other female mystics. Gerson's argument is centred on identifying and proving the origin of the gift of the Holy Spirit, and he argues that there are three ways to test spirits: by learning from the scriptures, by spiritual experience and by a special gift of the Spirit, which, he says, is 'granted by virtue of hierarchical office and spiritual gift'.[32] The work has been seen as a rejection of the Swedish petitions and a subtle refutation of the *Epistola solitarii*.[33] Gerson suggests that even though her Swedish supporters might be permitted to honour Birgitta, the French (whose interests had never been in harmony with Birgittine argument) should not have to, for to do so would jeopardise their reputation. He then discusses the mental states of 'visionary' men and women (against chapter 2 of the *Epistola solitarii*) and describes the behaviour expected of them and their advisers. He gives hints of the risks of heresy and vanity in the spiritual adviser, alluding to the active support Alphonso had given to Birgitta; and he points out that far from living a quiet life away from society, she always sought the centre of public life to utter her religious messages. As Eric Colledge puts it: 'Without saying it in so many words, *De probatione spirituum* makes clear beyond all doubt that Gerson did not believe that her inspiration came from God.'[34]

Because of the internal division and confusion within the papacy at the time of the canonisation, there remained a shadow of uncertainty over the legitimacy of Birgitta's canonisation and her supporters therefore sought reconfirmation at the Council of Constance, and their petitions were supported

31 Ullmann 1972, p. 299, summarises the situation: 'The one system was the denial of the other . . . sovereignty belonged to the pope alone (the papal-hierocratic standpoint); sovereignty belonged to the whole Church (the conciliar viewpoint). The one sovereignty was personal and individual; the other corporate and collectivist.'

32 See Caiger 1990, especially p. 396.

33 See Colledge 1956, pp. 44–5.

34 Colledge 1956, p. 46.

by, among others, King Henry V of England.[35] Even at this Council there were technical and legal objections (many of them relating to the renewal of indulgences and the confirmation of the Rule, which was proving even more contentious). The re-confirmation was finally agreed on 1 July 1419, by Pope Martin V, who had temporarily removed to Florence.

At the Council of Basle (1431–49) renewed criticism came when a committee of theologians submitted 123 articles from the Revelations asking for them to be censored on the grounds that they were heretical. One theologian, Mathias Döring, the author of an anti-Birgittine tract, *Probate spiritus*, even argued that the Revelations were the work of Mathias of Linköping. The Council withdrew some of the privileges from the order, and referred some of the revelations for revision and further clarification by 'expert' theologians in 1436. In particular the Council took exception to the claims made about the burial and bodily assumption of the Virgin, and the claim that only Christ and the Virgin have human bodies in heaven, as well as the apparent equating of Birgitta's words with the Gospels. The Spanish Dominican Juan Torquemada, however, who was Birgitta's most vigorous defender at the Council, said there was no cause for suspicion. Because the Council was schismatic, its decrees were not all upheld and Torquemada's *Defensorium* was accepted. Rumblings of discontent continued intermittently against Birgitta's canonisation and it was not until the post-medieval period, with Benedict XIV's pontificate (1740–58), that a bull 'De servorum Dei beatificatione et beatorum canonizatione' was issued which silenced the critics of the canonisation of the three great women saints of the later medieval period, Hildegard of Bingen, Caterina of Siena and Birgitta of Sweden.[36]

By canonising St Birgitta, the papacy had shown – however temporarily – that in its perception of sanctity it favoured a widowed woman from the high nobility who had spoken out prophetically in favour of the reform of the Church. Her canonisation legitimises for the first time the new tradition of the married saint, and in obtaining public and papal recognition, it ends what André Vauchez calls 'the "sexual taboo" in matters of sanctity'.[37] However, the fact that her canonisation had to be confirmed three times – by Boniface IX, the schismatic Pope John XXIII and Martin V – and yet still caused widespread rumblings of disapproval, is an illustration that this idea of sainthood was not universally and lastingly recognised by the Church at large, and that the canonisation was intricately connected with the rival obediences of the papacy as well as the disarray within the Church. The debates surrounding the canonisation further demonstrate that there was a suspicion of women who dared to speak out and challenge the established hierarchy of the Church. Indeed, as Jean Gerson pointedly comments in his polemical work *De examinatione doctri-*

35 See Höjer 1905, pp. 160–222.
36 See Vernet 1937– .
37 Vauchez 1993, p. 246.

narum in 1423, even Pope Gregory XI on his deathbed in 1378 appears to have regretted having been too attentive to female mystics when he listened to their advice and returned to Rome, thus sparking the Great Schism:

> Placed here on his deathbed, he bore witness in the presence of them all, that they should beware of all persons, both male and female, who related visions from their heads under the guise of religion. He himself had been led astray by such . . . with the result that he drew both himself and the Church to the peril of the now imminent Schism . . .'.[38]

38 My translation. 'Hic positus in extremis . . . protestatus est coram omnibus, ut caverunt ab hominibus, tam viris quam mulieribus, sub specie religionis visiones loquentibus sui capitis; quia per tales ipse seductus esset . . . ut se et Ecclesiam ad discrimen schismatis tunc imminentis traxerit . . .' (Quoted from Vauchez 1993, p. 328 note 37)

VII

The Birgittine Legacy

> Ego plantabo michi nouam vineam, vbi apportabuntur palmites et mittent radices . . . Ex. hac autem vinea multe vinee longo tempore arentes renouari incipient et facere fructum iuxta diem innouacionis sue.
>
> I will plant a new vineyard for myself, where vine branches will be brought to take root . . . From this vineyard, many other vineyards will be renewed, which have been arid for long, and they will bear fruit after the day of their renewal.
>
> (*Regula Saluatoris*, Prologue)

PROBABLY St Birgitta's most lasting achievement was her monastic foundation, the Ordo Sanctissimi Salvatoris. By introducing a completely new order, she leaves after her death an embodiment and furtherance of her own life and work. At first sight it may seem contradictory that so public a saint as Birgitta should have founded a monastic order which was strictly contemplative and played no part in society. Yet the Birgittine Order echoes aspects of its founder's life and keeps her legacy alive after her death. It was an aristocratic Order which, at least in its early history, drew its members from the highest social classes. Birgitta was never a popular saint of the countryside who appealed to all ranks of society. Her immediate appeal was to women of her own class and background, although as her cult grew she attracted women of more varying social origins.[1] In her Order women were given a central role to model themselves on the love of the Virgin, and the brethren preached the public message of reform which Birgitta had so ardently advocated during her lifetime.[2]

1 Many women flocked to Vadstena as pilgrims, and in many Birgittine houses – in Sweden, Denmark and Poland for instance – there is evidence that beguine communities sought the protection of the Birgittines and lived on the periphery of their enclosures. See further Morris 1999. On the social origins of Vadstena nuns see Wallin 1991.

2 The unusual architecture of the churches even reinforced this intention: with the nuns' and brethren's altars at either end, the nave was to be filled with the laity, to whom the brethren would preach in the vernacular language at appointed times and hereby bring the message of reform into the community at large.

Approval of the Order

The approval of the Rule and establishment of the Order proved even more challenging than the canonisation and passed through a similar number of lengthy and complex stages. Before her death Birgitta had asked Pope Urban V, some time after his return to Rome in 1367, to ratify the Rule, and Emperor Charles IV was asked to add his support to the request.[3] However, Urban V could not easily do so, as he had renewed a prohibition on the founding of independent orders which was first introduced at the Council of Lyon in 1274.[4] He stayed at Montefiascone during the summer, where Birgitta and Alphonso of Jaén also spent three months; and during this period count Niccolò Orsini was invited to modify the Latin of the Rule, which was not in keeping with curial style, after which the pope issued his bull of 5 August 1370, allowing for the provision of two distinct and separate monasteries within the Order, which was to be established under the Augustinian Rule. Thus Birgitta's original concept of a 'double' monastery was denied her and the primacy of Vadstena as a monastery for women was not acknowledged in the bull, for it elevated the brethren and confessor general to equal status with the nuns and abbess.

Birgitta is unlikely to have been satisfied with the bull, but she did not live to argue for further changes to be made. Katarina returned to Rome in 1375 to seek further modifications to the Rule (as well as to press for the canonisation), and a new bull was issued by Urban VI in 1378, which recognised not only the monastery but also the Order, as an order for women which included men, although still under the Augustinian Rule.

The first few decades of the Order's history were precarious, as a result of internal strife and uncertainties within the Church. Deliberations with the papacy continued, and the recognition of the universal Church was eventually given in the important *Mare Magnum* bull of Pope John XXIII, dated 1 May 1413, which was a confirmation of all previous papal bulls and established more explicitly the principle of the double monastery. But within a few years, in 1418, this and all the privileges granted to the Order by earlier popes were revoked by Pope Martin V on the grounds that double monasteries were canonically forbidden.[5] Letters were sent to the pope imploring him to reverse the decision, including a letter from King Henry V of England, who had just gained papal approbation for an English foundation. Amid many

3 Books IV 137, VIII 51. The history of the Birgittine Order is a vast subject that cannot be given justice in the space of a short chapter. The most important works in this area are by Höjer 1905, Cnattingius 1963, Nyberg 1965. For a useful brief survey and bibliography see *Medieval Scandinavia*, ed. P. Pulsiano, 1993, s.v. 'Monasticism'.

4 See further Eklund 1975, pp. 24–9.

5 See Ullman 1976.

uncertainties during the following years the prohibition was lifted gradually, and the pope restored the right to observe the 1378 version of the Rule to the monasteries individually, starting with the English house and ending with Marienkron in the Netherlands in 1427.

Opposition to the concept of the double monastery continued well into the fifteenth century, not least because central authority lay in the hands of a woman – the abbess – in every house. In 1422, two Birgittine brethren, Johannes Halewater and Johannes Serminius, who were associated with monasteries in Poland and Italy, complained about the rule of the monasteries by an abbess and there were further attempts to diminish the indulgences and to segregate brethren and nuns into completely separate communities, all of which finally resulted in the matter being raised at the Council of Basle. Birgitta's defenders of her Revelations at the Council also spoke in favour of the arrangements within the Order. An act of the Council in 1436 limited the privileges of the Order to its confessions and indulgences, but these decisions were lessened by the disputes of the Council and Pope Eugene IV subsequently accepted its decisions on these two points. In 1435, Eugene IV issued a bull which confirmed the double monasteries and, in answer to some of the criticisms of the Council of Basle, gave full recognition to the entire Order by the Church at large.

The most unusual – and contentious – feature of the Birgittine Order, then, was that it was a dual establishment for men and women. Chapter 1 of the Rule stipulates that it was to be primarily an Order for women, with the purpose of praising and honouring the Virgin: 'I wish to found this Order in honour of my beloved Mother, and first and foremost for women.'[6] However, the intended imbalance in numbers between the sexes laid down in the Rule makes the description of a double monastery a misnomer, and the preferable term *Gesamtkloster* has been used to suggest the separate coexistence of two forms of monastic life according the same Rule, in which the roles of the male and female elements varied.[7] The Rule (chapter 12) stipulates that the monastery was to be governed by an abbess, representing the Virgin, and that there should be a maximum of sixty nuns, a general confessor, representing St Peter, thirteen priests, representing the apostles and St Paul, four deacons, representing the four church fathers, Ambrose, Augustine, Gregory and Jerome, and eight lay brothers. This made eighty-five people in total, who were commensurate with the thirteen apostles (including Paul) and seventy-two disciples in Luke 10.17. In addition there was to be an unspecified number of servant brethren and sisters from outside the cloister.

Some have argued that Birgitta may have known of the French double monastery at Fontevrault, which she may have visited during her pilgrimage

6 'Hanc igitur religionem ad honorem amantissime Matris mee per mulieres primum et principaliter statuere volo.' Eklund 1975, p. 105.

7 Nyberg 1968, Nyberg 1988.

to Spain and used as an initial model for her foundation.[8] The community at Fontevrault was founded in c.1100 by Robert of Arbrissel and included men and women, although like the Birgittines, it was not, strictly speaking, a double order and the women outnumbered the men.[9] Robert appointed a woman to take overall authority as abbess, and he indicated his preference for a Martha-type of spiritual leader who had experience of a worldly life and practical management. The structured division of activities between men and women is also echoed in the Birgittine Rule. The Birgittine brethren were formally integrated into the constitution and thus the nuns did not have to rely on *ad hoc* arrangements with local clerics for the sacramental and administrative side of their monastic existence.

The Rule

With the constant revision in the statutes and the uncertainty about the status of the Order in its first few decades of existence, corresponding changes had to be made to versions of the text of the Rule itself, and there are a number of overlapping stages in the history of this text, which continued to be reworked and added to for many years after Birgitta's death.[10] There were also many additions to the Rule which came to be associated with or incorporated into later editions and translations of the Rule, including the constitutions written by Prior Petrus, who was charged with working out the practical implications and the execution of Birgitta's ideas. Many such additions are found in the *Extravagantes* chapters 1–46.

The Rule is in thirty-one chapters, and gives specific detail on the practical arrangements of the Order. It reflects Birgitta very much as the woman with an eye for practicalities and close detail, and it is characterised by common sense and expediency; 'everything should be reasonably executed' (chapter 6).[11] It also suggests a desire to contain the potential excesses and deprivations of cloistered females, by ensuring moderation in all things. For example, the elderly and infirm were allowed to relax the fasting regulations (chapter 9), and precautions had to be taken to ensure that there was no excess in fasting (chapter 24).

8 See for example Höjer 1905, p. 41.

9 See further Gold 1984, Thompson 1991.

10 Several versions of the Rule survive today. There was a distinction between the original revelation of the Rule, in which Christ spoke to Birgitta in the first person, and the Rule in which he spoke in the third person. A refinement of this crude distinction has introduced the descriptions of 'early version' which denotes Birgitta's own text, the 'authorised version' which is the version accepted in the bull of 1378, and the 'adapted version' which is a mixture of Birgitta's own text and the bull. See further Eklund 1975, p. 21, and Ellis 1996.

11 'Omnia enim racionabiliter debent fieri.' (Eklund 1975, p. 109)

The precepts of humility, chastity and voluntary poverty were the foundation virtues for the monastery; and it was forbidden to possess anything at all, or to touch anything made of gold or silver, unless it was for embroidery (chapter 2). The beds were to be made of straw, with two blankets and a linen-covered pillow but no sheets or mattresses were allowed (chapter 3). The sisters' clothes consisted of two white underskirts to be worn alternately for daily use, a grey tunic, the flaps of which could be buttoned up on the sleeve for manual work, and a cowl. In addition there was a full-length grey cloak – lined in winter with inexpensive sheepskin – which was not to be full and pleated, but close-fitting, and fastened with a wooden button. Their summer footwear was to be low shoes and knee-high stockings, and in winter, knee-high lined boots, and stockings. The head-dress, which became the distinctive feature of the Order's habit, was to be fastened with pins, and around the black veil there would be a white crown with an intersecting cross and a small piece of red material sewn into each intersection to look like the five drops of Christ's blood: a reminder of continence and chastity for all women who wore it (chapter 4). A similar cross symbol on the brethren's clothing was to be situated under the left arm of their mantle (chapter 13).

Chapter 5 concerns the liturgy and the shorter prayers that were to be recited on different occasions, all of them giving prominence to the Virgin Mary. Mary was to be praised with three readings from the *Sermo Angelicus* on feast-days; and every day at the beginning of vespers each side of the choir was to bow in humility to the other side. At the end of each Hour, the Ave Maria antiphon was to be sung. There would be a daily Mass to the Virgin, and on feast-days and on Saturdays after the Mass 'Salve Regina' would be sung (chapter 5). The rules of silence at different times of the day are covered in chapter 6 and the prohibition of communication with seculars in chapter 7. Between nones and vespers on Sundays and major feast-days the nuns were permitted to speak to lay people at a specially built window; they could open the window if they wished to be seen by relatives (chapter 8). Fasting regulations are laid down in chapter 9: Lenten fare (no animal fats or dairy products) during Advent and Lent and every Friday, and bread and water on the vigils of feasts; otherwise meat could be eaten four times a week.

Chapter 10 deals with the circumstances and conditions for entry, and the year-long period of probation; at which point the novice was to swear to the bishop that she had not been driven into the monastery by worldly trouble or debt. She had to enter the church behind banners depicting the crucifixion and the Virgin. Her ring was then consecrated, and the procedure for her profession is outlined in detail in the subsequent chapters.

Chapter 14 concerns the election of the abbess, who in turn had to appoint a confessor general; both offices were to be confirmed by the bishop. All the brethren had to obey the confessor general and the sisters had to obey the abbess, 'But the confessor, except when it concerns the judgements over the brethren and the observation of the Rule, shall do nothing without consultation with the abbess, for since she is the head of the monastery she should be consulted concerning its affairs and property.'[12] The priests' tasks were to preside at the services, to study and pray. Every Sunday they had to interpret the gospel from the day's Mass in their native tongue, 'in materna lingua', and on feast days they preached in public (chapter 15). All members of the monastery had to make confession to the confessor general three times a year, but more frequently if they needed (chapter 16); and they had to communicate every feast-day, on Maundy Thursday, Easter Day, Ascension Day, Whit Sunday and Christmas. Nuns who were especially pious and prayed with a true yearning could communicate every Saturday (chapter 17). Every Thursday a chapter for the correction of sins was to be held. Any sister who had sinned by having something she privately owned, which was reported by three witnesses, would not be permitted to go into church on the chapter day and Friday but had to lie in silence headlong in the passageway outside the church, and after vespers, the abbess would lead her to the altar to receive absolution (chapter 18). If gifts were offered by a nun's kinsmen, they could on no account be received, however rich and powerful the donor was: 'For just as a spark grows into a fire, so ownership causes damnation: it breaks the worthy unity of the monastery and destroys equity.'[13] The abbess had to set an example on the subject of ownership (chapter 19). The monastery was bound by an obligation of poverty, and chapter 20 deals with the donations that are part of a nun's entry requirement, and the way they were to be administered.

Chapter 21 explains that there were to be thirteen altars, and gives specifications about ornaments. Books for the purposes of teaching and studying were permitted. Chapter 22 concerns the legal age of entry and chapter 23 the daily occupations of the nuns; chapter 24 addresses the desirability for equal rationing between the nuns, regardless of their social origins. Chapter 25 describes the rules of enclosure, the separation of the sexes and the windows at which the nuns shall make confession, receive communion, and deal with secular matters – for this there was to be a rotating wheel built into the wall which could act as a point of communication. The bishop was the visitor, the king the defender, and the pope was the supreme authority of the institution (chapter 26). A grave always had to stand open at the monastery as a *memento mori*, which the nuns were to visit every day after terce, and in addition there was always to be a bier with some earth on it at the sisters' entrance to the church (chapter 27). The final chapters concern the way in which the Rule was

12 'Qui tamen confessor preter iudicia fratrum et conseruacionem ordinis absque consilio abbatisse nichil omnino faciet, que, quia caput monasterii est, de negociis et bonis monasterii ordinandis est consulenda.' (Eklund 1975, pp. 120–1)

13 'quia, sicut a scintilla augetur ignis, sic a proprietate dampnacio, que laudabilem in monasteriis rescindit vnitatem et communem corrumpit equitatem.' (Eklund 1975, p. 123)

revealed, and instruct Birgitta to obtain the pope's permission to establish the Order.

The Birgittine Rule was based broadly on the stipulations laid down in traditional monasticism, and it attempted to restore features of the ideal monastic community of early Christianity. It falls between the contemplative character of the older orders and the apostolic zeal of the mendicant orders, and displays a range of influences from other monastic statutes.[14] Often in the wording and phrasing there are echoes of the Benedictine Rule, which was the basis of the Cistercian Order (for example, there are Cistercian echoes in the tradition that the bishop shall induct the nun at her profession, and some of the indulgence privileges are similar), but there is also a considerable influence in practical details from Dominican tradition, which followed the Rule of St Augustine (for example, in prescriptions on clothing and the use of animal furs), as well as Franciscan tendencies (for example, in the precepts of humility, chastity and poverty).

In a number of ways, however, it introduces innovative elements, which, while not necessarily unparalleled in existing monasticism, are given a new emphasis. Although the Cistercians, for instance, made the Virgin their patroness, the Birgittines placed her in a position central to their entire monastic existence, from the liturgy (which was underpinned by the Marian *Sermo Angelicus*) to the architecture (as is suggested by the altar at the east end of the church for the nuns, dedicated to the Virgin).

Further, there was a difference in the intended roles of the nuns and brethren. The life of the nuns was completely cloistered and contemplative, whereas the brethren also fulfilled an important role as preachers, giving instruction and disseminating learned works in the vernacular.[15] They were allowed to leave the monastery only in their ministry, and for this reason their religious role – pastoral and homiletic – lacked the practical, outward-looking and itinerant character of, for example, the mendicant preachers. Nor were they, unlike the Cistercians, able to develop the economic side of their existence with material enterprises or cultivate local relations with the lay world outside.

Perhaps in part because of its eclecticism, the organisation of the Birgittine Order made it unwieldy to administrate and its development was hampered by a number of innate weaknesses in its constitution. A monastic community in which two sexes lived separately but within the same enclosure must have been cumbersome to manage and expensive to maintain. The segregation of the sexes had to be guaranteed as a matter of priority in the design of the

14 For a discussion of the monastic influences see Fogelqvist 1991.
15 Nyberg 1968.

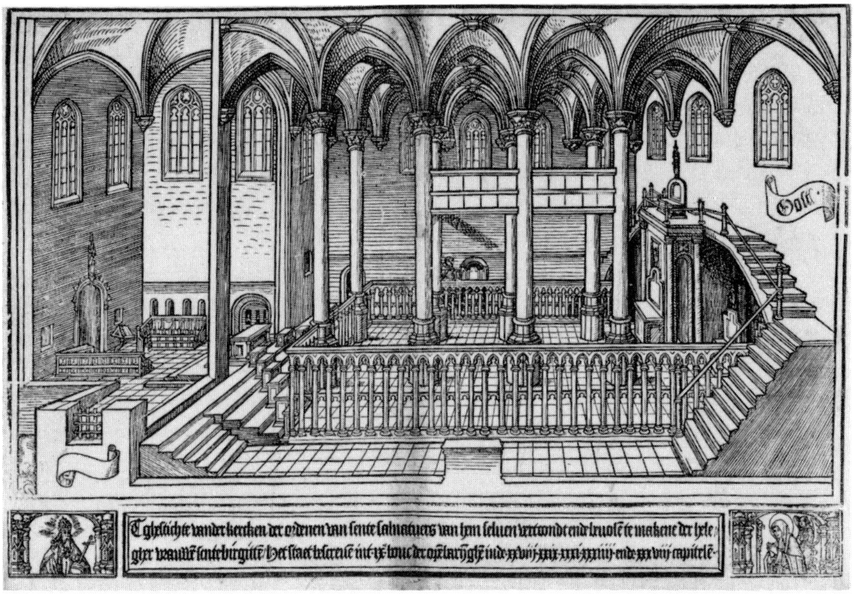

Plate 7. Dutch woodcut dating from c. 1500, giving a hypothetical reconstruction, according to Birgitta's stipulations, of the interior of a Birgittine church.
Source: Kungliga Biblioteket, Stockholm.

buildings, which often must have made local dioceses reluctant to support new establishments.[16]

Internal tensions were also possible as a result of the Rule's prescriptions, which stipulated a continuing link with the local diocese. Birgittine organisation was not heavily centralised, unlike the independent Cistercians or the mendicants who were relieved of ties with Church jurisdiction and had a hierarchical structure at the head of which was a *generale* and chapter. The Birgittines received visitations from the local bishop and the brethren's services were under episcopal authority and under the special protection of the king. Although attempts were made to establish a Birgittine constitution which might give the Order greater independence, there was insufficient support from the abbesses and local bishops, and the networks of newly-founded Birgittine communities therefore did not have regular, formalised, contact with each other.

16 The construction of Vadstena could be analysed with a view to establishing how gender stereotypes were enforced within the *Gesamtkloster*: see Gilchrist 1993, who develops a methodology for analysing monastic communities from an archaeologist's perspective.

Vadstena

After Birgitta's death a great impetus was given to Vadstena when her relics were translated there in 1374, and the beginnings of a community were forming well before official recognition was granted. Katarina and Peter of Skänninge became the first *de facto* abbess and confessor general respectively; although Katarina did not live to see the formal consecration of the monastery which took place on 23–24 October 1384, three and a half years after her death on 24 March 1381. The events of the inauguration are recorded in the *Diarium Vadstenense*:

> On Bishop St Severinus's day, which that year fell on a Sunday, the sisters' convent was inaugurated, in keeping with St Birgitta's constitutions, in Vadstena, in the presence of these honourable men, Archbishop Henrik of Uppsala, Bishop Tord of Strängnäs and Bishop Nikolaus of Linköping. The sisters who were then inducted and consecrated were forty-six in number. On the following day, i.e. on Monday, the brethren were inducted into their enclosure, nine priests and seven laymen. On the following Wednesday, two priests who had been sent out by the convent for certain reasons, were inducted in the presence of the aforementioned people.[17]

Clearly there was unease in Rome about the arrangements for both sexes on one site, in case it gave rise to scandalous gossip, and a decree was read out to the sisters and brethren on 25 October 1384 to the effect that the brethren were prohibited from entering the nunnery except in the two cases given in the Rule – to administer the sacraments to a sick nun and to bury a deceased nun – and their conduct in these cases was outlined. Likewise, the sisters risked excommunication and were reminded of eternal punishment if they pretended to be ill in order to have an excuse to meet any of the brethren. The brethren, in turn, were threatened with excommunication if they harassed the sisters during their confession.[18]

As Vadstena grew in importance, funds began to flow into the monastery;

[17] 'Item, die sancti Severini episcopi, cuius festum tunc cadebat in dominica, primo introductus fuit conventus sororum ad tenendum constituciones sancte Byrgitte in Vastenom presentibus venerabilibus patribus et dominis, videlicet Henrico archiepiscopo Upsalensi et Thordone episcopo Stræengianensi cum institutore domino Nicholao episcopo Lincopensi. Erant enim sorores in numero, que tunc introducte erant et consecrate, xlvi. Et sequenti die sive feria secunda introducti sunt fratres in curiam suam: presbiteri ix et frates layci vii. Et feria quarta in mediate proxima duo presbiteri, qui de conventu deputati fuerunt pro aliquibus causis ad tempus extra stare, introducti sunt presentibus patribus et dominis supradictis.' (Gejrot 1988, pp. 119–20)

[18] See Höjer 1905, pp. 89–100. Clearly, the relationship of the male community to the female one was not clearly enough defined in the constitutions, and it led to tensions in several monasteries. In Munkeliv, in Norway, on 1 January 1496 the *lagman* Erik Andersson wrote to Vadstena monastery saying 'the abbess who should rule most,

the first recorded one being the donation of gifts for entry by novices in 1375.[19] A significant number of privileges was also conferred on the monastery, which protected its property, granted exemptions from taxes, and helped to establish its economic independence. In 1378 permission to grant indulgences was given, which also meant a vast increase in wealth. During the 1380s there was a flow of funds to the monastery and no doubt the canonisation in 1391 helped put a seal on the establishment of the embryonic Order, which continued to be financed by bequests and donations of land, and led to its becoming one of the foremost monastic institutions in Scandinavia by the end of the middle ages.

Vadstena became completely infused with Birgitta's spirit after her death and a catalyst for increased communications between Sweden and the continent. It came to have a substantial library which compared favourably with other continental monastic libraries, and is estimated to have had about 1500 books by the beginning of the sixteenth century.[20] The nuns were active in copying didactic literature in the vernacular, and were permitted to have prayer books and other similar reading in their cells. The brethren's library was enriched by books sent or acquired from the centres of learning in Europe, such as Paris, Prague and Rostock. The monastic scriptorium acquired its own writing style, grammar, spelling system, handwriting habits and bindery. In addition, a Swedish school of sculpture, based mainly on northern German styles, was developed at the monastery; and the nuns engaged in embroidery which still survives today.[21] Vadstena's first printing press, introduced in 1495, was destroyed by fire in the same year, and the monastery had to rely instead on printers from Lübeck which became a focal point for the transmission of Birgittine texts in northern Europe.

The Order outside Sweden

Outside Sweden the Order was quick to become established.[22] The Birgittine following in Italy was particularly strong, and the first house there was Santa

she now rules least'; and there are similar complaints from Lublin. See Höjer 1908, pp. 187–8, and 62 note 2.

19 On the economic history see Norborg 1958, who discusses the poverty ideal in the Rule in relation to its implementation in practice.

20 The surviving collection, now mostly in Uppsala University Library, provides an early map of Swedish intellectual history. See Andersson-Schmitt, Hedlund et al. 1988–95. Vadstena language marks the beginnings of a continuous literary tradition in the Swedish language. It formed the basis of the sixteenth-century Bible translations and the language of these translations in turn laid the foundations of the modern Swedish language.

21 See further Lindblom 1965 and Lindgren 1991. On daily activities at Vadstena see also Rajamaa 1992.

22 See the 'family tree' in Sander Olsen 1991, pp. 346–8. For a survey of the history of the Order, see Nyberg 1974.

Maria in Paradiso, outside Florence, founded in 1394, which became a centre for the active organisation of the Order and the scholarly study of Birgitta's works.[23] Another of the earliest foundations was Gdańsk (Danzig) in 1396, through which the Swedish party had passed with the Saint's relics in 1373, on their way to Vadstena. It was here that the mystic Dorothea of Montau received a vision shortly before she died in 1394, in which St Birgitta called her to join her in heaven; two years later a Birgittine foundation in this prosperous town was authorised by Pope Boniface IX, which took the name Fons Mariae (Marienbrunn).[24]

As the Birgittine cult developed in Scandinavia, too, there were early foundations, though not all equally as successful. In Norway, the former Benedictine abbey of St Michael outside Bergen, known as Munkeliv, became a Birgittine foundation through the efforts of the Swedish Benedictine, Sten Stenarsson, who had been instrumental in the founding of Paradiso.[25] Munkeliv never prospered financially and appears to have had difficulty in recruiting Norwegians to join the Order: the first residents were Birgittine brethren from Denmark, and the high-born Norwegian women who wished to enter the Order chose Vadstena in preference to Munkeliv. In Finland, the abbey of Vallis Gratiae, Naantali (Nådendal) was founded in 1441 by a group of brethren from Vadstena, and it became the foremost cultural centre in the country, where the monk Jöns Budde, Finland's first named writer, produced an important body of mystical and devotional literature in translation.[26] In Denmark, Erik of Pomerania, ruler of the Union of the Scandinavian kingdoms, sent a colony of pioneers to Maribo on Lolland in 1413, which became a rich establishment and had a considerable reputation for preaching and for producing prayer books, as did its daughter-house at Mariager, in Jutland. Erik opened up new spheres of influence by incorporating Birgittine activities into his political programme, and using the foundations to consolidate and strengthen the Union.

The Danish houses were part of an important group of fully-integrated 'dynastic foundations', which were endowed by kings who sought to strengthen and consolidate their authority in the European sphere. Two other such foundations were Gnadenberg (near Nuremberg) in Bavaria, established in 1420 by Katerina, a sister of King Erik of Pomerania who was married to a Bavarian palatine duke, and the house founded by the ruler of the joint Polish-Lithuanian kingdom and a convert from paganism, Wladyslaw Jagiello, who won an unexpected victory over the Teutonic Knights at Tannenberg (Grünwald) on 15 July 1410. On the battlefield he sent a promise to the Birgittines of Gdansk, who by now were well-established, saying that he

23 See Nyberg 1996.
24 See Nyberg 1996, p. 10.
25 See Gunnes 1990.
26 Klockars 1979.

would improve their economic standing; and two months afterwards he sought permission to build an abbey on the battlefield site. When the site was lost to Poland in a subsequent peace treaty, the house was removed to Lublin.[27]

Another of the important dynastic foundations was Syon in England, established by King Henry V. A few months before he dealt the French nobility a devasting defeat at Agincourt in 1415 he laid the foundation stone of the monastery of Syon at Twickenham, on the opposite bank of the Thames from his own palace.[28] In May 1415, four consecrated nuns and a number of novices and priests left Vadstena to give instruction to the volunteers for the Birgittine Order in England, and the first members were professed in 1420. In 1431 the community moved a short distance down the Thames to Isleworth, into a larger building on the site of the mansion which is still called Syon House today. Syon monastery rapidly became one of the most richly endowed monastic centres in late medieval England, and an important place of pilgrimage. It attracted many distinguished secular scholars, such as Richard Whytford and Thomas Betson, and gained a reputation as a centre of book-learning and book production.[29]

Endowments from their dynastic patrons were often insufficient to maintain some of the complex monastic sites, which had to depend on political patronage and gifts from nearby towns for their continued prosperity. With the exception of Scandinavia, where towns were still small in size, there is a firm link in the history of the Birgittine Order between community and city, and the interaction with local economic life seems to have been a necessity for the survival of several monastic communities. This tendency can be seen especially in northern Europe, where houses were established in the urban and mercantile centres along the Baltic shores and in the Germanic regions with Hanseatic connections: houses such as Tallinn (Reval) founded in 1407, and Lübeck in 1415, for instance, owed their existence to the merchants of the city. The same pattern is seen in many other houses which are close to centres of trade and industry, such as the Dutch monasteries of Kampen, Gouda, Brielle and Dendermonde in Flanders.

The success of the Birgittine Order can be explained against the background of the general decline in monastic standards in the fifteenth century: in

27 See Cnattingius 1971–72.

28 See further Knowles 1961, pp. 175–82. His foundation, along with another new one, Charterhouse at Sheen, is referred to by Shakespeare in the prayer of Henry V before he goes into battle (*Henry V* IV i). On the Birgittine Order in England see Tait 1975, Ellis 1984, Johnson 1993.

29 Unlike Vadstena, however, there is little evidence that the nuns at Syon were involved in book production. See further O'Mara 1990, and (for a more general discussion on female scribal ability and activity in England) O'Mara 1996.

keeping with Birgitta's ambitions, it was seen as a fresh beginning and therefore attracted benefactors who were willing to lend it their financial support in preference to the more established orders. The total number of houses in the medieval period – both the fully developed *Gesamtkloster*, for men and women, and the smaller scale single-sex communities – was never large, certainly by the standards of mainstream monasticism, but for an innovative female foundation, it was impressive, and all the more so for the influence and support it gained from among the noble and royal houses of Europe.

The post-Reformation survival

The Birgittine heritage continued to spread beyond the Reformation, although in the nineteenth century the Order nearly became extinct. There are three branches of the Order in existence today. First, there is the unreformed branch which traces its roots back to the original Order and includes the Syon community, which went from England to the Netherlands at the Reformation and thence to Portugal, where it continued to recruit nuns from recusant English families until the convent was able to return to England in the mid-eighteenth century. The English house is the only one to have had an unbroken history since its foundation.[30] In Germany, the house at Altomünster in Bavaria belongs to the unreformed branch, and in the Low Countries there was the house at Mariënwater, near 's-Hertogenbosch, which from the eighteenth century continued as Maria Refugie at Uden in Brabant. Maria Hart in Weert, southern Netherlands, was founded from Uden at the beginning of the nineteenth century. The unreformed Birgittine Order was reintroduced to Sweden in 1963 on the same site as the medieval monastery in Vadstena, which had been closed in 1595; and it was upgraded to abbey status in 1992.

In the seventeenth century, in the Netherlands, there were schismatic groups of priests who moved away from the nuns and set up an Order of their own, with papal approval, under the name Novissimi Birgittani. The nuns meanwhile established convents of their own and had numerous houses throughout the Netherlands and northern France. A separate branch of the Order developed in Spain in the seventeenth century when the Spanish mystic Marina de Escobar (1554–1633) inspired the founding of a house in her home town of Valladolid, which had four other houses in Spain as well as a branch in Mexico, all of which are still in existence.

The third branch was founded at the beginning of the twentieth century by the Swede, Maria Elisabeth Hesselblad (1870–1957), who joined the mass emigrations from Sweden to the United States at the end of the nineteenth

30 See de Hamel 1991. The Birgittine house in England today is now situated at South Brent, Devon.

century. Having converted to Roman Catholicism in 1902, she travelled to Rome to the house where Birgitta had lived. The house had remained in Swedish hands since Francisca Papazzura had bequeathed it to Vadstena, and from 1692 to 1828 Birgittines from Altomünster lived there. It was later given to the parish of Santa Maria in Trastevere, and between 1855 and 1889 it was run by the Knights of the Holy Cross. At the time Elisabeth Hesselblad came to Rome, it was being used by Polish Carmelite nuns. She took up residence with this community and in 1906 the pope gave her permission to wear the Birgittine habit within the Carmelite community. She gradually developed the idea of re-establishing the Birgittine Order in the house in Rome, although she met with scant interest among the cloistered branches in Spain, the Low Countries, England and Germany. Intent upon establishing a reformed branch of the Order she sought papal support to enable the resident Carmelites to be rehoused. The new branch received an official confirmation in 1920 and in 1942 it was given permission to take the name of the Ordo Sanctissimi Salvatoris. Unlike the old Order, it did not adopt a cloistered life, but supported itself gaining a living mainly from running guest-houses. The reformed Birgittine Order was reinstated in Sweden in 1923 in a house in Djursholm, on the outskirts of Stockholm; and other houses were established as far afield as Lugano in Switzerland, Iver Heath, Uxbridge, in England, Mexico City, Darien, Connecticut, USA, and several locations in India. There are twenty-three houses belonging to this branch today.

St Birgitta's legacy: the active and contemplative life

The Birgittine Order embodies the twin roles of apostolic ministry and ascetic devotion, and a balance is struck between the hours spent in active work and private contemplation. This balance is seen in Birgitta's own life. For her, as she suggests in Book VI 65, there is no contradiction between the interior and exterior life and it is possible to live simultaneously an ascetic and active life in the world. Although she places the meditative life above the active life, in keeping with traditional Church teaching, at the same time she recognises the value of the active life, which is at its best when joined with the meditative life. Using the biblical story of Mary and Martha, Christ shows her how the two modes of life are not incompatible:

> Therefore I said in the Gospel that Mary made the best choice. Martha's part is good when she sorrows over the sins of her fellow men. Her part is also better when she works to make people live more wisely and honourably, and does this only and completely because of her love of God. But Mary's part is the best, when she alone sees the heavenly and the gain of souls. Then too, God goes into Martha's and Mary's house, when the mind is filled with good desire and freed from worldly unrest, when one thinks constantly of

God as if he were present, and when one not only meditates on his love but also works night and day.[31]

Birgitta's life spanned almost the entire fourteenth century, and it reflects the patterns of lay piety of her time, which had reached an unprecedented level of devotionalism. As we have seen, she undertook pilgrimages, self-mortification and fasting; she wore penitential clothing, revered relics, and helped the poor and sick. From her early childhood onwards, she showed a particular devotion to the Virgin, and to the Incarnation and the human life of Christ. She listened to the teachings and sermons of the learned clerics who surrounded her, engaged constantly throughout her life in private meditation and even composed a number of her own prayers.

Like other holy lay women of her time, she had lived a busy life in society, and was married with children. In canonising her, the Church showed, however temporarily, that marriage and widowhood were legitimate states in which women could achieve the highest recognition of the Church. Just as she modelled herself on the married saint Elizabeth of Hungary, so in turn she became an example in the later fourteenth and fifteenth centuries to Dorothea of Montau, Margery Kempe and possibly also the Roman noblewoman, Francesca Romana (d.1440), all of whom turned to a devout life during or after their marriages.[32]

Although she shares characteristics in common with her contemporaries and predecessors, there are a number of elements in Birgitta's devotionalism that distinguish her from her continental counterparts and that, together, can be said to constitute the unique nature of her spirituality.

First, she is a prophet of reform. At all stages of her life she observes a decline in moral standards and a falling away from the ideals taught by Christ; and she urges a return to the old values, advocating an ideal which is realisable by an imitation of early Christian modes of existence, and exemplified primarily in biblical models. She believes that a renewed world must come about essentially by means of personal reform, which is reflected through every level of society from the papacy downwards. Her programme for reform is essentially élitist and concerned with the leading groups in society, knights and secular leaders as well as clerics and prelates. As

31 'Ideo ego dixi in euangelio, quod Maria optimam partem elegit. Nam pars Marthe tunc bona est, quando dolet de peccatis proximorum. Est quoque pars Marthe tunc melior, quando laborat, quomodo homines sapienter et honeste viuant et subsistant, et hoc facit propter solius Dei dileccionem. Sed pars Marie optima est, quando ipsa sola celestia et animarum lucra contemplatur. Tunc quoque Deus domum Marthe et Marie ingreditur, quando mens repleta bonis affeccionibus et pacata a secularium tumultibus Deum quasi presentem cogitat et in eius dileccione non solum meditatur sed laborabat die ac nocte.' (Bergh 1991, p. 221)

32 See Damsholt 1991 on Francesca.

responsible leaders of people, such groups must set an example for their subjects or flocks to follow, and if the people at large fail it is because of the weakness of their leaders. She views the present Church as an institution which is filled with people who are Christians in name only, who violate, abuse and scorn their faith. Their forms of apostasy are sparked essentially by their worldliness, ambition, disobedience, anger, impatience and intellectual arrogance. In Birgitta's opinion, contemporary Christians also show a disregard for Christ and lack of contrition for their sins. They are indifferent to the punishments of the afterlife, and they neglect to care for others by setting a bad example and by acting unjustly. These repeated appeals for reform are at the core of her missionary calling.

Second, she anticipates the shift that took place in the later medieval period and coincided with the crises taking place within the Church, away from extreme affective states, towards a more active spirituality. She takes up the new challenge, prophesying imminent catastrophes with a political shrewdness which was combined with genuine spiritual maturity. To a greater extent than her male counterparts (and to the same extent as Caterina of Siena) Birgitta executed her missionary ambition amid the general climate of uncertainty in the fourteenth century. In having a privileged, direct and unfettered communication with God, she thus found the means of circumventing the established voice of authority within the Church. Potentially, of course, such women were a dangerous threat, because they voiced ideas which were not rooted in official doctrine. The opposition to them is well exemplified by the vilification of Birgitta before and after her canonisation, or indeed later, by Jeanne d'Arc, who was condemned as a heretic and witch in 1431. The shift towards an active mysticism in Birgitta's case was accompanied by a shift in the mystic's relationship with her confessors. She knew that women on their own were ineffectual in publicising the message of reform and that they had to be supported by male clerics who were preachers and well-connected theologians, and who would proclaim and promulgate the message of reform in the public sphere and outside the confines of the monastery. This fact is seen not only in the organisation of her order, but also in the recording of her divine revelations. Whereas her predecessors had enjoyed a relationship of obedience and submission to their spiritual directors, Birgitta co-operated actively with her confessors in producing a collaborative text of her revelations. This caused difficulties for the first time among Church authorities for what Vauchez describes as the 'access of women to the ministry of the Word – something that hitherto had always been denied them – as well as the entirely new question of the authenticity of private revelations and the faith that they should be accorded'.[33]

33 Vauchez 1993, p. 245.

Third, she anticipates and contributes to the rise in Marian devotion and to the Incarnation in the later middle ages. Mary was the central figure in the Order, in Birgitta's life, and in her revelations. In her capacity as wife and mother she showed exemplary conjugal and maternal devotion which was to translate into an ardent devotion to the Virgin, whom she regarded as her mentor and spiritual mother. Many of her revelations in praise of the Virgin demonstrate a deep spiritual maturity and lyricism; indeed, the *Sermo Angelicus* and many individual revelations dating from all the years of her calling can be said to belong properly to the mainstream tradition of late medieval European mystical writing.

St Birgitta's achievement is paradoxical: on the one hand she was conservative, with a deeply traditional view of the Church. From her native Sweden, where old ideals still resonated and gave a voice to women of her class, she exhibited elements of traditional values, mixed, as they undoubtedly were by the fourteenth century, with new continental impulses. On the other hand, she looked forward to the fifteenth century in her anticipation of propheticism and Marian devotion and for this reason she heralded new spiritual developments and appealed to her continental contemporaries. Furthermore, in her revelations as well as her life, she vacillated constantly between the extremes of tenderness, grim fantasy and visionary power.

After her death, the Birgittine spirit lived on for centuries in various ways, in the canon of saints, in the often-quoted prophecies, and perhaps most of all, in her monastic order. The Reformation obviously checked the spread of Birgittine influence in Sweden, although, as we have seen, it continued to be renewed in a variety of forms throughout Europe in the following centuries, not least in the past century, which has seen a steady increase of interest in the saint. August Strindberg caricatured her as domineering and self-righteous in his historical drama *Folkungasagan* in 1899, and two years later the atheist writer Verner von Heidenstam portrayed her as an embodiment of the neo-Romantic concept of 'genius'. The early feminist writer, Emilia Fogelklou, wrote a number of perceptive studies of Birgitta, emphasising her role as woman and mother.[34] A number of interpretative biographies of Birgitta were also published, beginning with a substantial work in French in 1882 by the Comtesse de Flavigny.[35] They in turn laid the foundations for the scholarly development of Birgittine studies. From having been promoted as a national, Catholic saint early in the twentieth century, in more recent years she has been

34 Modern feminist critics have been slow to study Birgitta except superficially, but see for example Bergom-Larsson 1981 and Witt-Brattström 1992.

35 The others have been Jørgensen, first published in Danish in 1941–43, Stolpe 1973, and a biography in German – Adalsten 1951.

studied by a wider international community, both lay and religious.[36] The burgeoning interest in all aspects of the life and work of this remarkable medieval woman is testimony to a living legacy that will surely continue to present her in new forms and open up new interpretations for years to come.

36 Indeed, at the time Sweden was applying for entry into the European Union, it was suggested that she might become the first female patron saint of Europe (see Rehnberg 1994; see too *Der Spiegel* 13 January 1997, p. 154), and this proposal is still being discussed in Rome today.

BIBLIOGRAPHY

Abbreviated references in the text refer to the following works and series:

AP	Collijn 1924–31.
DS	*Diplomatarium suecanum.*
KLNM	*Kulturhistorisk leksikon for nordisk middelalder.*
KVHAAH	Kungliga Vitterhets Historie och Antikvitets Akademiens Handlingar.
SFSS	Svenska Fornskriftsällskapets Samlingar.
SRS	*Scriptores rerum svecicarum medii aevi.*
Ex.	Book of *Extravagantes.*
SA	*Sermo Angelicus*

There is no complete translation of the Revelations into English but there are selections in Tjader Harris 1990. For a lavishly-illustrated translation into Swedish, see Lundén 1957–59. The Latin texts of the Revelations are published in the second series of the collections of Svenska Fornskriftsällskapet (SFSS). The following books have been published in modern critical editions:

Book I: Carl-Gustaf Undhagen, 1978.
Book III: Ann-Mari Jönsson, 1998.
Book IV: Hans Aili, 1992.
Book V: Birger Bergh, 1971.
Book VI: Birger Bergh, 1991.
Book VII: Birger Bergh, 1967.
Revelationes Extravagantes: Lennart Hollman, 1956.
Sermo Angelicus: Sten Eklund, 1972.
Quattuor Oraciones: Sten Eklund, 1991.
Regula Salvatoris: Sten Eklund, 1975.

Books II and VIII are still in preparation, by C.-G. Undhagen and H. Aili respectively.

Abergale, F.R. Johnatan. 'The Revelations and the Hundred Years' War'. In *Santa Brigida: Profeta dei tempi nuovi. Saint Bridget: Prophetess of New Ages*. Rome, 1991, pp. 901–6.

Acta sanctorum quotquot toto orbe colunter, published by the Bollandists. See especially on St Birgitta vol. IV, *Octobris*, 1868, Paris/Rome, pp. 368–560.

Adalsten, Karola. *Licht aus dem Norden. Die Heilige Birgitta von Schweden*. Emmendingen, 1951.

Aili, Hans. 'St Birgitta and the Text of the *Revelationes*. A Survey of Some Influences Traceable to Translators and Editors'. In *The Editing of Theological and*

Philosophical Texts from the Middle Ages. Ed. Monika Asztalos. (Acta Universitatis Stockholmiensis. Studia Latina Stockholmiensia 30). Stockholm, 1986, pp. 75–92.

Aili, Hans, Olle Ferm, and Helmer Gustavson. *Röster från svensk medeltid*. Stockholm, 1990.

Aili, Hans (ed.). *Sancta Birgitta. Revelaciones. Book IV.* (SFSS ser. 2, VII:4). Stockholm, 1992.

Aili, Hans. 'Petrus Olavi, f. i Skänninge' Petrus Olavi, f. omkring 1307'. *Svenskt biografiskt lexikon*. Stockholm, 1995, pp. 221–6.

Allmand, Christopher. 'Documents Relating to the Anglo-French Negotiations of 1439'. *The Camden Miscellany 24. Fourth Series*. London, 1972.

Allmand, Christopher. *The Hundred Years War.* Cambridge 1988.

Anderson, Iwar. *Vadstena gård och kloster.* Stockholm, 1972.

Andersson, Aron. *Birgitta och det heliga landet*. Stockholm, 1973.

Andersson, Ingvar. *Källstudier till Sveriges historia 1230–1436*. Lund, 1928.

Andersson-Schmitt, Margarete, Monica Hedlund et al. (eds.). *Mittelalterliche Handschriften der Universitätsbibliothek Uppsala. Katalog uber die C-Sammlung. I–VIII.* (Acta Bibliothecae R. Universitatis Upsaliensis 26). Stockholm, 1988–95.

Annerstedt, Claes (ed.). 'Chronicon de genere et nepotibus Sanctae Birgittae'. *Scriptores rerum svecicarum medii aevi*, III, part 2. Uppsala, 1876, pp. 207–16.

Armstrong, Charles A.J. *England, France and Burgundy in the Fifteenth Century.* London, 1983.

Atkinson, Clarissa W. *Mystic and Pilgrim: the 'Book' and the World of Margery Kempe.* Ithaca, New York, 1983.

Atkinson, Clarissa W. *The Oldest Profession. Christian Motherhood in the Middle Ages.* Ithaca, New York, 1991.

Authén Blom, Grethe. *Norge i union på 1300-tallet. Kongedømme, politikk, administrasjon og forvaltning 1319–1380. I–II.* Trondheim, 1992.

Barraclough, Geoffrey. *The Medieval Papacy.* London, 1968.

Beckwith, Sarah. *Christ's Body: Identity, Culture and Society in Late Medieval Writings.* London, 1993.

Bergh, Birger (ed.). *Den heliga Birgittas Revelaciones Bok VII.* (SFSS ser. 2, VII:7). Uppsala, 1967.

Bergh, Birger (ed.). *Sancta Birgitta. Revelaciones Book V. Liber Questionum.* (SFSS ser. 2, VII:5). Uppsala, 1971.

Bergh, Birger. 'Birgittas djävulsskildringar'. *Credo. Katolsk tidskrift* 54 (1973), pp. 108–16.

Bergh, Birger (ed.). *Den heliga Birgitta. Revelaciones Bok VI.* (SFSS ser. 2, VII:6). Stockholm, 1991.

Bergh, Birger. 'Birgittabilden i kanonisationsakterna'. In *Heliga Birgitta – budskapet och förebilden*. Ed. Alf Härdelin and Mereth Lindgren (KVHAAH, Konferenser 28). Stockholm, 1993, pp. 289–98.

Bergh, Birger (ed.). *Magister Mathias Lincopensis. Testa nucis and Poetria.* (SFSS ser. 2, IX:2). Lund, 1996.

Bergom-Larsson, Maria. 'Brinnande och förnuftig'. In *Nordisk Kvindelitteraturhistorie I.* Ed. Elisabeth Møller Jensen. Stockholm, 1981.

Billing-Ottosson. 'Magister Mathias' Apokalypskommentar: edition av kap.1 och 2 med inledande anmärkningar, handskriftsklassificering och kommentar till texten'. Uppsala University M.A. thesis, 1960.

Blamires, Alcuin. *Woman Defamed and Woman Defended. An Anthology of Medieval Texts*. Oxford, 1992.

Boland, Paschal. *The Concept of 'Discretio Spirituum' in John Gerson's 'De probatione spirituum' and 'De distinctione verarum visionum a falsis'*. (The Catholic University of America. Studies in Sacred Theology, 2nd series, 112). Washington, 1959.

Bolton Holloway, Julia. 'Saint Birgitta of Sweden, Saint Catherine of Siena: saints, secretaries, scribes, supporters'. *Birgittiana* 1 (1996), pp. 29–46.

Børresen, Kari Elisabeth. 'Birgitta's Godlanguage: exemplary intention, inapplicable content'. In *Birgitta, hendes værk og hendes klostre i Norden*. Ed. Tore Nyberg. Odense, 1991, pp. 21–72.

Brilioth, Yngve. *Svensk kyrka, kungadöme och påvemakt 1363–1414*. (Uppsala universitets årsskrift 1925, Teologi 1). Uppsala, 1925.

Brodd, Sven-Erik, and Alf Härdelin (eds.). *Maria i Sverige under tusen år. Föredrag vid symposiet i Vadstena 6–10 oktober 1994. I–II*. Skellefteå, 1996.

Bygdén, A., N.-G. Gejvall and C.-H. Hjortsjö. *Les reliques de sainte Brigitte de Suède*. Lund, 1954.

Bynum, Caroline Walker. *Holy Feast and Holy Fast. The Religious Significance of Food to Medieval Women*. Berkeley, Los Angeles and London, 1987.

Bynum, Caroline Walker. *Fragmentation and Redemption. Essays on Gender and the Human Body in Medieval Religion*. New York, 1992.

Caiger, S.J. 'Doctrine and Discipline in the Church of Jean Gerson'. *Journal of Ecclesiastical History* 41:3 (July 1990), pp. 389–407.

Carlsson, Sten, and Jerker Rosén. *Svensk historia I. Tiden före 1718*. Stockholm, 1962.

Christiansen, Eric. *The Northern Crusades: the Baltic and the Catholic Frontier 1100–1525*. London, 1980.

Clover, Carol J. 'Regardless of Sex: men, women, and power in early northern Europe'. *Speculum* 68 (1993), pp. 363–87.

Cnattingius, Hans. *Studies in the Order of St Bridget of Sweden. The Crisis in the 1420s*. (Acta universitatis Stockholmiensis. Stockholm Studies in History 7). Stockholm, 1963.

Cnattingius, Hans. 'Birgittinerorden i Polen'. Kungl. *Vetenskapssamhällets i Uppsala årsbok* 15–16 (1971–72), pp. 21–83.

Colledge, Eric. '*Epistola solitarii ad reges*: Alphonse of Pecha as Organizer of Birgittine and Urbanist Propaganda'. *Mediaeval Studies* 18 (1956), pp. 19–49.

Collijn, Isak (ed.). *Acta et processus canonizacionis beate Birgitte*. (SFSS ser. 2, I). Uppsala, 1924–31.

Collijn, Isak. *Birgittinska gestalter: forskningar i italienska arkiv och bibliotek*. Uppsala, 1929.

Collijn, Isak (ed.). *Processus seu negocium canonizacionis B. Katerine de Vadstenis, efter Cod.Holm. A93* (SFSS ser. 2, III). Uppsala, 1942–46.

Collijn, Isak (ed.). *Birgerus Gregorii, legenda sancte Birgitte*. (SFSS ser. 2, IV). Uppsala, 1946.

Collins, A.J. (ed.). *The Bridgetinne Breviary of Syon Abbey*. (Henry Bradshaw Society 96). Worcester, 1969.

Cornell, Henrik. 'The Iconography of the Nativity of Christ'. *Uppsala Universitets årskrift* 3 (1924), pp. 1–45.

Costello, Melanie Starr. 'Women's Mysticism and Reform: the Adaptation of Biblical Prophetic Conventions in Fourteenth Century Hagiographic and Visionary Literature'. Ph.D. Northwestern University, 1989.

Cousins, Ewart. 'The Humanity and Passion of Christ'. In *Christian Spirituality: High Middle Ages and Reformation*. Ed. Jill Raitt, Bernard McGinn, and John Meyendorff. (World Spirituality: an Encyclopedic History of the Religious Quest 17). New York, 1987, pp. 375–91.

Cross, J.E. 'St Eric of Sweden'. *Saga Book of the Viking Society* 15 (1957–61), pp. 294–326.

Curry, Anne. *The Hundred Years War.* London, 1993.

Damsholt, Nanna. 'A Glimpse into Women's Life in the Rome of St Birgitta'. In *Birgitta. hendes værk og hendes klostre i Norden*. Ed. Tore Nyberg. Odense, 1991, pp. 73–82.

Davies, Horton and Marie-Hélène. *Holy Days and Holidays. The Medieval Pilgrimage to Compostela*. Lewisburg, 1982.

de Hamel, Christopher. 'The Medieval Manuscripts of Syon Abbey, and their Dispersal'. In *Syon Abbey. The Library of the Bridgettine Nuns and their Peregrinations after the Reformation*. Ed. John Martin Robinson. London, 1991, pp. 48–132.

Dictionnaire de spiritualité ascétique et mystique. Paris, 1937– .

Dinzelbacher, Peter. 'Saint Bridget and Mysticism of her Time'. In *Santa Brigida: profeta dei tempi nuovi. Saint Bridget: Prophetess of New Ages*. Rome, 1991, pp. 338–72.

Diplomatarium suecanum. Stockholm, 1829– .

Duby, George. *Love and Marriage in the Middle Ages*. Cambridge, 1994.

Duffy, Eamon. *The Stripping of the Altars. Traditional Religion in England c.1400–c.1580*. New Haven and London, 1992.

Edbury, Peter W. *The Kingdom of Cyprus and the Crusades, 1191–1374*. Cambridge, 1991.

Eklund, Sten (ed.). *Den heliga Birgitta. Opera minora II. Sermo Angelicvs*. (SFSS ser. 2, VIII:2). Uppsala, 1972.

Eklund, Sten (ed.). *Den heliga Birgitta. Opera minora I. Regvla Salvatoris*. (SFSS ser. 2, VIII:1). Stockholm, 1975.

Eklund, Sten. 'A Re-assessment of the Old Swedish Bridgettine Text Corpus'. *Kungl. Humanistiska Vetenskaps-Samfundet i Uppsala. Årsbok* (1983–84), pp. 5–24.

Eklund, Sten (ed.). *Sancta Birgitta. Opera minora III. Quattuor oraciones*. (SFSS ser. 2, VIII:3). Stockholm, 1991.

Ekwall, Sara. *Vår äldsta Birgittavita och dennas viktigaste varianter.* (KVHAAH. Historiska serien 12). Stockholm, 1965.

Ekwall, Sara. 'Årscykeln i Acta et Processus canonizacionis b. Brigide'. *Personhistorisk tidskrift* 69 (1973), pp. 1–9.

Ekwall, Sara. 'Den heliga Birgittas makes dödsår än en gång'. *Personhistorisk tidskrift* 72 (1976), pp. 32–5.

Elliott, Dyan. *Spiritual Marriage: Sexual Abstinence in Medieval Wedlock.* Princeton, 1993.

Ellis, Roger. ' "Flores ad fabricandam . . . coronam": an investigation into the uses of the Revelations of St Briget of Sweden in fifteenth-century England'. *Medium Ævum* (1982), pp. 163–86.

Ellis, Roger *Viderunt eam filie Syon: the Spirituality of the English House of a Medieval*

Contemplative Order from its Beginnings to the Present Day. (Analecta Cartusiana 68). Salzburg, 1984.

Ellis, Roger. 'The Swedish Woman, the Widow. The Pilgrim and the Prophetess: Images of St Bridget in the Canonization Sermon of Pope Boniface IX'. In *Santa Brigida: Profeta dei tempi nuovi. Saint Bridget: Prophetess of New Ages.* Rome, 1991, pp. 93–120.

Ellis, Roger. 'The Divine Message and its Human Agents: St Birgitta and her Editors'. In *Studies in St Birgitta and the Brigittine Order I.* Ed. James Hogg. Salzburg, 1993.

Ellis, Roger. 'The Visionary and Canon Lawyers: Papal and other Revisions to the *Regula Salvatoris* of St Bridget of Sweden'. In *Prophets Abroad. The Reception of Continental Holy Women in Late-Medieval England.* Ed. Rosalynn Voaden. Cambridge, 1996, pp. 71–90.

Erbe, Theodor (ed.). *Mirk's Festial. A Collection of Homilies by Johannes Mirkus (John Mirk).* (Early English Text Society, Extra Series 96). London, 1905.

Evans, G.R. *The Thought of Gregory the Great.* Cambridge, 1986.

Fennell, John. *The Emergence of Moscow 1304–1359.* London, 1968.

Ferm, Olle. 'Heliga Birgittas program för uppror mot Magnus Eriksson'. In *Heliga Birgitta – budskapet och förebilden.* Ed. Alf Härdelin and Mereth Lindgren. (KVHAAH, Konferenser 28). Stockholm, 1993, pp. 125–43.

Flavigny, Comtesse de. *Sainte Brigitte de Suède, sa vie, ses révélations et son œuvre.* Paris, 1892.

Fogelklou, Emilia. *Birgitta.* (First published 1919). Stockholm, 1955.

Fogelklou, Emilia. *Bortom Birgitta.* Stockholm, 1941.

Fogelqvist, Ingvar. 'The New Vineyard. St Birgitta of Sweden's Regula Salvatoris and the Monastic Tradition'. In *In Quest of the Kingdom. Ten Papers on Medieval Spirituality.* Ed. Alf Härdelin. Stockholm, 1991, pp. 203–44.

Fogelqvist, Ingvar. *Apostasy and Reform in the Revelations of St Birgitta.* (Bibliotheca Theologiae Practicae 51). Stockholm, 1993.

Foote, P.G., and D.M. Wilson. *The Viking Achievement.* London, 1970.

Foote, P.G. (ed.). *Olaus Magnus. A Description of the Northern Peoples. Rome 1555.* 1. (Hakluyt Society, 2nd series, 182). London, 1996.

France, James. *The Cistercians in Scandinavia.* (Cistercian Studies Series 131). Kalamazoo, 1992.

Fritz, Birgitta. 'Kung Magnus Erikssons planer för Vadstena klosterkyrka – och Birgittas'. In *Kongsmenn og Krossmenn. Festskrift til Grethe Authén Blom,* ed. Steinar Supphellen. Trondheim, 1992, pp. 115–29.

Fröjmark, Anders. *Mirakler och helgonkult. Linköpings biskopsdöme under senmedeltiden.* (Studia historica upsaliensia 171). Uppsala, 1992.

Gejrot, Claes (ed.). *Diarium Vadstenense. The Memorial Book of Vadstena Abbey.* (Acta universitatis stockholmiensis. Studia Latina Stockholmiensia 33). Stockholm, 1988.

Ghotan, Bartholomaeus, *Revelationes S. Birgitte. Impressit B. Ghotan,* Lübeck, 1492.

Gilkær, Hans Torben. *The Political Ideas of St Birgitta and her Spanish Confessor, Alfonso Pecha. Liber celestis Imperatoris ad Reges: A Mirror of Princes.* (Odense University Studies in History and Social Sciences 163). Odense, 1993.

Gilchrist, Roberta. *Gender and Material Culture. The Archaeology of Religious Women.* London, 1993.

Gräslund, Anne-Sofie. 'Gud hjälpe nu väl hennes själ'. *Tor* 22 (1988–89), pp. 223–44.

Gold, Penny Schine. 'Male/Female Cooperation: the Example of Fontevrault'. In *Distant Echoes. Medieval Religious Women I*. Ed. John A. Nichols and Lillian Thomas Shank. (Cistercian Studies Series 71). Kalamazoo, 1984, pp. 151–68.

Götlind, Anna. *Technology and Religion in Medieval Sweden*. (Avhandlingar från historiska institutionen i Göteborg 4). Falun, 1990.

Graef, Hilda. *Mary. A History of Doctrine and Devotion I*. London and New York, 1963.

Greenspan, Kate. 'The Autohagiographical Tradition in Medieval Women's Devotional Writing'. *a/b: Auto/Biography Studies* 6 (1991), pp. 157–68.

Gunneng, Hedda, and Birgit Strand. *Kvinnans ekonomiska ställning under nordisk medeltid. Uppsatser framlagda vid ett kvinnohistoriskt symposium i Kungälv 8–12 oktober 1979*. Lindome, 1981.

Gunnes, Erik. 'The Foundation of the Brigittine Monastery of Munkeliv, and its Struggle for Existence'. *Collegium medievale. Interdisciplinary Journal of Medieval Research* 3 (1990), pp. 111–22.

Halborg, John, E. 'A Possible Gestation of Bridget's Vision of the Nativity'. In *Studies in St Birgitta and the Brigittine Order. 1*. Ed. J. Hogg. (Analecta Cartusiana 35:19). Salzburg, 1993, pp. 85–90.

Härdelin, Alf. ' "Guds brud och egendom." Om "nunnebilden" i Birgittinregelns nunnevigningsrit'. In *Heliga Birgitta – budskapet och förebilden*. Ed. Alf Härdelin and Mereth Lindgren. (KVHAAH, Konferenser 28). Stockholm, 1993, pp. 203–12.

Härdelin, Alf and Mereth Lindgren (eds). *Heliga Birgitta – budskapet och förebilden* (KVHAAH, Konferenser 28), Stockholm, 1993.

Hedlund, Monica. 'Vadstena kloster – ett fönster mot England'. *Annales academiæ regiæ scientiarum upsaliensis* 28 (1989–90), pp. 84–96.

Hedlund, Monica. 'Vadstenapredikanter om Birgitta'. In *Heliga Birgitta – budskapet och förebilden*. Ed. Alf Härdelin and Mereth Lindgren. (KVHAAH, Konferenser 28). Stockholm, 1993, pp. 311–27.

Henning, Sam (ed.). *Upplandslagen enligt Cod. Holm. B199 och 1607 års utgåva*. (SFSS 240). Uppsala, 1967.

Hill, G. *A History of Cyprus II*. Cambridge, 1948.

Hogg, James, ed. *Studies in St Birgitta and the Birgittine Order, I–II*. (Analecta Cartusiana 35:19). Salzburg, 1993.

Högman, Bertil (ed.). *Heliga Birgittas originaltexter*. (SFSS 205). Uppsala, 1951.

Hohmann, Thomas (ed.). *Heinrichs von Langenstein 'Unterscheidung der Geister' Lateinisch und Deutsch: Texte und Untersuchungen zu Übersetzungsliteratur aus der Wiener Schule*. Zurich, 1977.

Höjer, Torvald. *Studier i Vadstena klosters och birgittinordens historia intill midten af 1400-talet*. Uppsala, 1905.

Höjer, Torvald. 'Ett vittnesmål af den heliga Katarina af Sverige om Urban VI: s val 1378'. *Historisk tidskrift (Sweden)* (1907), pp. 41–44.

Höjer, Torvald. 'Till kännedom om Vadstena klosters ställning som religiös institution'. In *Historiska studier tillägnade Professor Harald Hjärne på hans sextioårsdag den 2 maj 1908*. Uppsala, 1908, pp. 59–106.

Holland Smith, John. *The Great Schism 1378. The Disintegration of the Papacy.* London, 1970.

Hollman, Lennart (ed.). *Den heliga Birgittas Reuelaciones extrauagantes.* (SFSS ser. 2, V). Uppsala, 1956.

Imsen, Steinar. 'Late Medieval Scandinavian Queenship'. In *Queens and Queenship in Medieval Europe.* Ed. Anne J. Duggan. Woodbridge, 1997, pp. 53–71.

Johnson, Elizabeth. 'Marian Devotion in the Western Church'. In *Christian Spirituality: High Middle Ages and Reformation.* Ed. Jill Raitt, Bernard McGinn and John Meyendorff. (World Spirituality: an Encyclopedic History of the Religious Quest 17). New York, 1987, pp. 392–414.

Johnson F.R. 'English Defenders of St Bridget'. In *Studies in St Birgitta and the Brigittine Order,* I. Ed. James Hogg. (Analecta Cartusiana 35:19). Salzburg, 1993, pp. 263–75.

Jónsson, Guðni. *Konunga Sögur* 2. Reykjavík, 1965.

Jönsson, Ann-Mari. 'Den heliga Birgittas skrinläggning'. *Kyrkohistorisk årsskrift* 87 (1987), pp. 37–53.

Jönsson, Ann-Mari. *Sancta Birgitta. Revelaciones. Book III.* (SFSS ser. 2, VIII:3). Uppsala, 1998.

Jönsson, Arne. *Alfonso of Jaén. His Life and Works with Critical Editions of the 'Epistola Solitarii', the 'Informaciones' and the 'Epistola Serui Christi'.* (Studia graeca et latina lundensia 1). Lund, 1989.

Jönsson, Arne. 'Birgitta i Birgittalegenderna'. In *Heliga Birgitta–budskapet och förebilden.* Ed. Alf Härdelin and Mereth Lindgren. (KVHAAH, Konferenser 28). Stockholm, 1993, pp. 35–48.

Jönsson, Arne. *St Bridget's Revelations to the Popes. An edition of the so-called 'Tractatus de summis pontificibus'.* (Studia graeca et latina lundensia 6). Lund, 1997.

Jørgensen, Johannes. *Saint Bridget of Sweden I–II.* Translated by Ingeborg Lund. London, 1954.

Karlsson, K.H. (ed.). 'Lars Romares berättelse om den heliga Birgittas kanonisering'. *Samlaren* 22 (1901), pp. 1–15.

Keen, Maurice Hugh. *Chivalry.* New Haven, Connecticut, 1984.

Kemp, Eric Waldram. *Canonization and Authority in the Western Church.* London, 1948.

Kerby-Fulton, Kathryn. *Reformist Apocalypticism and Piers Plowman.* (Cambridge Studies in Medieval Literature 7). Cambridge, 1990.

Kieckhefer, Richard. *Unquiet Souls. Fourteenth-century Saints and their Religious Milieu.* Chicago and London, 1984.

Kleinberg, Aviad M. 'Proving Sanctity: Selection and Authentication of Saints in the Later Middle Ages'. Viator 20 (1989), pp. 183–205.

Klemming, G.E. (ed.). *Heliga Birgittas Uppenbarelser.* 5 vols. (SFSS fasc. 29, 30, 34–38, 62, 65, 81, 83). Stockholm, 1857–84.

Klockars, Birgit. *Biskop Hemming av Åbo.* (Skrifter utg. av Svenska litteratursällskapet i Finland 379). Helsinki, 1960.

Klockars, Birgit. *Birgitta och böckerna. En undersökning av den heliga Birgittas källor.* (KVHAAH, Historiska serien 11). Stockholm, 1966.

Klockars, Birgit. 'De tidigaste Birgittabilderna'. *Historisk tidskrift (Finland)* (1966), pp. 139–46.

Klockars, Birgit. *Birgitta och hennes värld.* (KVHAAH, Historiska serien 16). Stockholm, 1971.

Klockars, Birgit. *Birgittas svenska värld.* Stockholm, 1976.

Klockars, Birgit. *I Nådens dal: klosterfolket och andra c.1440–1590.* (Svenska litteratursällskapet i Finland). Helsinki, 1979.

Knowles, David. *The Religious Orders in England, II.* Cambridge, 1961.

Koch, Helga. 'Gud og menneske hos Birgitta'. *Dansk teologisk tidsskrift* 50 (1987), pp. 161–83.

Koch, Helga. 'Lignelses-, symbol- og billedsprog hos Birgitta. Visdommens efterfølgelse som Imitatio Christi et Mariae'. In *Birgitta hendes vaerk og hendes klostre i Norden.* Ed. T. Nyberg. Odense, 1991, pp. 471–89.

Koht, Halfdan. 'Magnus Erikssons giftermål med Blanche av Namur'. *Historisk tidskrift (Norway)* 5:5 (1924), pp. 566–82.

Krötzl, Christian. 'Om nordbornas vallfarter till Santiago de Compostela'. *Historisk tidskrift (Finland)* 72 (1987), pp. 189–200.

Krötzl, Christian. 'Parent-Child Relations in Medieval Scandinavia According to Scandinavian Miracle Collections'. *Scandinavian Journal of History* 14 (1989), pp. 21–37.

Kulturhistorisk leksikon for nordisk middelalder. Copenhagen, 1956–78.

Kumlien, Kjell. *Sverige och hanseaterna: studier i svensk politik och utrikeshandel.* (KVHAAH, Historiska serien 86). Stockholm, 1953.

Leclercq, Jean. *The Love of Learning and the Desire for God. A Study of Monastic Culture.* London, 1974.

Lerner, Robert E. 'Medieval Prophecy and Religious Dissent'. *Past and Present* 72 (1976), pp. 3–24.

Liedgren, Jan. 'Magister Mathias' svenska kungörelse om Birgittas första stora uppenbarelse. Ett förbisett dokument i Riksarkivet'. In *Meddelanden från Svenska riksarkivet för år 1958.* Stockholm, 1961, pp. 101–16.

Liedgren, Jan. 'Två birgittinska data'. *Personhistorisk tidskrift* 70 (1974), pp. 51–4.

Lind, John. 'The Russian Sources of King Magnus Eriksson's Campaign against Novgorod – Reconsidered'. *Mediaeval Scandinavia* 12 (1988), pp. 248–72.

Lindblom, Andreas. 'Birgittas sista färd'. *Rig* (1955), pp. 33–68.

Lindblom, Andreas. *På Birgittas vägar.* Stockholm, 1962.

Lindblom, Andreas. *Kult och konst i Vadstena kloster.* (KVHAAH, Antikvariska serien 14). Stockholm, 1965.

Lindblom, J. *Prophecy in Ancient Israel.* Oxford, 1962.

Lindgren, Mereth. 'De heliga änkorna: S. Annakultens framväxt, speglad i birgittinsk ikonografi'. In *Den monastiska bildvärlden i Norden. Föredrag vid det 10: e nordiska symposiet för ikonografiska studier i Vadstena 1990.* Ed. Catherine Bonnier, Mereth Lindgren and Marian Ullén. Stockholm, 1990, pp. 52–72.

Lindgren, Mereth. *Bilden av Birgitta.* Höganäs, 1991.

Lindkvist, Thomas and Kurt Ågren. *Sveriges medeltid.* Stockholm, 1985.

Lindroth, Sten. *Svensk lärdomshistoria. I. Medeltiden, Reformationstiden.* Stockholm, 1975.

Löfqvist, Karl-Erik. *Om riddarväsen och frälse i nordisk medeltid. Studier rörande adelsståndets uppkomst och tidigare utformning.* Lund, 1935.

Lokrantz, Margherita Giordano. 'Intorno al viaggio italiano di Birgitta de Svezia: il soggiorno milanese (autunno 1349)'. In *Vestigia: Studi in onoer de Giuseppe Billonovich*. Ed. Rino Avesani. Rome, 1984, pp. 387–98.

Losman, Beata. 'Birgitta, en kvinnlig väckelsepredikant'. In *Förändringar i kvinnors villkor under medeltiden: uppsatser framlagda vid ett kvinnohistoriskt symposium i Skálholt, Ísland 22–25 juni 1981*. Ed. Silja Aðalsteinsdóttir and Helgi Þorláksson. Reykjavík, 1983, pp. 82–104.

Lundén, Tryggve. *Den heliga Birgitta. Himmelska uppenbarelser*. Malmö, 1957–59.

Lundén, Tryggve. *Nikolaus Hermansson biskop av Linköping. En litteratur- och kyrkohistorisk studie*. Lund, 1971.

Lundén, Tryggve. *Den heliga Birgitta och den helige Petrus av Skänninge. Officium parvum beate Marie Virginis I–II*. (Acta Universitatis Upsaliensis. Studia Historico-Ecclesiastica Upsaliensia 27). Lund, 1976.

Lundén, Tryggve. *Sveriges missionärer, helgon och kyrkogrundare*. Storuman, 1983.

Magnus, Olaus. *Historia de gentibus septentrionalibus*. Rome, 1555. (Republished by Gregg International Publishers, Farnborough, 1971.)

McGuire, Brian Patrick. 'Spiritual Life and Material Life in the Middle Ages: a Contradiction?' In *Mensch und Objekt im Mittelalter und in der frühen Neuzeit: Leben–Alltag–Kultur. Internationaler Kongress Krems an der Donau 27. bis 30. September 1988*. (Österreichische Akademie der Wissenschaften, Philosophisch-Historische Klasse, Sitzungsberichte 568; Veröffentlichungen des Instituts für Realienkunde des Mittelalters und der frühen Neuzeit 13). Vienna, 1990, pp. 300–10.

Meech, Sanford Brown. *The Book of Margery Kempe*. (Early English Text Society 212). London, 1940.

Moberg, Lennart. 'Heliga Birgittas första uppenbarelse i Magister Mathias svenska version'. *Studier i nordisk filologi 62 (Skrifter utgivna av Svenska litteratursällskapet i Finland 490)*. (1980), pp. 193–211.

Moberg, Lennart (ed.). *Konungastyrelsen. En filologisk undersökning*. (SFSS 255). Uppsala, 1984.

Montag, Ulrich. *Das Werk der heiligen Birgitta von Schweden in oberdeutscher Überlieferung*. (Münchener Texte und Untersuchungen zur Deutschen Literatur des Mittelalters 18). Munich, 1968.

Morris, Bridget (ed.). *Book V of St Birgitta's 'Uppenbarelser' Edited from MS Cod. Ups. C61*. (SFSS 260). Lund, 1991.

Morris, Bridget. 'Labyrinths of the Urtext'. In *Den heliga Birgitta – budskapet och förebilden*. Ed. Alf Härdelin and Mereth Lindgren. (KVHAAH, Konferenser 28). Stockholm, 1993, pp. 23–34.

Morris, Bridget. 'Swedish Foreign Policy of the 1340s in the Balance: an Interpretation of Book IV chapter 2 of St Bridget's Revelations'. In *Studies in St Birgitta and the Brigittine Order, I*. Ed. James Hogg. Salzburg, 1993, pp. 180–91.

Morris, Bridget. 'Four Birgittine Meditations in Medieval Swedish'. *Birgittiana* 2 (1996), pp. 167–86.

Morris, Bridget. 'Birgittines and Beguines in Medieval Sweden'. *New Trends in Feminine Spirituality. The Holy Women of Liège and their Impact*. Ed. J. Dor, L. Johnson and J. Wogan-Browne (Medieval Women: Texts and Contexts, 2). Turnhout, 1999, pp. 157–73.

Nelson, Axel. 'Lagman Birgers begravningskostnader'. *Upplands Fornminnesförenings tidskrift* 10 (1925–26), pp. 12–18.

Nicholas, David. *Medieval Flanders*. London and New York, 1992.

Nieuwland, Jeanettte. 'Birgitta's View of Marriage: Theory versus Practice'. In *Birgitta, hendes vaerk og hendes klostre i Norden*. Ed. Tore Nyberg. Odense, 1991, pp. 83–92.

Norborg, Lars-Arne. *Storföretaget Vadstena kloster. Studier i senmedeltida godspolitik och ekonomiförvaltning*. (Bibliotheca historica Lundensis 7). Lund, 1958.

Nordenfalk, Carl. 'St Bridget of Sweden as Represented in Illuminated MSS'. In *Essays in Honour of Erwin Panofsky, I*. Ed. Millard Meiss. New York, 1961, pp. 371–93.

Nyberg, Tore. *Birgittinische Klostergründungen des Mittelalters*. (Biblioteca historica Lundensis, 15). Lund, 1965.

Nyberg, Tore. 'De birgittinska ordensmännens uppgift'. In *Kyrkohistorisk årsskrift* 68 (1968), pp. 22–37. (Reprinted in Nyberg 1991.)

Nyberg, Tore. 'The Development of the Order of St Birgitta'. In *Birgitta. Una santa svedese*. Rome, 1974, pp. 135–79.

Nyberg, Tore. 'Das Gesamtkloster als Rechtseinheit im Lichte der Klosteridee Birgittas'. *Zeitschrift der Savigny-Stiftung für Rechtsgeschichte, Kanonistische Abteilung* 74 (1988,) pp. 357–90.

Nyberg, Tore. 'Introduction'. In *Birgitta of Sweden. Life and Selected Revelations*. Ed. Tjader Harris. New York, 1990, pp. 13–53.

Nyberg, Tore. 'Birgitta som mor. Den heliga Katarina av Vadstena'. In *Birgittinsk festgåva. Studier om Heliga Birgitta och Birgittinorden*. Ed. Tore Nyberg. (Skrifter utgivna av Svenska kyrkohistoriska föreningen 46). Uppsala, 1991, pp. 36–55.

Nyberg, Tore. *Birgittinsk festgåva. Studier om Heliga Birgitta och Birgittinorden*. (Skrifter utgivna av Svenska kyrkohistoriska föreningen 46). Uppsala, 1991.

Nyberg, Tore, ed., *Birgitta, hendes vaerk og hendes klostre i Norden* (Odense University Studies in History and Social Sciences 150). Odense, 1991.

Nyberg, Tore. 'The Thirteen Apostles in the Spiritual World of St Bridget'. In *Studies in St Birgitta and the Birgittine Order, I*. Ed. James Hogg. (Analecta Cartusiana 35). Salzburg, 1993, pp. 192–208.

Nyberg, Tore. 'Autour de la Sacralité Royale en Scandinavie'. In *Annuarium historiae conciliorum* 27–8 (1995–96), pp. 177–92.

Nyberg, Tore. 'Paradiso'. *Birgittiana* 1 (1996), pp. 9–14.

Obrist, Barbara. 'The Swedish Visionary: Saint Bridget'. In *Medieval Women Writers*. Ed. Katharina M. Wilson. Manchester, 1984, pp. 227–51.

Öberg, Jan. *Kring Birgitta*. (KVIIAAH, Filologiskt arkiv 13). Stockholm, 1969.

O'Mara, V.M. 'A Middle English Text Written by a Female Scribe'. *Notes and Queries* 105 (1990), pp. 396–8.

O'Mara, V.M. 'Female Scribal Ability and Scribal Activity in Late Medieval England: the Evidence?' *Leeds Studies in English*, new series 27 (1996), pp. 87–130.

Ortved, Edward. *Cistercieordenen og dens klostre i norden I*. Copenhagen, 1927.

Paravicini, Werner. 'Das Haus Namur im Ostseeraum'. In *Mare Balticum. Beiträge zur Geschichte des Ostseeraumes in Mittelalter und Neuzeit. Festschrift zum 65.*

Geburtstag von Erich Hoffmann. (Kieler Historische Studien 36). Sigmaringen, 1992, pp. 165–93.

Petroff, Elizabeth Alvilda (ed.). *Medieval Women's Visionary Literature*. New York and Oxford, 1986.

Pezzini, Domenico. 'The Italian Reception of Birgittine Writings'. In *The Translation of the Works of St Birgitta of Sweden into the Medieval European Vernaculars*. Ed. Bridget Morris and Veronica O'Mara. Turnhout, 1999 (forthcoming).

Piltz, Anders. *Prolegomena till en textkritisk edition av magister Mathias' 'Homo Conditus'*. Uppsala, 1974.

Piltz, Anders. *Magistri Mathiae canonici Lincopensis opus sub nomine Homo conditus vulgatum*. (SFSS ser. 2, IX:1). Stockholm, 1984.

Piltz, Anders. 'Magister Mathias of Sweden in his Theological Context: a Preliminary Survey'. In *The Editing of Philosophical and Theological Texts from the Middle Ages*. Ed. Monica Asztalos. Stockholm, 1986, pp. 137–60.

Piltz, Anders. 'Uppenbarelserna och uppenbarelsen: Birgittas förhållande till bibeln'. In *Birgitta. Hendes værk og hendes klostre i Norden*. Ed. Tore Nyberg. Odense, 1991, pp. 447–69.

Piltz, Anders. 'Inspiration, vision, profetia: Birgitta och teorierna om uppenbarelsen'. In *Heliga Birgitta – Budskapet och förebilden: Föredrag vid jubileumssymposiet i Vadstena 3–7 oktober 1991*. Ed. Alf Härdelin and Mereth Lindgren. (KVHAAH, Konferenser 28). Stockholm, 1993, pp. 67–88.

Pulsiano, Phillip, et al. (eds.). *Medieval Scandinavia. An Encyclopedia*. New York and London, 1993.

Pipping, Rolf (ed.). *Erikskrönikan*. (SFSS 231). Uppsala, 1963.

Rahmqvist, Sigurd, and Lars-Olof Skoglund. *Det medeltida Sverige: 1: Uppland, 5 Attundaland: Lyhundra, Sjuhundra*. Stockholm, 1986.

Rajamaa, Ruth, *Systrarnas verksamhet, undervisning och uppfostran i Vadstena kloster 1384–1595*, Stockholm, 1992.

Reeves, Marjorie. *The Influence of Prophecy in the Later Middle Ages. A Study in Joachimism*. Oxford, 1969.

Reeves, Marjorie. 'The Medieval Heritage'. In *Prophetic Rome in the High Renaissance Period*. Ed. Marjorie Reeves. Oxford, 1992, pp. 3–21.

Rehnberg, Anna Maria. 'Evig mamma som rörde om i Europa'. *Svenska Dagbladet* 25.05 (1994), p. 5.

Renouard, Yves. *The Avignon Papacy 1305–1403*. (Translated by Denis Bethell). London, 1970.

Riehle, Wolfgang. *The Middle English Mystics*. London, 1981.

Roberts, Michael. *Essays in Sweden's History*. London, 1967.

Roelvink, Henrik. 'Andlig släktskap mellan Franciskus och Birgitta'. In *Heliga Birgitta – budskapet och förebilden*. Ed. Alf Härdelin and Mereth Lindgren. (KVHAAH, Konferenser 28). Stockholm, 1993, pp. 99–122.

Roschini, Gabriele M. *La madonna nelle 'Rivelazioni di S.Brigida' nel sesto centenario della sua morte (23 luglio 1373)*. Rome, 1973.

Rosenthal, Joel T. *The Purchase of Paradise. Gift Giving and the Aristocracy, 1307–1485*. London and Toronto, 1972.

Sahlin, Claire. ' "His Heart was my Heart": Birgitta of Sweden's Devotion to the Heart of Mary'. In *Heliga Birgitt – abudskapet och förebilden*. Ed. Alf Härdelin and Mereth Lindgren. (KVHAAH, Konferenser 28). Stockholm, 1993, pp. 213–27.

Sahlin, Claire. 'Birgitta of Sweden and the Voice of Prophecy: a Study of Gender and Religious Authority in the Later Middle Ages'. Harvard Ph.D. dissertation (unpublished). 1996.

Sahlin, Claire. 'Gender and Prophetic Authority in Birgitta of Sweden's *Revelations*'. In *Gender and Text in the Later Middle Ages*. Ed. Jane Chance. Gainesville, 1996.

Sahlin, Claire. 'The Virgin Mary and Birgitta of Sweden's Prophetic Vocation'. In *Maria i Sverige under tusen år. Föredrag vid symposiet i Vadstena 6–10 oktober 1994, I*. Ed. Sven-Erik Brodd and Alf Härdelin. Skellefteå, 1996, pp. 227–54.

Sahlin, Claire. 'Submission, Role Reversals, and Partnerships: Birgitta and her Clerical Associates'. *Birgittiana* 3 (1997), pp. 9–41.

Sahlin, Claire. 'The Prophetess as Preacher: Birgitta of Sweden and the Voice of Prophecy'. *Medieval Sermon Studies*. Hull, Autumn: 1997, pp. 29–44.

Sander Olsen, Ulla. 'Arbejdspraksis og arbejdsetos i birgittinernes nonnekonvent'. In *Birgitta, hendes værk og hendes klostre i Norden*. Ed. T. Nyberg. Odense, 1991, pp. 329–48.

Santa Brigida: Profeta dei tempi nuovi. (Saint Bridget: Prophetess of New Ages). Proceedings of the International Study Meeting, Rome October 3–7, 1991, Rome, 1991.

Sawyer, Peter and Birgitta. *Medieval Scandinavia. From Conversion to Reformation circa 800–1500*. Minneapolis, 1993.

Schmid, Toni. 'Den heliga familjen i revelation och liturgi. Ett bidrag till kännedom om birgittinsk tankevärld och birgittinskt inflytande'. *Samlaren* (1933), pp. 107–21.

Schmidtke, J.A. 'Saving by Faint Praise: St Birgitta of Sweden, Adam Easton and Medieval Antifeminism'. *American Benedictine Review* 33 (1982), pp. 149–61.

Schück, Henrik. 'Rosa rorans: Ett birgitta-officium'. *Meddelanden från det litteraturhistoriska seminariet i Lund* 2. Lund, 1893, pp. 29–53.

Schück, Henrik (ed.). 'Två svenska biografier från medeltiden'. *Antiqvarisk tidskrift för Sverige* 6 (1895), pp. 295–312.

Scott, Franklin D. *Sweden. The Nation's History*. Minneapolis, 1977.

Scriptores rerum svecicarum medii aevi I–III. Ed. E.M. Fant et al. Uppsala, 1818–76.

Seidlmayer, Michael. 'Ein Gehilfe der hl. Birgitta von Schweden: Alfons von Jaen'. *Historisches Jahrbuch der Görres-Gesellschaft* 50 (1930), pp. 1–18.

Shahar, Shulamith. *The Fourth Estate. A History of Women in the Middle Ages*. London and New York, 1983.

Sjöholm, Elsa. *Sveriges medeltidslagar. Europeisk rättstradition i politisk omvandling*. (Skrifter utg. av Institutet för rättshistorisk forskning 41). Lund, 1988.

Southern, R.W. 'Aspects of the European Tradition of Historical Writing: 3. History as Prophecy'. *Transactions of the Royal Historical Society*, 5th series, 22 (1972), pp. 159–80.

Stolpe, Sven. 'Birgitta och politiken'. In *Opuscula ecclesiastica. Studier tillägnade Gunnar Rosendal den 4 april 1972*. Ed. Oloph Bexell. Uppsala, 1972, pp. 359–73.

Stolpe, Sven. *Birgitta i Sverige I. Birgitta i Rom II*. Stockholm, 1973.

Strömberg, Bengt. 'Magister Mathias' ställning till tidens heretiska strömningar'. *Svensk teologisk kvartalskrift* 19 (1943), pp. 301–22.

Strömberg, Bengt. *Magister Mathias och fransk mendikantpredikan*. (Samlingar och studier till Svenska kyrkans historia 9). Stockholm, 1944.

Sundén, Hjalmar. *Den Heliga Birgitta: ormungens moder som blev Kristi brud*. Stockholm, 1973.

Svanberg, Jan. 'De allra äldsta bilderna av den heliga Birgitta och hennes vision av Jesu födelse'. *Kungl. Vitterhets Historie och Antikvitets Akademiens årsbok* (1997), pp. 132–46.

Tait, M.B. 'The Brigittine Monastery of Syon Abbey'. D.Phil. thesis (unpublished). University of Oxford, 1975.

Thompson, Sally. *Women Religious. The Founding of English Nunneries after the Norman Conquest*. Oxford, 1991.

Thorell, Olof. *Fem Moseböcker på fornsvenska. Enligt Cod. Holm. A1*. (SFSS 212, 218, 223). Uppsala, 1959.

Tjader Harris, Margaret. *Birgitta of Sweden. Life and Selected Works*. New York, 1990.

Ullmann, Walter. *The Origins of the Great Schism*. London, 1967.

Ullmann, Walter. *A Short History of the Papacy in the Middle Ages*. London and New York, 1972.

Ullmann, Walter. 'The Recognition of St Bridget's Rule by Martin V'. In *The Papacy and Political Ideas in the Middle Ages*. Ed. Walter Ullmann. London 1976, pp. 190–201.

Undhagen, Carl-Gustaf (ed.). *Birger Gregersson, Birgitta-officium*. (SFSS ser. 2, VI). Uppsala, 1960.

Undhagen, Carl-Gustaf. 'Une source du prologue (chap. 1) aux Révélations de Sainte Brigitte par le cardinal Jean de Turrecremata'. *Eranos* 58 (1960), pp. 214–26.

Undhagen, Carl-Gustaf (ed.). *Sancta Birgitta Revelaciones Book I, with Magister Mathias' Prologue*. (SFSS ser. 2, VII:1). Uppsala,1978.

Vadstenabrödernas predikan. Meddelanden. (Department of Classical Philology, University of Uppsala). Uppsala, 1994– .

Vauchez, André. *La sainteté en occident aux derniers siècles du Moyen Age*. Rome, 1988. Also in English translation *Sainthood in the Later Middle Ages* (translated by Jean Birrell), Cambridge, 1997.

Vauchez, André. 'Saint Bridget's Revelations in France at the End of the Middle Ages'. In *Santa Brigida: Profeta dei tempi nuovi. Saint Bridget: Prophetess of New Ages*. Rome, 1991, pp. 176–87.

Vauchez, André. *The Laity in the Middle Ages. Religious Beliefs and Devotional Practices*. Edited and introduced by D.E. Bornstein, translated by M.J. Schneider. Notre Dame and London, 1993.

Vernet, F. 'Brigitte de Suède'. In *Dictionnaire de spiritualité ascétique et mystique*. Paris, 1937– , cols. 1943–58.

Voaden, Rosalynn. 'Women's Words, Men's Language: *Discretio Spirituum* as Discourse in the Writing of Medieval Women Visionaries'. In *The Medieval Translator V*. Ed. Roger Ellis and René Tixier. Turnhout, 1996, pp. 64–83.

von der Hardt, Herman (ed.). *Consilium pacis de unione ac reformatione Ecclesiae II*. Frankfurt and Leipzig, 1697.

von der Hardt, Herman (ed.). *Res concilii oecumenici Constantiensis II*. Frankfurt, 1697.

von Heidenstam, Verner. *Heliga Birgittas pilgrimsfärd*. Stockholm, 1901.

Wåhlin, Lars (ed.) *Magister Mathias. Copia exemplorum*. (Introduction by M. Andersson-Schmitt). (Studia seminarii latini upsaliensis 2). Uppsala, 1990.

Wallin, Curt. 'Vadstenanunnornas sociala proveniens'. In *Birgitta, hendes vaerk og hendes klostre i Norden*. Ed. Tore Nyberg. Odense, 1991, pp. 291–322.

Weinstein, Donald, and Rudolph M. Bell. *Saints and Society. The Two Worlds of Western Christendom, 1000–1700*. Chicago and London, 1982.

Wernstedt, Folke. *Äldre svenska frälsesläkter. Ättartavlor utgivna av Riddarhusdirektionen*. Stockholm, 1957, 1965.

Wessén, Elias. *Svensk Medeltid II. Birgitta-texter*. (KVHAAH, Filologisk-filosofiska serien 10). Stockholm, 1968.

Wessén, Elias. *Svensk Medeltid III. De fornsvenska handskrifterna av Heliga Birgittas Uppenbarelser*. (KVHAAH, Filologisk-filosofiska serien 16). Stockholm, 1976.

Westman, K.B. *Birgitta-Studier, I*. Uppsala, 1911.

Wiktorsson, Per-Axel. 'Fornsvenska texter bland medeltida pergamentsomslag', (SFSS ser. 3, *Smärre Texter och undersökningar*, 2, ed. Börje Tjäder). Uppsalla, 1988, pp. 86–110.

Witt-Brattström, Ebba. 'Fräckt, Birgitta!' *Bonniers Litterära Magasin* 61:3 (1992), pp. 6–11.

Wollin, Lars. 'Birgittine Biography at Vadstena – a Bilingual Affair?' In *The Translation of the Works of St Birgitta of Sweden into the Medieval European Vernaculars*. Ed. Bridget Morris and Veronica O'Mara. Turnhout, 1999 (forthcoming).

Wood, Diana. *Clement VI. The Pontificate and Ideas of an Avignon Pope*. Cambridge, 1989.

GLOSSARY OF NAMES

Scandinavians are listed under their first name, rather than their patronymic.

Nola, 99
Novgorod, 83
Öland, 142
Olaus Magnus, 7, 15, 19
Olof Skötkonung, 24
Olof, St, 15, 27
Omberg, Östergötland, 72, 74
Orekhov (Nöteborg), 83
Orsini, family, 95, 100
Orsini, Golicia, 148
Orsini, Latino, 148
Orsini, Niccolò, 99, 101 n. 36, 116, 161
Orsini, Selena, 100
Orvieto, 138
Ostia, 150
Oxford, 148
Palazzo della Cancellaria, Rome, 99
Palestine, 126
Papazurra, Francisca, 99, 141, 148, 173
Paradiso, Florence, house of, 170
Paris, 28, 58, 153, 157, 169
Patriarch of Constantinople, 83
Paul, St, 42, 162
Paulus, Cistercian monk, 74
Pavia, 100
Pecha, Fernán Rodriguez, 118
Peder Lykke, archbishop of Lund, 156
Pedro I, king of Spain, 119
Pedro of Aragon, Infante, 97 n. 11
Perugia, 154
Peter I, king of Cyprus, 126–8
Peter II, king of Cyprus, 126, 128–9
Peter Olafsson, Magister, of Skänninge, 8, 101, 103, 105, 110, 122, 141, 145, 168
Peter Olafsson, Prior, of Alvastra, 8, 72, 74, 79, 82, 101, 113 n. 63, 114, 122, 141, 145, 147, 163
Peter Tyrgilsson, bishop, 79
Peter, St, 42, 95, 98–9, 162
Petrarch, 95–7, 116
Petrus Amelius, Patriarch of Grado, 151 n. 15
Petrus Frijs, 141
Petrus Jacobi Papazzuri, 99
Petrus of Dacia, 27
Petrus of Orvieto, bishop, 146
Philip IV, the Fair, king of France, 30
Philippe VI, king of France, 80–2
Pocius de Péret, 114
Poitou, 126
Poland, 142, 162, 171
Portugal, 172
Prague, 28, 157, 169
Praxedis, Spanish anchoress, 122
Querini, Pietro, Venetian pilgrim, 16 n. 4
Ragnhild Erlandsdotter, 34
Ragnvald, prior of Alvastra, 75 n. 40
Richard I, king of England, 126
Rimbert, 23
Riseberga, Cistercian convent, 48, 110
Robert of Anjou, 122
Robert of Arbrissel, 163
Robert of Artois, 82
Robert of Geneva, cardinal, 146
Robert of Namur, 58
Rolle, Richard, 2
Rome, 48, 50, 52, 60–1, 93–117, 119, 124, 138 n. 51, 139, 143, 145–8, 159, 161
Rörik Matsson, 34
Rostock, 169
Saldaña, León diocese, 119
San Antonio de Vienna extra Muros, Naples, church of, 138–9
San Eligio, Naples, church of, 139 n. 55
San Giorgio Maggiore, Naples, church of, 139 n. 55
San Giovanni in Laterano, Rome, church of, 148
San Lorenzo in Damaso, Rome, church of, 99, 105
San Lorenzo in Panisperna, Rome, house of, 100, 141, 150
San Paolo fuori le Mura, Rome, church of, 100 n. 24, 101
San Pietro (St Peter's) Rome, church of, 116, 150
San Pietro in Vincoli, Rome, church of, 114
San Sebastiano, Rome, church of, 111
Santa Maria del Carmelo, Naples, church of, 139 n. 55
Santa Maria in Trastevere, Rome, church of, 148, 173
Santa Maria Maggiore, Rome, church of, 98, 146
Santa Maria Novella, Florence, church of, 139
Santa Maria Rotunda, Rome, church of, 100
Santiago de Compostela, 59, 113, 120
Sebastian, St, 95
Segovia, 118
Serminius, Johannes, Birgittine brother, 162

INDEX OF MANUSCRIPTS

The Latin manuscripts of the *Revelaciones* are found in national and university libraries across the world; for details see the introductions to the critical editions published by Svenska Fornskriftsällskapet. The Swedish collections divide broadly into two groups: manuscipts written in the vernacular which are mostly held in Kungliga Biblioteket, Stockholm, and manuscripts written in Latin which are in the so-called 'C-collection' in Uppsala Universitetsbibliotek. The C-collection is the repository of what remains of the Vadstena library (see further the eight-volume catalogue by Andersson-Schmitt, Hedlund et al., eds, 1988–95).

The most important Birgittine manuscripts include the following:

Autographs
MS A65, Kungliga Biblioteket, Stockholm. Two fragments in Birgitta's own hand. (See Högman 1956.)

Latin manuscripts
Two early Latin manuscripts which are among the most complete and best preserved:
Kalmar, Stifts- och Gymnasiebiblioteket, c. 1380–91; which belonged to Vadstena monastery; and Lund Universitetsbibliotek, MS 21, 'Codex Falkenberg', written by brother Johannes Johannis of Kalmar at the end of the fourteenth century.

Another important manuscript is British Library, MS Harley 612, mid fifteenth century. It originated at the English house of Syon, and contains a *Defensorium* of St Birgitta written by Galfridus of Byland during the Council of Basle.

The first printed edition of the *Revelaciones* was that of Bartholmaeus Ghotan in Lübeck, 1492.

Manuscripts in Medieval Swedish
There are some 15 manuscripts containing all or parts of a translation of Birgitta's *Uppenbarelser* into Swedish. There are essentially two traditions, one a close rendering of one or more (unidentified) Latin texts, the other a slightly more idiomatic rendering of the same translation. These traditions are best exemplified respectively by MS C61, Uppsala Universitetsbibliotek, c.1500, only part of which has been edited (see Morris 1991) and MS A 5a, Kungliga Biblioteket, Stockholm, c. 1425 (see edition by Klemming 1857–84).

The earliest known fragment of the translation into Swedish is:
Kungliga Biblioteket, Stockholm, MS A110 ('Codex Oxenstierna') dating from c.1385.

The 'Birgittiner-norske' text, MS Skokloster 5 (now in Riksarkivet, Stockholm), reflects an early (possibly pre-Latin) stage in the transmission of the Birgittine texts (see Wessén 1968).

Other manuscripts mentioned in the present book:
Corpus Christi College, Cambridge, MS 404
Kungliga Biblioteket, Stockholm, MS A 36
Lincoln Cathedral Chapter Library, MS 114
Uppsala Universitetsbibliotek, MS C2
Uppsala Universitetsbibliotek, MS C15
Uppsala Universitetsbibliotek, MS C 621

GENERAL INDEX